BLIND

CORNERS

Adventures on Everest
and the World's Tallest Peaks

Geoff Tabin

The Lyons Press
GUILFORD, CONNECTICUT

AN IMPRINT OF THE GLOBE PEQUOT PRESS

To my wife, Jean, who supports me in my work in Asia and tolerates my climbing habit; my babies, Sara Elizabeth and Daniel Reid Tabin, who are just beginning their own adventures; and to the memory of Daniel Reid and all of my climbing partners and friends who have perished in the pursuit of adventure.

Copyright © 2002 by Geoffrey Tabin

ALL RIGHTS RESERVED. No part of this book may be reproduced or transmitted in any form by any means, electronic or mechanical, including photocopying and recording, or by any information storage and retrieval system, except as may be expressly permitted by the 1976 Copyright Act or in writing from the publisher. Requests for permission should be addressed to The Globe Pequot Press, P.O. Box 480, Guilford, CT 06437.

The Lyons Press is an imprint of The Globe Pequot Press.

10 9 8 7 6 5 4 3 2 1

Printed in the United States of America

Library of Congress Cataloging-in-Publication Data is available on file.

ISBN 1-58574 344 5

CONTENTS

FOREWORD

Geoff Tabin's story is an astonishing mixture of wild adventure and the overcoming of formidable challenges. One cannot help feeling that the major battle is always with himself. He has an incredible desire to stretch himself to the utmost—almost, one feels, beyond his natural abilities. But somehow with considerable courage and great determination he nearly always achieves his objective despite frostbite and exhaustion and returns safely to the bottom of the mountain.

Geoff has climbed Mount Everest up the Southeast ridge and almost succeeded on the formidable East Face. Many of his greater efforts have been in the remote and inaccessible parts of the globe. He has climbed new routes on Mount Kenya near the equator and battled his way through the jungles of Irian Jaya to reach the summit of Carstensz Pyramid. He has climbed the isolated summit of Mount Vinson in the Antarctic.

Geoff has a vast respect—and rightly so—for Dan Reid, who died on Mount Kenya in September 1991. I met Dan Reid when I joined his team for the first climbing exploration of the Kangshung Face of Mount Everest and we subsequently became friends. I also first met Geoff on this same trip. Dan was an astonishing man both as a climber and a human being. In a way Dan was a role model for Geoff. They were both incredibly determined and a little crazy. They both permitted no challenge to stop them from reaching their goals—and took enormous risks in their achievements.

Geoff is a strange conglomeration of success and brilliant failure. He has met many strange personalities and seems to have enjoyed them all. But there is no questioning his courage and determination.

SIR EDMUND HILLARY

ACKNOWLEDGMENTS

I am grateful to many people for their help and input. First and foremost I appreciate the support of my family. In particular, my brilliant oldest daughter, Livia Demarchis, read the manuscript, served as a sounding board and provided fantastic help in the initial editing process. I also appreciate the support of my wife, Jean, my stepdaughters Ali and Emilia, my brother Cliff Tabin, and parents, Julius and Johanna Tabin, who encouraged me and tolerated my wanderings.

This book would not have come into existence without my agent Susan Golomb who got the project started; Tom McCarthy, my editor at Lyons Press; or Tom Todd, who initially approached me to write a book. Ken Banta, Rick Telander, Richard Stengel, Nanette Varian, Michael Lewis, John Harlin, Phil and Marcia Lieberman, Bob Shapiro, George Lowe, Brad Werntz, Beth Peterson, Matthew Childs, Neal Beidelman, Dominic Eisinger, Cliff Tabin, and Carl Tobin read various sections of the manuscript and provided valuable suggestions. Gwynn Travis helped with typing. Thank you all.

I also owe a debt of gratitude to all of the great adventurers who went before me, inspired me, and showed me the way. Finally, I appreciate the help of all of my climbing and ophthalmic partners and companions who shared my journeys, both those named in this book and those of you who are too boring to mention . . .

INTRODUCTION

My name is Geoff Tabin. I like to climb.

I remember a Far Side cartoon in which two gorillas are sitting around an enormous bunch of bananas. One of the gorillas turns to the other and says, "Yeah, I know we all like bananas, but with me it goes a bit deeper than that." That's how I feel about climbing.

So how much do I like climbing? Enough that it has consistently caused me to make life-changing decisions that appear senseless and irrational to the outside observer. I quit medical school—twice—to attempt a new route on Mount Everest that most climbing experts felt was impossible, suicidal, or both. I quit a residency in orthopedic surgery to climb when everyone told me I would absolutely be ruining my life. A feature article in *Sports Illustrated* once described me as "cheerfully oblivious to all of society's norms."

Yet somehow, at age forty-six, I seem to have found my niche. I'm the father of a wonderful family, a wife and five children. I hold down a day job as a tenured associate professor of surgery and ophthalmology at the University of Vermont College of Medicine, and I'm a co-director of the Himalayan Cataract Project, an effort to eradicate preventable and treatable blindness in the Himalayan region. And still, I like to climb.

Over the last three decades, I have made the first ascents of difficult technical rock, ice, or mountaineering routes on all seven continents, and I have become the fourth person to climb to the highest point on each continent. Along the way I've had the privilege of hanging out with some of the world's most bizarre and, by most of society's standards, crazy, people. I'm not a particularly gifted, natural climber—so what gives? How has this all been possible?

First and foremost, I must acknowledge a specter of luck. Yet I firmly believe that you make your own "luck" through preparedness. Fate definitely favors the prepared mind and body. I've made a lot of my own luck through what some would consider a fanatic dedication to training and a commitment to doing my best. I was fortunate that early in my climbing career, climbers more gifted, more skilled, and more experienced than I tempered and mentored my youthful exuberance. Also, I was not afraid to take chances. Even when the possibility of success was remote and the odds were stacked against me, I took on challenges. Usually I failed. But I kept on trying. With climbing, it was easy to keep trying because I loved what I was doing. The feeling of accomplishment and empowerment achieved from putting maximum effort into an impossible challenge drove me. I never felt I was torturing myself through training. In fact, I never felt I was training at all; I was following a passion. I always opted to climb one more pitch and come down in the dark instead of calling it a day before the sun set. I often pushed a little harder, went a bit farther, and ended up bivouacking out in the cold instead of making it down from a climb for the night. I loved training on rock walls until my fingertips and forearms began to cramp.

Above all, my decisions in climbing and in life have been defined by a willingness to fail. The essence of adventure is that the outcome is uncertain. I have continually taken on challenges without having much, if any, idea what I was getting into. I have turned blind corners and dealt with whatever came. When faced with difficult choices, such as whether to stay in medical school or drop out to go climb, the overriding thought in my decision making was not, *Is this sensible?* but rather, *Will I regret not doing this?* And once I had made a decision, I focused all my passion on living in the moment, without regrets or regards for past or future consequences.

Some people view adventure sports as simply a way to get an adrenaline rush. One burst of adrenaline leads to the next, and adventure sport junkies need to keep getting a "fix." Perhaps the real answer to why the chicken crossed the road was because it had drifted over the line into "cheap" thrills and was looking for an adrenaline high. Imagine a small excitement-seeking chicken crouched by the side of the road, its heart beating wildly, waiting for a big truck. Addicted to danger, its pulse soars to more than two hundred as it sees the oncoming headlights of an eighteen-wheeler glaring through the night sky. At the last possible moment the bird sprints forward and darts across the pavement, missing the wheels by less than an inch. The exhausted chicken feels more alive than ever before as it pants in the grass on the far side of the road. What's next? Perhaps sprinting underneath the wheels, letting the truck pass, and then dashing out to the other side. Then it's a two-lane highway, then a four . . . This analogy is a far cry from the adventures my climbing friends and I seek. Although I have had several partners and acquaintances who have died in the pursuit of the sports they loved, I cannot think of a single one who sought risk purely for risk's sake or for the instantaneous burst of adrenaline. The closest I have come to the media image of extreme sports was as a member of the Oxford Dangerous Sports Club. In 1979 we invented bungee jumping. On the television show *That's Incredible* I jumped from the Royal Gorge Bridge in Cañon City, Colorado, tethered to a long elastic cord. This event led to the popularization of this nonskill activity. But even the activities of the Oxford Dangerous Sports Club had a higher intensity and purpose than the momentary adrenaline rush gained by stepping off a bridge.

I do not believe any of my deceased climbing partners lived in a way that beckoned death, but rather in a way that maximized life. The freedom of the mountains and the ability to confront the unknown is a metaphor for the freedom of the human spirit. The core of this attitude is beautifully captured in Felice Benuzzi's book *No Picnic on Mount Kenya*. Benuzzi was an Italian climber who was placed in a prison in British East Africa during World War II. He escaped with the sole purpose of climbing Mount Kenya. He had an incredible adventure on the mountain and then returned voluntarily to prison because he saw there was no chance of escape back to Italy. Benuzzi liked to climb. He was willing to take a great risk, but he was no fool. What makes the Benuzzis of the world seek adventure? Some scientists have hypothesized that it is genetic. They suggest that there is a "danger gene" some of us have inherited that programs us to seek risk rather than security. Others say risk-taking behavior is a result of upbringing. In my case maybe it was the radiation to my dad's testicles.

My father, Julius Tabin, is a nuclear physicist who earned his doctorate at the University of Chicago before World War II. He worked on the first nuclear reactor and went with his mentor, Enrico Fermi, to work on the atomic bomb with the supersecret Manhattan Project in Los Alamos, New Mexico. After the initial and successful test explosion, Julius was the first person to go into White Sands to gather samples and test the radioactivity. He received a near-lethal dose of radiation. Because of likely damage to his sperm it was suggested that he not have children. After the war Julius taught at MIT in Boston but he was unable to continue nuclear studies because of radiation danger. He earned a law degree at Harvard before returning to Chicago, where he married my mother, a clinical child psychologist.

Despite all warnings my parents had two sons. My dad had us hiking and skiing shortly after we learned to walk and encouraged my brother, Cliff, and me in all sports. Although I was never the most talented, I did well because I worked a bit harder than anyone else. I threw a ball against the garage door for hours by myself. I hit tennis balls, late into the night, against a backboard illuminated only by a street-light fifty feet away. My dedication led to my winning several state championships in tennis. And when I started rock climbing as a teenager, it became my way of life.

At college I began reading mountaineering and adventure writing. My heroes became the people who asked *Why not?* rather than *Why?* I read and reread the adventures of Gaston Rebuffat, Heinrich Harrer, Hermann Buhl, H. W. Tilman, Eric Shipton, Reinhold Messner, Chris Bonington, George Leigh Mallory, Walter Bonatti, and others, including many explorers who never climbed. Ernest Shackleton, T. E. Lawrence, Vladimir Rawicz, Sven Heiden, Wilfred Thesiger, and Lewis and Clark became my role models. Among these men, my favorite to read about was Sir Richard Francis Burton. Born in Hertfordshire, England, in March 1821, Burton was described in his lifetime as an adventurer, linguist, scholar, rogue, sexual deviant, and genius. He lived a life that epitomized turning blind corners and facing the unknown. Burton left Oxford University without a degree and went to India, where he lived with Muslims and learned Iranian, Hindustani, and Arabic. He then posed as an Afghan physician on a hajj and journeyed to the forbidden cities of Mecca, Medina, and Harar. Had he been discovered he would certainly have been killed. Burton explored the blank areas on the map of central Africa and discovered Lake Tanganyika, the source of the Nile. He mastered twenty-five languages and shocked and outraged the staid Victorian world with his sexual views. By being the first to translate the Kama Sutra of Vatsayana, the Anga Ranga, and the Enchanted Garden into English, Burton brought Eastern erotica to the Western world. Burton's was a life that invited emulation. But how do you live a life of adventure in our modern world of global positioning satellites and mass communication?

There are plenty of modern-day explorers who have merged their passions with successful careers. Wade Davis—a disciple of the godfather of ethnobotany, Richard Shultes—experienced, like his mentor, years of wild adventure and exploration in South America. He researched hallucinogens and stimulants as well as native reme-dies among some of the most primitive people in the world. He followed his wander-lust to become a respected professor, best-selling author, and one of the foremost ecologists working to preserve our planet. Robert Sapolsky spent his twenties living with baboons and wandering in Africa. Jane Goodall spent her time with chimps; Galen Rowell has equal talent for both climbing and photography; Yvon Chouinard had a flair for designing better climbing tools and clothing; David Breashears is a brilliant climber and cinematographer. All of these individuals have been able to make their passion for adventure part of successful lives. Others, like Dan Reid and Lou Reichardt, combined their avocation with their vocation with an equal intensity in the pursuit of climbing and medicine or research. Dan became a top heart surgeon and Lou, a respected neuroscientist. As a college student I did not think much about the future or how I would combine climbing with a mainstream career. My simple answer for the short-term future was to climb. I had vague ideas that I might become a mountain guide. I liked sciences and, in an abstract way, thought of medicine as a way to spend my life helping people. I completed the minimal course requirements to apply to medical school.

The single event that most altered my life was being awarded a Marshall scholarship to spend two years at Oxford University after college. At Yale, in addition to climbing virtually every day, I was twice the captain of the tennis team. Both my tennis coach and academic adviser nominated me for a Rhodes scholarship. Yale also put my name in for the Marshall, which was the British government's thank-you gesture for the Marshall recovery plan after World War II. It gave the same stipend as the Rhodes and had similar selection criteria, but placed more emphasis on academics. The standard joke at Oxford was that a Rhodes couldn't read and a Marshall couldn't run. To my great surprise I found myself with two fully funded years at University College, Oxford, where I was to study philosophy. Moreover, Oxford has a scholastic calendar with an eight-week term followed by a six-week break, then another eight-week term with another six-week break, and a final eight-week term with a long summer vacation. Twenty-eight weeks of paid climbing for two years! Term time consisted of reading about an open-ended philosophical question and then arguing with a tutor, over sherry, for two hours per week. By scheduling my tutorials on back-to-back days I could climb in the Alps and all over Britain during term and keep up with my studies by bringing books along.

Three days after my arrival in England I was in the University College common room and heard a voice complaining, "Doug, don't you know anyone who climbs? My gear is all packed in my car. I really want to climb!"

I sidled up and introduced myself to a tall, thin man. Thirty minutes later Bob Shapiro and I were off to rock climb on the sea cliffs of Cornwall. Bob became my regular climbing partner, though I also hung out with and climbed with Simon Richardson and other members of the Oxford Mountaineering Club. As it turned out the faculty adviser to the mountaineering club was David Cox, who was also the vice master of my college. Professor Cox had been a bold climber in his day, but contracted paralytic polio while exploring in India. He went on to become president of the Alpine Club and maintained a keen interest in climbing. He often invited me to "high table" dinner to talk climbing.

"High table" is a multicourse gourmet feast in which the Oxford dons sit dressed in full academic regalia on a raised platform above the students, who eat the worst of British institutional food. The banquet starts with sherry and appetizers. This is followed by white wine with a fish course, red wine with a meat course, dessert wine with the fruit and cheese, and finally brandy, port, and cigars. During these intoxicating dinners Professor Cox would discuss my most recent ascents and regale me with stories of his climbs with Odell and Tilman in the 1930s. We became good friends. Dr. Cox told me about a bunch of Oxford fellowships that fund exploration. One was the "A. C. Irvine grant for Oxford gentlemen to enjoy strenuous holidays in mountains abroad," given in memory of Andrew Irvine, who died on Everest with George Leigh Mallory in 1924. Professor Cox controlled the purse strings; the more exotic the locale we chose, the more money he could give.

Bob Shapiro and I had similar attitudes and made a near-perfect team. Our climbing skills and personalities blended perfectly. It was a true partnership where we worked together without ego or competition. Together Bob and I pushed beyond what either of us might have done alone, whether on a one-day ascent in Wales or a two-month trip to climb a big wall in the jungles of New Guinea. We entered the realm of true adventure by setting out on improbable journeys—the kind where we didn't know if we could even reach our mountains, let alone climb them. Bob was more calculating and did the majority of the research and preparations. He planned our routes. I had the damn-the-torpedoes-full-speed-ahead enthusiasm to get up them. At the core we were always having fun together, and we both liked to climb. Before returning to America we planned a final dream trip. We received an A. C. Irvine grant, an Oxford Exploration Society grant, and an American Alpine Club grant, but we were still short on funds. A bit of serendipity led to *Sports Illustrated* picking up our tab and sending a reporter, Sam Moses, along on our quest to make the first ascent of the North Face of Carstensz Pyramid in Irian Jaya, New Guinea. It turned out to be the greatest pure adventure of my life.

We were incarcerated briefly in Indonesia before returning to America where I enrolled, a week late, at Harvard Medical School. At the end of my first year, in 1981, I was invited to join an American team that was going to try to make the first ascent of the East Face of Mount Everest. The trip was fully sponsored by ABC Television and several major equipment companies. It would be the first American climbing expedition in Tibet. Moreover, my teammates would be many of my climbing heroes.

I didn't think much about the consequences and left in an instant when I was asked to join the team as a last-minute substitute. We didn't get very close to the top of the mountain. Several of the most famous members of our team had ferocious arguments over where to climb. Others decided the entire face was suicidal. Still, for me, it was a great adventure. We eventually discovered a route that several of us believed could be climbed, although it would be an order of magnitude more difficult than any other path up Everest. After the expedition ended I joined one of my teammates, George Lowe, in climbing a nearby twenty-thousand-foot peak and then attempting a winter ascent of the highest mountain completely within Tibet. When I returned to America, I found myself out of medical school. The dean was incredulous. "You can't send a letter saying you're going to Tibet and then just leave!" I reapplied. After a long interview during which I assured a faculty committee that I did indeed want to be a doctor, I was allowed to return on probation.

Still, there was unfinished work to be done on the East Face of Mount Everest. Six members of our 1981 trip were going back and had secured National Geographic sponsorship. I completed a formal application for a leave of absence from medical school to return to Tibet. A few nights later I received a phone call. "Hello, is this Geoff Tabin?" the caller inquired.

"Yes," I answered.

"You are an idiot!"

"Excuse me?" I asked, confused.

"I cannot believe Harvard Medical School ever admitted anyone as dumb as you," he continued. "This is Dr. Mike Wiedman and I was reviewing your file. There's no way you will be given time off to climb. You'll face the dilemma of either never being a doctor or not going to Everest. Anyone with half the intelligence required to be admitted here should know that if you apply to do research, Harvard will give you money. I happen to be a professor of ophthalmology and am interested in the physiology of high altitude as it relates to the eye. I took the liberty of withdrawing your application for a leave of absence. Come to my house for dinner tomorrow night and we will discuss your research on high-altitude retinopathy to be conducted in Tibet on the East Face of Mount Everest!"

This led to the best team experience of my life and a wildly successful expedition. We made the first ascent of the East Face of Mount Everest by a route that is still, by far, the most difficult on the mountain and remains unrepeated after nearly twenty years. I received full credit for three months of a research elective, published a major academic article, and graduated from Harvard Medical School. Thinking of a possible career in sports medicine, I began a prestigious residency in orthopedic surgery. I did enjoy medicine and surgery, but I had more passion for climbing. I remember distinctly one morning during my third year in which several multiple trauma cases had arrived at our hospital around midnight. I had spent the rest of the night performing surgery to piece together a leg and pelvis. At six o'clock in the morning at X-ray rounds I showed the results of my work. The other residents looked at me with genuine envy.

"Excellent work! Gosh, what a great night you had! I didn't get to pin a pelvis until I was a fourth year," our chief resident told me.

I had been awake for twenty-six straight hours and had at least ten more hours of work ahead of me before I would have a chance to sit down. I was then planning to drive most of the night for big weekend climbing plans. This was going to be my only full weekend off that month. I would gladly have traded the pelvis surgery for a few hours of sleep. A few weeks later I got another phone call inviting me to join yet another sponsored climb in the Himalayas. Everyone I knew, including the few who had previously supported my decision to leave medical school, told me to finish my residency. It would only be two years. Then, they argued, I could write my own ticket. But I had seen how the conveyor belt to success works. The farther you get along the road, the harder it is to step off. My heart told me to climb. Now.

For the next several years I mainly climbed and explored. I became the fourth person to climb the highest mountain on all seven continents. I supported myself— relatively well—by working as a mountain guide, as well as giving slide shows about my climbs and motivational lectures to corporate groups about climbing Mount Everest. I wrote for several magazines, including serving as the "adventure" columnist for *Penthouse*. I also worked as a general doctor in both Africa and Nepal. In these developing countries most of the problems I faced were public health issues. I treated children dying from malnutrition and diarrhea, giving them intravenous medications and sending them out healthy only to see them return a few weeks later just as ill. This process often continued until I would helplessly watch a baby die. Infections that were easily treatable in the developed world killed the elderly. Then I watched a miracle. A Dutch team performed cataract surgery, and I saw a woman from our village who had been totally blind have her sight restored. She went from living the life of a neglected houseplant—kept in a dark corner of the house and occasionally carried out to spend a few hours in the sun or go to the bathroom—to having her life fully restored. She was no longer a burden and could return to being an active member of the family, cooking and caring for her grandchildren. I suddenly had a passion and direction in medicine.

When I returned to America, serendipity stepped in again. I had just decided that I would like to be an ophthalmologist. Eye surgery, however, is one of the most competitive fields in medicine. Having quit a residency and medical school twice, it was unlikely that any residency program in America would accept me. I was in Snowbird, Utah, with my girlfriend, Beth Peterson, who was then a fellow in plastic surgery in her home state of North Carolina. She rode the chairlift with a man who identified himself as a doctor. Beth said she was also a doctor. Later in their conversation she said she was with her boyfriend. He asked if I was also a doctor.

She replied in her southern drawl, "'Well, he graduated from Harvard Medical School, but he's just a *bum!* All he does is climb mountains."

To which her chairlift companion replied that he was an ophthalmologist and that he had just read a fascinating article about high-altitude retinopathy. Beth told him it was my paper he had read. We had dinner together that night. He described to me a position had just opened at the Brown University residency where he taught. I was on my way to guide a trip on Mount McKinley in Alaska. I flew from Salt Lake to Anchorage via Providence, Rhode Island, to interview for the job. Thanks to my "research" on the East Face of Mount Everest, I was given the residency.

I completed my training in America and faced the difficult question of how I could make a dent in the blinding diseases of mountainous Asia. It seemed like a bigger obstacle than any mountain I had faced. Serendipity led me to Professor Hugh Taylor, in Melbourne, Australia, who invited me to join him for a fellowship in corneal surgery. Taylor is one of the leading lights in international ophthalmology and had been a protégé of Fred Hollows, an iconoclastic and inspirational ophthalmologist who advocated training and empowering local doctors. Taylor sent me to Nepal to work at a high-volume cataract surgery camp with Dr. Sanduk Ruit as part of my fellowship year. Ruit is a master surgeon who had spent a year perfecting his microsurgical technique with Hollows in Sydney. He took modern, state-of-the-art cataract surgery with a lens implant and adapted it to Nepal. Ruit was performing perfect cataract surgery in seven minutes at a cost of twenty dollars. I was an instant convert to his methods and stayed in Nepal after my fellowship to work with him for a year. This also gave me the time and connections to explore and climb virgin peaks in remote areas.

I then returned to a faculty job at the University of Vermont College of Medicine. Before I left Nepal, Ruit and I vowed to work to overcome needless blindness in the Himalayan regions in our lifetime. We formed the Himalayan Cataract Project to teach other doctors in the region modern surgical techniques. Now in our eighth year, we are starting a full residency-training program in Nepal and are active in Tibet, Bhutan, Sikkim, India, and northern Pakistan. Soon after moving to Vermont I met an incredible woman who was a fellow ophthalmologist. Jean was a widow with three young girls. Turning perhaps my biggest and scariest blind corner yet, we fell in love and got married. At age forty I went from being a single degenerate with girlfriends on three continents to being a married degenerate with three daughters. We have gone on to have another daughter and a son.

Despite the family and the day job I still manage to keep climbing and to work in Asia several months of the year, something many people told me would be impossible. Serendipity again has led to my continued climbing. The most important factor has been a loving and tolerant wife. The next was that my youngest stepdaughter, Ali, turned out to be an amazingly gifted climber, and quickly became my excuse to get out and climb. Daddy–daughter bonding time meant exploring the local rock faces. Ali began climbing with me when she was eight. By the time she was eleven she could follow anything I could lead. At thirteen she scaled rock climbs more difficult than I had ever climbed. I now had to train to keep up with her. In a way things have come full circle for me. My job, work in the Himalayan regions, my family, and climbing have blended perfectly. Apart from my wife and children, most of my closest friends are my climbing partners and others who have taken on big risks and seemingly impossible challenges.

On September 11, 2001, I was sitting in a large boisterous restaurant in Kathmandu with Dr. Ruit and Narayan Shresta, the chief of police for the eastern region of Nepal. We had just finished dinner and were discussing the growing Maoist movement in the rural areas of Nepal and the problems in the Nepalese economy in the wake of the massacre of the royal family a few months earlier. In the midst of our conversation a nursery rhyme chirped from Mr. Shresta's polyester coat pocket—the prestigious sound of upper-class mobile phones in Nepal. He answered and then left the table to better hear his call. A few moments later he returned. He smiled at me and then said casually, "Well, doctor, I am now knowing you are also having problems in your country. I am hearing that both of your World Trade Centers are falling down and they are attacking your Pentagon. So, as I was saying, in the eastern region we are now approaching the Maoists on a village-by-village basis . . ."

His words did not really register. I assumed it was a misunderstanding. I had been working in Biratnagar seven years earlier when satellite television first reached Nepal. A panicked man from one of Nepal's wealthiest and best-educated families had rushed into my room. He was terrified. He told me that space aliens had attacked the United States and destroyed the White House. He was so upset that I called my dad, waking him at three in the morning to confirm that he was still alive and America still existed. It turned out that the television channel, which had been broadcasting CNN, was now showing the movie *Independence Day*. I reassured the man, and we calmly sat and watched Will Smith save the world.

I returned to my hotel on September 11 and this time watched the real CNN. To my horror I saw the events unfold on live television. I spoke to my wife on the phone. The next morning I departed with Dr. Ruit for Taplejung, a remote mountain village nestled under the shadow of Kanchenjunga, the world's third highest mountain, and a place where no one had ever been freed from the darkness of cataract blindness.

I thought for only a few minutes about whether we should alter the way we live because of terrorism. My philosophy remains the same. As long as we are alive we have choices. Any choice entails risks. I am already aware that this life we have is precious and short. We must maximize every moment. In the pages of this book you will hear stories about people who dream, who follow their hearts, and dare to be different. Despite tragedy, the joy of life remains. I continue to wonder what is around the next blind corner.

And I still like to climb.

QUEST
FOR
ADVENTURE

"Say, Geoff, wanna climb the North Face of Carstensz Pyramid?" I knew that in order to climb the two-thousand-foot, sheer rock wall to the highest point between the Andes and the Himalayas, we'd have to trek through dense jungle inhabited by the cannibalistic Dani tribesmen, among the most primitive people on earth. I also knew that because of terrorist activity, the Indonesian government had closed all access to the region of Irian Jaya, New Guinea, where the mountain is located. Finally, I didn't have enough money for the airfare to Jakarta, let alone to Irian Jaya.

It didn't take me long to reply. "Yes!"

My friend Johnny Petroske characterizes his need for great adventures as "feeding his rat." I know what he means. Floundering, way over my head, calms my wanderlust for a while. But inevitably, a gnawing starts in my gut. It gets stronger and stronger until the only thing I can do is set out in search of yet another wild adventure. My rat will be temporarily sated. But he always returns, fatter and more demanding.

I like a good adventure. The satisfaction of turning blind corners, relying on my wits and skills to succeed is, to me, the essence of adventure. In our mechanized world of processed food, electric socks, and in-flight entertainment, real adventures can be difficult to find. The expanding "adventure travel" industry offers exotic and sometimes strenuous trips all over the world. But they do not offer adventure. Your guide makes the decisions and ensures your safety. Pay your fee and enjoy the ride—in our litigious society, the outcome must never be left in doubt. You will see tigers and mountain peaks, but you won't get the feeling of accomplishment and joy that comes from doing it yourself. Then again, if you don't take a risk, you won't get hurt. Adventure, by definition, risks failure.

Society evolved to protect us from adventure. Thomas Hobbes wrote that life in the state of nature is "nasty, brutish, and short." For example, in the Masai tribe of Africa, very few warriors seek adventure vacations. After a hard week of fending off leopards with their short spears, they prefer to unwind in a nice quiet hut with plenty of fresh urine, cow's blood, and milk to drink. Still, the Masai do send their children out to kill a lion as part of a rite of manhood. Austrian explorer Heinrich Harrer said, "No man can summon all his strength, all his will, all his energy, for the last desperate move, till he is convinced the last bridge is down behind him and there is nowhere to go but on." Adventure tells you what you are capable of in ways that our civilization can't encompass.

We can only guess at the last words uttered by Bill Dunlop, a truck driver from Portland, Maine. Dunlop set out in July 1983 to discover his limits by circumnavigating the globe in a nine-foot sloop, and was last seen somewhere in the South Pacific in June 1984. He is presumed dead. Bill exemplifies the fine line that can exist between adventure and suicide.

When I agreed to join climber Bob Shapiro on an illegal excursion to scale the death wall in the middle of the jungle, I had spent seven years honing my rock and ice climbing skills, had acquired new route experience on the equatorial rock faces of Mount Kenya, and was familiar with Indonesian bureaucracy as the result of a month of wandering in Java and Bali. Bob was the perfect partner. In addition to being a superb mountaineer, he had excellent third-world jail experience. So even though I couldn't predict exactly what obstacles and dangers lay around the next turn, I foolishly thought it was likely that together we could surmount them.

One of my favorite parts of any adventure is the moment I become committed to it. There is a heady mix of tension, excitement, and fear. Then incredible things start happening as a cascade of unexpected events propels me into the mess of my own design. I have a deep respect for Goethe's couplet: "Whatever you can do, or dream you can, begin it. Boldness has genius, power, and magic in it." Word of our plans spread, and grants began to materialize from exploration and climbing foundations.

We were cruising. We had an objective that we could conceivably meet and that would push us to our limit, and we were now able to afford it. Mistakes in calculating these basic considerations can be costly. Ask Warren Pearson. A middle-aged man with a cardiac condition, Pearson decided to sail solo to Antarctica. For four years he secretly read everything he could about seamanship and the South Pole. Meanwhile he spent forty thousand dollars building a boat, fearing all along that if his wife found out she would veto the trip because of his ailing heart. Finally, in 1985, with no hands-on sailing experience, Pearson set out from Australia in a thirty-seven-foot ketch bound for Cape Denison, Antarctica. In the first minor storm he lost his engine and rudder. Sixty miles from shore his boat floundered and sank, and Pearson was scooped up by a passing freighter.

I had the ideal teammate in Bob—our climbing skills were similar and I knew him well enough to know I could count on him in times of stress. This was the best-case scenario and I did not have to resort to H. W. Tilman's approach. The taciturn British explorer who crossed Africa alone on a bicycle in 1933, and reached twenty-eight thousand feet on Mount Everest wearing tweeds in 1938, claimed that any enterprise that could not be planned on the back of an envelope should not be done. When he needed a crew to sail to the Arctic in 1957, Tilman found his shipmates by placing an ad in the *London Times* that read, "Hands wanted for long voyage in small boat; no pay, no prospects, not much pleasure."

Adventures can also result from conceiving new ways to tackle old problems. Larry Walters received an FAA citation for violating controlled-airspace laws after he soared to sixteen thousand feet in a lawn chair rigged with forty-two helium-filled weather balloons. Using a pellet gun, the intrepid Walters popped the balloons, one by one, to engineer his safe return to terra firma. This spirit comes from the same vein as Thor Heyerdahl, who sailed a balsa wood raft called the *Kon-Tiki* four thousand miles from Peru to Easter Island. Adventures that delve into the unknown have allowed people to fly, explore outer space, and plumb the oceans' depths. The pioneers of these new ideas have traditionally been called insane and suicidal by the general populace, before they have proven that their dreams can be achieved.

Facing the unknown, head-on, fuels additional curiosity that benefits all areas of life. Following the flow of an adventure can help turn life's misfortunes into opportunities. Heinrich Harrer was a young mountaineer from Austria when he climbed the North Face of the Eiger in 1938. Hitler hailed this first ascent of the "death wall of the Alps" as proof of Aryan superiority, and Harrer became a national hero. But Hitler decided it was important for the "fatherland" to have the altitude record, which then belonged to H. W. Tilman, who had ascended 25,800-foot Nanda Devi in the Himalayas in 1936. A German Himalayan expedition was organized to climb 26,400-foot Nanga Parbat, with Harrer as a lead climber. While the team was trekking through British-ruled India, World War II broke out, and the Germans were arrested and placed in a prison camp. Harrer then moved on to a much greater adventure. First he tunneled out of jail. Then he fled, without equipment, over twenty-one-thousand-foot Himalayan passes into Tibet, where, disguised as a Sikh, he eventually reached the Forbidden City of Lhasa. Harrer became one of the few Westerners to reach the Tibetan capital since Francis Younghusband had entered by force in 1903. He rose from destitute vagabond to tutor for the fourteen-year-old Dalai Lama, remaining as a modern Connecticut Yankee in King Arthur's court for seven years. He brought his practical knowledge of Western civilization to the isolated Tibetans while learning about their culture and exploring uncharted mountains.

Adventure stems from the state of mind that says, "I want to see what is around the next turn."

—

Bob and I thought that we had everything under control for our journey to the Carstensz Pyramid. We were joined by Sam Moses, a reporter from *Sports Illustrated* magazine and a serious climber. In Jakarta we obtained permission to fly to Jayapura, the center of government in Irian Jaya, and amassed letters of recommendation from the American ambassador, the Indonesian Sports Federation, and the minister for Irian Jaya affairs, each with a fancy letterhead. We expected to plunk the impressive stationery down in front of the local officials and immediately be issued a Surat Jalan, or permit to visit the island's interior.

Unfortunately, upon reaching Jayapura, we found that we had succeeded only in making ourselves too important for anyone to risk his career by giving a Surat Jalan allowing dignitaries to visit an area where they would certainly die. The Indonesians had been engaged in low-level warfare with the Dani tribe for several years: The Javanese occasionally got excited and machine-gunned a few Dani, who retaliated by blow-darting stray soldiers. Bob and I had been told by missionaries that "round eyes" are relatively safe. We tried to convince the local officials that we would be responsible for our own asses, but to no avail. The chief of police said that he needed permission from the mayor, who said that he needed permission from the military commander, who in turn needed permission from the chief of police.

We were at a roadblock of the type that can either make or break an adventure. The more frequently I have landed in situations where the choices are to think fast on my feet or sink, the better I have become at sizing up the options. For role models on how to handle these situations I look toward the British Burgess twins. They can quick-think their way out of jams better than anyone I know—maybe because they tend to get into more sticky situations than anyone else. Wearing long blond Prince

Valiant haircuts and standing an imposing six foot three with identical well-defined musculature, Adrian and Alan Burgess are a well-known sight from Lima to Kathmandu. They have been traveling and climbing full time for twenty years with no visible source of income. But many of their wildest adventures have taken place off the slopes. Recently the pair were descending from a difficult ascent of Fitzroy in Patagonia when they were pinned down for a week by a storm and ran out of food three days before it was safe to leave their ice cave. Returning to base camp, they discovered that they had been robbed. All their food was gone. The emaciated climbers were still two days' walk from the nearest town when they saw a flock of sheep. While Adrian started building a fire, Alan grabbed an ewe. Before reaching camp, a gaucho with a rifle rode up on him.

To be caught red-handed in a lawless land stealing another man's animal meant it was sink-or-swim time. Al quickly dropped his pants, secured his grip on the sheep's sides, and pressed the animal back into his groin. Keeping his head down, Al thrust his pelvis back and forth to simulate bestial sex until the horseman's angry voice went silent and, after what seemed to be an eternity, changed to laughter. Burgess kept the motion going until he heard the giggling gaucho ride away. Then he and his twin had dinner.

My party did not have to act quite so quickly or spectacularly. We had time to explore all of our possibilities. We thought that once we were out of Jayapura, we would be safe from government restrictions. Without the proper papers, however, we couldn't even leave the airport. Fortunately, I learned that some missionaries kept private landing strips. One immediate hurdle that Bob and I had to cross was Sam's refusal to do anything illegal. He was particularly stubborn on this point and is much larger and stronger than me or Bob. Luckily, he is also trusting, and he doesn't read Indonesian. One official had already offered to give us a Surat Jalan to fly to Wamena, the only Dani village where military protection could be assured. Wamena was several hundred miles from where we wanted to go, but the official said that there was a mountain nearby. After I gave him a bribe of fifty dollars, he gave me the Surat Jalan to Wamena: I showed it to Sam and told him we had permission to go to Carstensz Pyramid. Next, Bob and I had to find a bush pilot willing to fly us there.

Our savior came in the form of Leroy Kelm, a solidly built man with silver muttonchop sideburns who flies for the Missionary Air Fellowship and Seventh-Day Adventists. Since there are no roads in Irian Jaya, except in the vicinity of Jayapura, Leroy brings supplies to jungle villages and missionaries, flying daily over uncharted territory and visiting Stone Age cultures. At night he returns to his tidy home with his own landing strip, hangar, and manicured garden, and to his wife and daughter.

Leroy was intrigued by our plans and agreed to fly us as near to Carstensz Pyramid as possible. He regretted that we couldn't land at the Dani village of Ilaga, ten days' walk from the mountain. "All I have left is my Aero Commander," he explained. "I had a small Cessna I could have gotten in there, but I crashed it in the jungle a couple of months ago. The closest I can get with the bigger plane is Mulia, a couple of days farther out from Ilaga." We said that would be fine, but then he added, "The folks in Ilaga are at war with Mulia because of a few women and pigs that were stolen in a raid last month."

Realizing that it was our only option, we decided to go for it. Taking off at dawn, we were happy to find clear skies and spectacular views of the rugged jungle landscape. There were occasional clearings with grass huts, called *awis,* which looked like fat haystacks sunk in deep valleys. Leroy agreed to fly us over Carstensz Pyramid for an aerial view and to locate the path we would follow to reach it. We flew over a small cluster of huts that, he told us, was Mulia, and passed Ilaga a few minutes later. Leroy again lamented crashing his other plane, reiterating the problem of walking from Mulia. After we had circled the peak, he said, "Aw, what the heck, I'll try to put her down in that potato patch," pointing to a tiny clearing on a hillside above Ilaga. "I sure do wish I hadn't crashed the Cessna," he repeated, while he sent the Aero Commander into a deep dive. My terror mounted as Leroy began muttering the Lord's Prayer under his breath while we neared a muddy field.

We touched down neatly enough, but the look on Leroy's face told us that something was seriously wrong. The plane did not slow down, but instead skidded on the mud as if it were an icy highway.

We slid a couple hundred feet, with the drop at the end of the clearing looming larger and closer at an alarming rate. Then we veered toward an embankment, sliding diagonally until the tires started sinking in the mud. The plane spun violently to a halt, the left wingtip a mere fifteen feet from a drop-off into dense jungle.

I was still shaking like a leaf in a tornado when, twenty minutes later, Leroy turned the plane and prepared to say good-bye. "I can't believe you're going to trek from here and try to climb that mountain wall," he said. "That is absolutely the craziest thing I have ever heard of! Actually, I take that back—when I was home visiting my sister last year I saw some guys on television jump from a bridge, attached to long rubber bands. That was the craziest thing I've ever seen! But this is close."

Bob told him that I was the man he had seen bungee jumping on television. Without batting an eye Leroy said, "That figures," and left us to our adventure.

2

LEARNING
THE
LIMITS

To have a great adventure, and survive, requires good judgment. Good judgment comes from experience. Experience, of course, is the result of poor judgment. I finished high school in Illinois as a romantic dreamer in search of a quest. Like many teenagers, I had the ability to focus intensely on the present, maximizing the moment with little thought for long-term consequences. I headed for college thinking that I would devote my energies to the noble art of healing. However, I spent the first three months of my freshman year exploring the social opportunities, learning about my classmates, playing tennis, and searching for a romantic calling. Then reality hit. Exams approached and I hadn't opened a book in weeks.

I sat in the library, depressed and too overwhelmed to even start my work, when I saw a title on a bookshelf in front of me, *True Mountain Disaster Stories*. I began to read. After a couple of hours of learning about people freezing to death in crevasses, crawling off mountains with broken legs, and watching their friends swallowed by avalanches, I felt better. My problems were relatively minor. I focused on my work and got it done. From then on, whenever I felt down, I'd drift over to the Michael Ellenwood Curtis collection of mountaineering literature at the Yale Cross Campus Library. My habit grew to four hours a day as I became acquainted with mountaineering and adventure. Mountaineering became a romantic ideal for me. The pure, simple quest of man against nature and the struggle to ascertain one's own limits seemed a worthy goal. My reading also enthralled me with the variety of cultures, religions, and environments on our planet. I dreamed of the Alps, Africa, Antarctica, South America, and the Himalayas. H. W. Tilman, Heinrich Harrer, and Sir Richard Francis Burton became my heroes.

I finished my freshman year playing number one on the Yale varsity tennis team and contemplated playing on the pro tour. That summer I went to Europe with my doubles partner from junior tennis, Chuck Meurisse, to play the satellite tennis circuit. I lost consistently and watched the struggles of players, much better than I was, languishing on the minor-league tour. After losing in the qualifying round for the Swiss Grand Prix tournament in St. Moritz I noticed a sign advertising a "Climbing Week," celebrating the centenary of the Swiss Mountain Guides' associa-tion. I went to the guides' office, where I used my German-English dictionary to discern that they had "very strenuous," "strenuous," and "not so strenuous" tours available. I read the lists of the mountains and routes each group would climb. Unfortunately, I couldn't resist showing off my knowledge of the history of moun-taineering in the Alps, and asked, "Will the climb of the North Face of Piz Palu be via the Bonnati route?" The man said "Ja!" clearly excited to see that I knew the route. He promptly signed me up for the "most strenuous" tour.

No one else in my group of eight clients and four guides spoke English. The first day we hiked for eight hours up to a hut. During dinner the head guide gave a short speech in German. After the meal the rest of my group went to sleep. I was optimistic, because I clearly wasn't as tired from the day's walk as they were. It was only six o'clock in the evening and I was wired on excitement and nerves. At around eleven o'clock I tried to get some sleep. In the Alpine huts everyone sleeps together on long mattresses. This hut was crowded; it was impossible to lie down without bumping up against your neighbor. In addition, lots of people were snoring loudly, and many had been in the mountains for several weeks without bathing—the hut had a very ripe aroma. I lay awake until about half of the people got up at around midnight. I spread out and quickly fell asleep. The next thing I knew, a flashlight was shining in my face. Three angry people were swearing at me in German. My watch said it was two o'clock. Everyone else in my group had his backpack on and was ready to go. I struggled with my things in the dark and finally staggered out into the cold, starry night forty minutes later.

We walked uphill for a few hours until we reached the base of a glacier. Everyone quickly put on his crampons. Not only did I not know how to put on crampons, but I hadn't adjusted my pair to fit my boots. The guide fumbled with wrenches to adjust them in the dark while everyone began to get cold. A similar, but shorter fiasco occurred when it was time to tie into the rope. I was handed the middle of the rope and stared at it, dumbly, until the guide came over and tressed me up while muttering under his breath. By first light we were climbing an ice slope and it began to snow lightly. I became increasingly more nervous as the angle steepened. My calves began to burn and I started to get out of breath. Finally the slope eased and we pulled onto a flat area just as the storm increased into a blizzard.

This must be the summit, I thought. I was thrilled to have climbed my first mountain and relieved that I would be able to do the climbing on this tour. Gleefully, I took out my instamatic camera for a summit shot. I handed the camera to the man next to me, smiled broadly, and motioned for him to take my picture. *"Sheistmeister mensch!"* he said, turning away with a look of disgust. No one else in the group seemed very happy either. Oh well. *They must be mad because the storm obscures the view,* I thought. We ate a little chocolate and bread and started down, descending to a different hut. (Mountaineering huts are positioned in key places throughout the Alps and are used by anyone needing shelter or a rest.)

In this hut I met a man who spoke English. From him I learned that my group had not even attempted our proposed climb. We had hiked near the base, but because of me, we arrived too late to make the ascent. I had earned the affectionate nicknames of *"Dumsheist"* and *"Sheistmeister mensch"* from my companions. The storm kept me hutbound with eleven people who hated me for the next three days. My interpreter asked me about my climbs in America and wondered how I had gotten onto the "expert" course with no experience. I told him that I thought that I had signed up for the "strenuous tour." He laughed in amazement, and then explained the mistake to my guides. Three were in favor of sending me down. The youngest guide, Sepp, found my situation amusing and indicated that I should climb with him alone. I contemplated my options. I was in the mountains and had a guide willing to take me. I decided to follow the road to its conclusion. When the weather cleared my terror gave way to increasing enthusiasm as Sepp hauled me up the next three climbs to complete the tour.

I returned to Yale for my sophomore year with a short memory for the bad moments. I was happy to have made a few summits and survived and had no plans to climb ever again. Then, at a party, I heard an attractive woman talking about hiking in the Alps. She fit another of my romantic ideals and, in an effort to meet her, I casually mentioned that I'd done some mountain climbing in the Alps. She was not impressed and walked away, leaving me face to face with a fanatic. His eyes were fully dilated, his veiny forearms bulged, and talk of climbing brought out a manic grin. Henry Lester was gesticulating in the air about routes in the Shawangunks. He was excited to hear about my climbs. The next thing I knew Henry had decided that we had to go rock climbing together, tonight! We drove to the Shawangunk Mountains in the Catskill region of New York, the mecca of rock climbing on the East Coast. Henry soon found out that I was totally clueless. He was shocked to see me take out my hiking boots. It became clear that there were two choices: Either Henry would beat the shit out of me and leave me on the side of the road, or I would buy a pair of rock climbing shoes and endeavor to have Henry teach me to climb.

Henry taught me how to tie into the rope and belay my partner for safety. He then led up an overhanging face as if he were dancing up the stairs. I was unable to find any holds. I followed with a lot of help from the rope. Henry was a patient teacher. After one weekend I was enthralled with rock climbing: It is a combination of chess, vertical ballet, and gymnastics. You have to mentally figure out how to use the array of holds the mountain offers you, then perform the moves, which involve a harmony of strength, balance, and weight transfer. Climbing demands a total focus of the mind and body onto the moment: You are a being, stuck to a wall, where the entire universe boils down to reaching the next hold. There is no future or past, only now. Once I was able to climb a route of one difficulty, Henry moved things up a level so that I was always struggling at my limit. Henry trained like a maniac. I fell under his influence. I did pull-ups on small edges, traversed a rock wall climbing sideways until my forearms cramped. I eventually built up to the point where I mentally willed my fingers to hang on for half an hour after the cramps began. I went to Ragged Mountain, a small nearby crag, and set up top-ropes to safely practice at my limit most afternoons. When winter came, Henry and I went to New Hampshire to climb frozen waterfalls.

In my senior year Yale nominated me for the Rhodes scholarship and Marshall scholarship competitions, which provide two years of funded study in England. The criteria for selection were outlined in Cecil Rhodes's will as "citizenship, leadership, academic aptitude, and love of vigorous life." I was awarded a Marshall scholarship to study philosophy at Oxford University and deferred medical school. With my next two years fully funded, I was able to spend the summer after graduation doing nothing but climbing. I started in Yosemite Valley and hit most of the classic western rock climbing areas. I also climbed a few mountain routes in Colorado and Wyoming. By the time I left for England I was leading routes just below the top level in American rock climbing and had survived most of the stupid mistakes a beginner can make in the mountains.

During my first day at University College, Oxford, I met Bob Shapiro. Twenty minutes later we were off for the sea cliffs of Cornwall. Bob turned out to be an ideal partner. He had read many of the same romantic adventure books and is more than simply a dreamer—he is a doer. We followed a book called *Hard Rock* that describes the most famous climbs in Britain, ticking off the classics. To this point all of the climbs I had done were listed in guidebooks. I knew their difficulty, and I knew what I was getting myself into. Bob convinced me that real adventure involves going places where you don't know what you might encounter. For our first long vacation Bob tried hard to get me to hitchhike with him from England to the west coast of Africa, with stops to climb desert spires in the Sahara and to ride camels with the Bedouin. I turned him down to go on a trip to Thailand, Malaysia, and Indonesia with Ed Hundert, the smartest person I've ever met, and Jerry Howe, an ex–football player whose quiet craziness fed off my enthusiasms. The combination of our personalities and talents pushed the three of us into an exploration of ourselves and an expansion of our minds through the seamy underbelly of Southeast Asia.

Returning to Oxford for our second year, Bob and I renewed our climbing with a passion in both England and the Alps. Bob also found several indigenous trust funds that are remnants of the days when it was considered a sacred duty of Oxford gentlemen to go off and civilize people around the world. The vice master of our college, David Cox, steered us to the "A. C. Irvine Grant for Oxford gentlemen to explore strenuous holidays in mountains abroad."

Two of my favorite books from my Yale reading days were *White Nile* by Alan Moorehead, about the exploration of central Africa and the search for the source of the Nile (which led to the discovery of the Mountains of the Moon), and H. W. Tilman's *Snow on the Equator;* I particularly enjoyed his account of his climbs in the Ruwenzori Range. Bob and I received an A. C. Irvine Grant to go to Uganda to do technical climbing in the Ruwenzori. Unfortunately, political problems arose. The civil war that would lead to the fall of Idi Amin broke out a month before our departure. Bob, who had already spent time in African jails after illegally entering Benin on the national holiday celebrating the slaughter and ouster of all white people from Benin, thought it might still be safe in the mountains. The U.S. State Department, however, said, "Absolutely not! The remnants of Amin's troops are in the foothills of the Ruwenzori." So at the last minute we changed our plans to go to Tanzania, climb Mount Kilimanjaro, and then on to Kenya to do a technical ascent on Mount Kenya. The day before our departure the border between Tanzania and Kenya closed, so we opted to just go to Kenya. I knew that Mount Kenya was a huge mountain with no easy way to the top. Our goals were modest. We hoped to just get to the top of the mountain. We ended up making the first ascent of the hardest rock climb on Mount Kenya. This was a trip that changed my climbing focus and expanded my horizons into the realm of true adventure.

3

DAYENU—MIND
EXPANSION ON
MOUNT KENYA

Dayenu is a Hebrew word that translates to "it would have been enough" and was important to Moses, the first great Jewish alpinist, in his discussions with God. *Dayenu* is also relevant to me, and to Bob Shapiro, a modern Jewish alpinist with whom I had the pleasure of climbing on Mount Kenya during December and January 1980.

We intended to do the normal route and hoped to try a few of Mount Kenya's classics. I would have settled for the normal route only. It was my first journey to a big mountain, and just being there would have been enough. And even if I failed to acclimatize and couldn't get up anything, we still would be seeing a bit of Africa. *Dayenu*.

We flew via Cairo and opted for a stopover. Checking our equipment at the airport, we ventured into three of the most action-packed, outlandish days and nights imaginable. The details are not important. Suffice it to say that it was A-5 living, the Great Pyramid was ascended, and, in a region known as "The Mountain," a man named Mohammed got us acclimatized to an altitude higher than Messner will ever know (without oxygen). What the hell were we going to Kenya for? *Dayenu*.

Our descent from the heights of Cairo proved to be an epic. African airlines strictly enforce a twenty-kilo-per-man weight limit. To our horror, we discovered that it would cost two hundred dollars to get our equipment to Nairobi, which was more cash than we had. We hastily ducked out of the check-in line and retreated to a deserted corner of the airport to regroup. The strategy was clear: cut down on apparent weight. We emptied the haul sack on the ground and dressed ourselves in long underwear, wool pants, gaiters, mountain boots, wool sweaters, and, of course, our ceremonial necklace of Chouinard stoppers and hexes (part of Bob's religion). And we would not feel safe without hard hats on; this was, after all, 1980, and we were flying on a Boeing 727, which is a jet, like a DC-10. (There had already been two crashes that year.) Finally, we crammed the rest of our heavy hardware into carry-on luggage.

Confident of shedding the required weight and as inconspicuous as a Ubangi warrior in Phoenix, Arizona, we returned to the check-in counter. The Egyptians may never have seen climbing equipment, but they did recognize a financial opportunity. The supervisor came over and said that he admired our sense of adventure, while asking for a bit of *backsheesh*. Sweating profusely from the heat, we happily paid the five-dollar bribe and were off to Kenya.

East Africa is a tourist paradise. We spent our first eight days on a superb photographic safari. In the game parks we got to know John Rutt, an American climber who also hoped to climb on Mount Kenya but didn't have a partner. John had climbed at Hell's Gate Forge with Vince Fayad, one of the best local climbers. The three of us visited Vince at the Mountain Club of Kenya before heading to the mountain. He was extremely helpful, telling us all the routes that were in condition and giving us recommendations. Vince also cautioned us not to be too confident: Due to weather and altitude, only a small percentage of competent climbers reach the summit, and even fewer do more than one route.

The next day John, Bob, and I arrived in Naro Moro, where the approach to the mountain starts. This is also where the logistical hassles begin. It is possible to go by car for seventeen miles up a dirt track to the Met Station at ten thousand feet. Unfortunately, the Naro Moro River Lodge has a monopoly on four-wheel-drive transportation and charges seventy dollars for the forty-minute journey. We thus had to spend a full day trying to hitch a ride. The next problem was getting our things up the mountain. We had three weeks' worth of food in addition to all of our climbing and camping gear. The porters charge higher rates in the Christmas season. Being on a low budget, we decided to make two carries each rather than pay for the porters. We divided our gear into three heavy and three light sacks and began hiking with the heavier ones.

The trail up Mount Kenya is phenomenally beautiful, passing through a bamboo forest, thick rain forest, and then into an area called the vertical bog. It is as unpleasant as the name implies. We trudged in constant drizzle and mud above the ankle for over an hour. This steep section finally gives way to the lovely Teleki Valley with giant groundsel and lobelia plants. As dusk approached, we arrived at the Teleki hut at 13,500 feet, where we spent Christmas Eve.

Our Christmas present was a spectacular view of the peaks and a three-hour slog to base camp. We pitched our tents in a beautiful meadow, bordered by a glacial stream, directly below Midget Peak at 14,500 feet. I had a bit of altitude sickness, and all three of us were exhausted. After a short discussion—"What do you guys think about getting porters to bring up the rest of our gear?" "Definitely." "I'm for it"—we reached the hard question of who would go to get them. Twenty minutes later I walked down to the porters' shelter near Klarwill's hut at 13,650 feet and hired three men. We had to pay double rates because of Christmas but, lazing about all afternoon and evening, we gloated that we were paying ourselves three dollars an hour to take it easy. A real bargain.

In the morning we felt better and decided to attempt the normal route the following day. We hiked to Point Lenana at 16,355 feet, which is the fourth highest peak and attainable without technical climbing. We descended to Top Hut, where we spent a restless night. At five o'clock we crossed the Lewis Glacier. As the first rays of sun warmed the rock, John, Bob, and I tied into our ropes and began to climb the "normal route." The guidebook time is four and a half hours to the summit of Nelion, and our 6 A.M. start placed us there just before five in the afternoon. Unfortunately, we never got seriously off route, encountered bad weather, or suffered from the altitude, and thus were left without an excuse for our slow time.

We decided to spend the night in the four-man Lobonar shelter, a structure that Ian Howell made thirteen solo ascents of the mountain to build. After that much effort, we felt obliged to stay. Also, our tired bodies weren't fit for the descent even if we had time for it. Lastly, we stayed on Nelion in the hope of crossing over to Batian, the higher of Mount Kenya's twin summits, in the morning. Expecting to be able to descend the same day, we had not brought any extra clothing or food, and the twelve hours of darkness seemed interminable. Rising directly on the equator, the sunlight temperature on Mount Kenya is very warm. At night, however, you realize that you are above seventeen thousand feet—the temperature is well below freezing. Searching for extra padding to stuff down our clothes for insulation, we discovered a hut register and read about Ian Allen and Ian Howell doing the first ascent of Equator, a very hard line on the Diamond Buttress, the day before. Shivering and rubbing our feet with tired hands, we wondered what kind of supermen could climb that hard at this altitude.

In the morning our frozen bodies were greeted by swirling powder snow and a two-inch blanket on the top. Batian was out of the question. With the first slowing of the storm at eleven o'clock we began the descent. By noon the sun was shining brightly. The horrors we feared never came about. Back at camp we gorged ourselves to celebrate the first big-mountain ascent made by John and me. *Dayenu.*

As the sun went down, we watched a waterfall flowing down the Diamond Couloir and realized that if we wanted to try an ice route we would have to go soon. The next morning Bob and I departed camp at five o'clock to attempt the classic Ice-Window Route. It follows a hidden gully just right of the Diamond Couloir. The paths merge at the top of the Chouinard-Covington headwall. The Window is not as desperate as its neighbor, averaging fifty-five-degree mixed rock and ice climbing with only one short vertical section on its thousand-foot length. Ideal ice conditions on this side of the mountain are in the July-to-October season, and we encountered soft-fading ice in places and verglassed rock for three hundred feet.

Enjoyable climbing led us into the spectacular ice cave that gives the route its name. We entered a vast cavern guarded by sixty-foot icicles, climbed to the back, and chopped a window out of the other side. Being the first party on the route since September, we had to hack through three feet of solid blue ice. The exposure is incredible as you wriggle out of the window to stand near the top of the Diamond Couloir's headwall with 180 feet of vertical ice beneath. Happily it soon leans back to the comfortable sixty degrees of the Diamond Glacier, which leads to the Gate of the Mists.

Not wishing to endure another uncomfortable night out, we carried food, a stove, extra clothing, and sleeping bags on the climb. The heavy packs slowed us down and we again reached the summit just before dark, prepared for the bivouac. We were not, however, prepared for the company. This we found aplenty in the shelter. Four Italians who spoke no English smiled at us as we pushed the aluminum door open. We spent a warm but contorted night. The next morning the sun shone brightly and we crossed over to Batian for photographs on the highest summit of Mount Kenya.

Back at camp we celebrated the classic ascent with cold Jell-O crystals and straight glucolin—our MSR stoves refused to work with the fuel we bought in Kenya. The next day, while festering in the sun, we decided that two summit climbs were enough. We would do a rock route on Point John and one on Midget Peak and then head down to the outcrops where we belonged. The next afternoon Bob and I climbed the easy South East Gully to the top of Point John. On the way back to camp Bob noticed a beautiful slab that seemed to lead nowhere. Just our type of climb.

At noon the next day I began the first pitch with John belaying and Bob taking photographs of our first, first ascent. The climbing was delicate, but on balance, gradually steepening from seventy-five degrees to near vertical at the stance 150 feet up. I considered abseiling off, but the dihedral above looked like it might go and I only had a single rope. Thus I brought Bob up and set out on the next pitch. It was difficult, with loose rock, and I laced it with runners. The excitement of whether the route would go, combined with the increase in commitment, added an element I had never before experienced in climbing.

After 150 feet I arrived at a stance and pondered the alternatives. It looked feasible to move up and right into an easy gully but then the route would lead nowhere, giving a hard four-hundred-foot start to an easy gully climb. The other choice was to move left on nearly nonexistent holds and try to gain an overhanging crack that might lead to the South Ridge. I asked Bob if he wanted to lead. He generously said that since this was my first, first ascent I could do all the leading. Thanks a lot.

I went up twenty feet and placed a thumbnail-sized metal wedge into a crack, clipped the rope to it, and decided to try to reach the overhanging crack. I could see two very thin holds and, rechecking my "protection," moved left. I told Bob to watch me, and that after I fell I would pendulum to the crack. More microedges, the size of the edge of a quarter, materialized, and twenty-five feet later my nervous body reached the crack, where I happily slotted a "Friend," a self-camming anchor, and moved up on good jams to a hanging belay. The next pitch followed the crack for a few feet and then moved left again on a vertical face with large incut holds for the full 165-foot length of my rope to a nice roomy ledge. Bob and I were ecstatic. After one short enjoyable pitch we joined the classic Grade IV South Ridge.

The Tabin-Shapiro direct start provided us with a strong feeling of creative accomplishment. Moreover, we came to the happy realization that ordinary mortals can safely do serious technical climbing at altitude. *Dayenu.*

Back in camp we were racing with adrenaline; our natural high lasted all night. The next day Bob opted for a rest and John and I decided to do an afternoon ascent of Midget Peak. Approaching the gully between Point John and Midget, I noticed a possible line leading up and right and suggested that we give it a try. We checked the guidebook to make certain that it was not there, and set off. The second pitch went back slightly left, and after five long pitches we were on the summit. The climbing was not overly hard. Nor was the climbing overly pleasant, with sharp, prickly lichens cutting our fingers on many holds and some loose rock. Still, the same thrill of adventure made the route worthwhile.

Climbing technically difficult rock following a guidebook never gave this sense of accomplishment. In two days my climbing horizons had been broadened from a rock gymnastics approach to an understanding of the thrills of commitment and the unknown that a big mountain can provide. Our trip to Mount Kenya was successful in mental as well as physical accomplishments. *Dayenu.*

Back at camp I encountered one stoked Bob Shapiro. He had been receiving propaganda all day from Vince Fayad, who was now camped directly below us. Vince had done the second ascent of the Diamond Buttress Original Route with Ian Allen and described it as the best hard rock route on the mountain. In addition to the route's quality, he convinced Bob that doing the fourth ascent would be a great way to end an already successful climbing holiday. Knowing that I was on a first-ascent kick, Bob quickly pointed out that ours would be the first all-American and first Jewish rope on the Diamond Buttress. Enough said.

We set out to do the type of climb that one week before we had believed was only accessible to a strange breed of superhuman high-altitude hardmen. The psychological barriers were broken down. A solid week of sunshine put the rock in perfect condition for free climbing. The first two pitches yielded interesting and sustained difficult rock climbing. Surprisingly we felt as comfortable as if we were at sea level, and our confidence grew. On the third pitch I encountered a fixed piton, clipped the rope into it, and turned a six-foot overhang with large incut holds. When Bob joined me at the belay he said that I had just freed the aid overhang. "Bullshit," I said. Bob, who had been given the route description by Vince, was certain it was the aid overhang and decided we should try to free the entire route. I was dubious, as a massive roof loomed a few hundred feet higher.

Two pitches later I found myself 130 feet above Bob with nowhere to go. I was hanging from a single finger wedged in a crack just above a fixed piton and could see no useful holds above me. After ten minutes my arms were pumped and my mind was gripping up. Finally, I downclimbed twenty-five feet and brought Bob up. "You better lead this crack, I can't do it," I muttered. Bob claimed that this was the tension traverse and it was time to move right. "Bullshit," I said. Bob was insistent. I protested that we were getting off route, believing that we hadn't even reached the aid overhang.

Bob led off, ending all discussion. After clipping the rope into a piton, he moved right on fingernail edges and reached the next dihedral without coming off. He gave a whoop of joy. "We freed the tension traverse," he happily yelled back, adding, "Very thin stuff." "Bullshit," I said. "It was thin," Bob insisted. "I believe that, but I don't think this is the route," I yelled.

By now the rope was tugging at me and I had no choice but to follow. I was not convinced we were on route until we reached the "three-star" bivy ledge that I had heard Vince describe. I gave out a whoop and yelled, "Bob, we freed the Diamond Buttress."

Over dinner we happily discussed the day's accomplishments. According to Vince, we were above the four hardest pitches and all of the aid. All of the previous parties had spent two nights on the face. We decided that if we dropped our extra hardware and bivy gear down the Diamond Couloir, we could get up and off the same day. After a spectacular starry night Bob brought his very full pack to the couloir, and we watched our extra gear fall and land on the glacier below. This done, we set off with only one light load, which the second carried.

At noon we began to regret our decision, finding ourselves still far below the summit. The second day's climbing was sustained and hard with a less obvious line to follow. We got slightly off route and had to turn a strenuous overhang and climb two energy-sapping steep cracks, all above 16,500 feet. When we finally reached the easy summit ridge it was after four in the afternoon. We still had four easy full-rope-length runouts to the summit of Batian, the descent into the Gate of the Mists, and the climb back up to Nelion, before starting the descent. We arrived on Nelion, exhausted, shortly after five. With only cagoules to go over our sweaters, we were not eager to spend the night and immediately headed down. This was our third descent, and knowing exactly where to find the abseils, we reached the Lewis Glacier just before dark.

It was not the first ascents or the freeing of the buttress that was most mean-ingful, but the psychological breakthrough we made. We discovered that after fifteen days of climbing above fourteen thousand feet we could acclimatize like the mythi-cal supermen. We gained the confidence to extend ourselves on a big mountain in a remote setting. We realized that the most difficult obstacles to surmount in climb-ing, as in life, are mental. All this, and all we had dreamed of was making it to the summit of Mount Kenya. *Dayenu!*

4

THE WORLD'S MOST DARING SPORTSMAN

In 1933 H. W. Tilman decided he'd like to check out the beach at Cameroon. Only problem was, at that moment Tilman happened to be at his beachfront home in Mombassa, about three thousand miles away. To reach Cameroon's sandy shore required the first east-to-west traverse of Africa through the dense, uncharted jungles of Uganda and the Congo. Tilman was undeterred. Alone on his bicycle, armed only with a machete, he rode off into the sunset, probably pausing each afternoon at four for tea. A little more than two months later he reached his destination. At the age of fifty-six, with almost twenty-five years of exploration in Africa and the Himalayas behind him, the irrepressible old codger then bought a boat and, over several expeditions, eventually sailed it around the world. He even made a trip to the South Pole, which he reached just before his sixty-ninth birthday.

The decline of the British Empire and an increasingly well-charted globe have made the Tilmans of this world a dying breed. Once, an Oxford education, tweed trousers, two pairs of socks, and a heavy coat were all a British gentleman explorer needed to make an all-out assault on the summit of Mount Everest. These days it seems to require a six-figure budget, international sponsorship, and a small army of Sherpas to get that far. Indeed, "the right stuff" is in distressingly short supply. Or seems to be, anyway, until you cast your eye toward one David Kirke and that cradle of the eccentric idle rich, the university town of Oxford, England.

Kirke does not look like an adventurer or a hero of any kind. In fact, seen in his army-surplus coat (secured with safety pins) after a typical Friday evening at a smoky Oxford pub called "The Bear," he looks as though he might need help walking home. With a slight beer drinker's paunch, bristling gray-flecked beard topped by bulging eyes, and receding brown curls, he seems the quintessential upper-class twit gone to seed. Which he is. But he also happens to be the roguish kingpin of the world's only club devoted exclusively to those sports and diversions so dangerous, so improbable, so utterly outlandish that no one else would even think of them, let alone try them. As founder, director, idea man, and prime mover of the Oxford Dangerous Sports Club, Kirke is out to prove that the call of the wild still comes through loud and clear. He continually demonstrates that neither skill nor experience is needed to set a hang gliding record, fly an airplane, climb a mountain, scale a live volcano, or leap from a high-speed train. As Kirke carries his celebration of the dilettante to manic extremes, his actions tend to confirm what his friends cheerfully admit: He is, by all standards, deranged.

Even in his upbringing, the thirty-four-year-old Kirke seems to have been molded as a Victorian adventurer. With an education in self-reliance through his early years, Kirke proceeded, well prepared, to Oxford. He spent three undistinguished years there, as befits a man of good taste, leaving with a "gentleman's third" in English literature to take up journalism in London. Whatever the initial romance of a profession that involved watching other people do exciting things, Kirke found early on that he much preferred being watched himself. Helped by the fact that no one seemed to think he was destined to be a great journalist, Kirke packed his bags in 1970 and returned to Oxford.

There, with Christopher Baker and Ed Hulton, two friends who share a bit of that wild gleam that lights Kirke's eyes, he set about experimenting with adventure. Where some Oxonians become self-taught experts in dead languages or Australian wines, he would make himself the world expert on what he calls life-questioning sport.

The first step was to sample the traditional dangerous sports. During the summer of 1977, with no expertise and little equipment, Kirke clambered to the top of the Matterhorn. That August, without ceremony or training, he and Baker launched themselves down the Landquart in Switzerland, thus becoming the greenest of novices ever to survive what is probably Europe's most treacherous stretch of white water.

The reckless successes began piling up as Kirke, fired by his growing enthusiasm for danger, looked for ever-greater potential disasters. Later that summer, though he lacked a pilot's license, he somehow rented a small airplane, which he managed to get airborne and return safely to earth without ever having flown one of the contraptions before.

The birth of the Oxford Dangerous Sports Club, however, was delayed until October, when Kirke planned his first group activity: champagne brunch for six, followed by a jump from Rockall, a sixty-three-foot sea stack off the coast of Scotland. After a climb that was treacherous in itself, Kirke's little party looked down to where the ebb and flow of crashing waves created a cycle of filling and emptying pools— one instant safely full, the next nothing but bare rock for a diver to land on. Deciding that discretion was, indeed, the better part of valor, several would-be members of Kirke's new club turned around and risked the climb back down. Two people finally jumped, and Kirke himself dived headfirst into the freezing water, though he had never even jumped from a high board before. All that finally marred this true baptism of the club was that the boys already knew how to swim.

The following summer, for Kirke and his club, was devoted to experimentation. Having by then tried all traditional dangerous sports of importance, they felt it was time to move on, to invent new ones. In addition to the simple thrill that novelty provided—and it was becoming increasingly hard to thrill Kirke—there was an increased element of risk involved. Danger was relatively easy to evaluate when you knew what had happened before; it assumed mysterious dimensions, however, when the odds were unknown. It was at about this time that the calculations for all the group's events—the crucial calculations of speed, velocity, impact, and so forth that determined survivability—were turned over to Simon Keeling and Alan Weston, two of Kirke's buddies who had taken their respective Oxford degrees in engineering and computing, and who thus could be counted on to produce reasonably reliable estimates. However, because the dangerous sportsmen were not about to let the tedious certitude of modern science interfere with the spirit of their challenge to nature, they adhered to a policy of undertaking only adventures never before attempted, so that there would always be an element of uncertainty involved.

Thus did various bobsled runs in France and Switzerland take on new dimensions in the summer of 1979, when negotiated atop a block of ice fitted with a seat. Wheelchairs turned nearly lethal as they were moved out of hospital corridors and onto steep hillsides for the purpose of quick descent. During the traditional running of the bulls through the narrow Spanish streets of Pamplona, Kirke and company substituted skateboards for foot speed. And in what was planned as the climax of the summer, the tuxedo-clad sportsmen were to have parachuted into the Longleat animal park's lion enclosure, each armed with a revolver containing only one bullet. The fact that this event never came off probably had more to do with lack of organization than with lack of nerve.

Exactly what makes Kirke tread the edge of the great abyss with such regularity is impossible to say for sure. When he is not risking a final farewell, his daily schedule borders on the unbearably routine—a sort of burlesque of life in Oxford. Emerging every day about noon from his chaotic apartment, where books are strewn all over and trophies of dangerous ventures litter the shelves, he ambles to the center of town in time for lunch at The Bear. There, surrounded by his cronies, the world's most daring sportsman sits eating omelets and drinking pints of beer until the sun goes down. Then it's off to his club, where he can sit in a leather wing chair and read the papers with England's finest, warmed by frequent doses of good Scotch.

Now, admittedly, this is not the regimen of either genius or fitness. And indeed, Kirke takes unconcealed pride in the fact that he is usually at least five years the senior of his fellow Dangerous Sports Club members and apparently in the worst shape of all. He also takes pride in the fact that while climbing Kilimanjaro, he went straight to the nineteen-thousand-foot summit without missing a stride, while his young companions wheezed and gasped their way up behind him.

The secret of his stamina and of his remarkable ability to survive the unsurvivable is neither training nor any particular talent, but a psychological toughness that produces unparalleled performances through the sheer force of his will. Kirke assumes he will survive and, believing it, he does. With heroes of the era of the amateur—with men like Scott in the Antarctic and Stanley in Africa—he shares a mental determination that enables him to endure horrendous pain and to think clearly in the most disconcerting of crises. "Everyone has a certain level of anxiety," he says. "I direct my anxiety into the events I attempt. The rest of my life is very calm."

Maybe so, but to the impartial observer, Kirke's behavior is not as calm as he claims. A man who prefers extremes in every aspect of life, Kirke replaces the disintegrating army coat and safety pins each evening with an equally battered black tie and tails. He throws a succession of extravagant parties that seem to keep him stylishly in the hole. It may ultimately be more accurate to say that Kirke's "events" are the safety valve for anxieties and preoccupations that are larger than life.

But whatever the cause, there can be no doubt that by the fall of 1978, the manic gleam in Kirke's eyes had inspired a full-fledged organization of dangerous sportsmen and assorted hangers-on. With the trio of Baker, Weston, and Keeling forming the core of the club around Kirke, the sportsmen were beginning to stir interest in wider circles. Since their personal resources were rapidly dwindling and their schemes growing exponentially more expensive, that was a very good thing. Late in 1978 they enlisted the support of an independent film-production company and the BBC for a hang gliding expedition off Mount Kilimanjaro. Kirke had never bothered to master the sport, of course, but his smooth talking and confident air convinced the men holding the purse strings that he was a champion.

The expedition served to clinch Kirke's status as a legend among the cognoscenti and, at the same time, proved a disaster for the BBC. Loaded down with hang gliding apparatus, supplies, and the obligatory formal wear, two of Kirke's companions abandoned the attempt during the tortuous ascent. Weston, the only experienced hang glider in the group, got to the top but crashed on takeoff, destroying his glider and injuring his ankle. Kirke, meanwhile, managed a takeoff, then bounced his wingtip off the mountainside, swooped upward, and screamed back toward earth in a nylon-and-metal-tubed power dive leftward. The BBC captured approximately twelve seconds of filmed flight, which depicted the Kirke posterior disappearing into surrounding clouds. But what was the end of a short film clip best forgotten by the BBC was only the beginning for Kirke. Once enveloped by clouds, he continued to fly through the mist without a compass or an altimeter, eventually coming in for a gentle landing on a coffee plantation twenty-five miles away.

The Kilimanjaro exploit proved to be a crucial watershed in the history of dangerous sports. With it came a greater cohesiveness of the group and, symbolic of that new clubbiness, an official club tie (a silver wheelchair on black background). It also established the club as a media darling—and, just as important, convinced the sportsmen that anything they did was a media event. Kirke continued to indulge a mania for secrecy about preparations for the group's events, but he was increasingly receptive to the idea of coverage once the events were under way, particularly if that meant money. And finally, it was Kilimanjaro that first prompted him to speculate seriously about what was to become the club's most famous invention—a modern variation on an ancient puberty ritual that would be suitable for mass-media coverage.

I met Kirke around this time. Bob Shapiro and I had just returned from our successful climbing trip to Mount Kenya and were fired up for more equatorial ice climbing adventures. We had both read Heinrich Harrer's book *I Came from the Stone Age* about his exploration and climbs in the Carstensz Range of Irian Jaya, New Guinea. His encounters with the Stone Age Dani natives had me mesmerized, and I'd long dreamed of going there. The Indonesian government had closed access to the region, however, and the plan was on indefinite hold. About this time British climber Peter Boardman, who had just returned from Irian Jaya, gave a slide show about his trip. One look at his slide of the unclimbed two-thousand-foot rock wall on the North Face of Carstensz Pyramid was enough. Bob and I immediately began applying for grants.

A few evenings later we were at The Bear discussing the possible trip. David Kirke and Alan Weston, a classmate of mine in University College, sat at our table. "New Guinea?" Kirke asked, his interest piqued. "You must try vine jumping!"

He explained in detail a curious New Guinea rite of passage in which boys tie springy vines to their ankles, then leap from high trees. They hurtle, headfirst, toward the ground until the vine snaps them to a mind-jolting halt inches from the forest floor.

"Only we'll need something better than vines," Kirke said, almost to himself. He had already forgotten our climbing trip and was busily planning the details of his next "event." We were soon joined by Simon Keeling and many pints of beer. Before dawn it was jointly decided that bungee cord would be the perfect modern urban vine and that bridges should substitute for platforms in tall trees.

The first jump, on April Fools' Day, 1979, was from one of England's highest suspension bridges, the 245-foot Clifton Bridge in Bristol. One end of the bungee was tied to the bridge, the other to an improvised harness designed by Keeling and Weston. With champagne toasts, Kirke, Weston, Keeling, and Tim Hunt—younger brother of champion race-car driver James Hunt—all stepped off. Like tuxedo-clad yo-yos, the dangerous sportsmen dropped the full length of their cords, stretched another 100 feet waterward, and bounced back up nearly 200 feet; then it was down and up and down again, in bounces of decreasing magnitude, until they hung, limp but ecstatic, 120 feet below the bridge. It was only after Weston had popped the cork on the celebratory champagne he'd carried along on the leap that the remaining members of the party hauled them back up to the bridge.

Arrested and photographed, the sportsmen had achieved both of their objectives: They had garnered national publicity, and all four jumpers were alive, which proved that their new sport could be played. After another trial leap that October from the Golden Gate Bridge in San Francisco, Kirke decided they were ready for the big time.

What he had his eye on was nothing less than the world's highest suspension bridge. Like a toothpick slung across a funnel, the 1,260-foot Royal Gorge Bridge spans the Arkansas River just outside Cañon City, Colorado. The gap, which is about eight hundred feet wide at the top, narrows to less than sixty feet at the base. Without even having seen the bridge, the sportsmen were eager to jump from it. Keeling and Weston got to work on their computations. After much deliberation, they announced that a bungee cord 415 feet long, with Kirke attached, could be expected to stretch at least that distance again; Kirke would be subjected to a deceleration force of five gs and would pass out on the rebound.

Kirke was intrigued. "This will require total control, mental and physical, and you won't know the result until you wake up. How excellent!" he exclaimed. "If you do everything correctly up to the point you pass out, then you'll survive, but if you don't—if you make a mistake—then you'll die not even feeling your own death." But even as they indulged in such existential reflection, Kirke and his friends lost no time wrapping up the publicity and the dollar side of the expedition.

Back in early 1980 *That's Incredible!* —the now notorious ABC show that specialized in videotaping self-inflicted mutilation for mass consumption—had a lot less to its discredit than it soon would. Kirke was convinced that anything called *That's Incredible!* simply had to need his kind of adventure. As it turned out, he was right.

Kirke and the producers agreed on an eighteen-thousand-dollar fee to fill the club's coffers. Fill them, that is, so they could be emptied again. For, in the spirit of the club, Kirke ordained that every cent of the take would be spent on the jump itself and associated celebration.

The television company scheduled the filming for March 6, 1980, and requested three jumpers. Kirke decided to do it his way or not at all. He insisted on flying over as many of the club members as wanted to go, and most of them converged on London first for a preflight party. From Paris came Hunt and Hubert Gibbs, a shy young musician who was to be the jump's official pianist. From Ireland came ex-Oxonian Anthony Murphy and his wife, Sophia. Oxford yielded Murphy's brother Rob, Kirke, and me, rock climber extraordinaire. I was in charge of tying the bungee cords. Kirke and I had become good friends. We enjoyed living vicariously through each other's brand of adventure. Recently he had consulted me on harnesses and knot tying for his bungees.

On the morning of the scheduled departure, a mildly intoxicated David Kirke pounded on my door at three o'clock. "Geoff," he stated matter-of-factly, "do come along to America and have a bit of sport with us."

"Huh?" I muttered. "What time is it?"

"Nearly half three," Kirke replied. "Our flight to San Francisco leaves from Heathrow at ten."

"David, I can't. I have a tutorial at eleven o'clock this morning and exams coming up," I argued.

"Pitch it!" he demanded. "We quite need you to fix the harnesses and handle the safety angle. I will pick up all of your expenses. What do you say?"

I thought to myself for a moment. *Will I regret this more if I do it or if I don't do it?* An instant later, now fully awake, I said, "Okay I'm with you."

David smiled his broad grin. "Excellent! See you at the airport in a few hours." He handed me a club tie, shook my hand, then vanished back into the parties of the night.

Finally, tired and drunk from their various preliminary celebrations, the party converged on San Francisco five days before the scheduled jump. Weston was to meet up with the crew at the jump site, but Paul Foulon, Weston's stepbrother and the group's second American, drove down from Portland in his pickup—bringing with him the bungees used in the Golden Gate jump the year before.

"Every event may be my last," Kirke declared, before we set out for Colorado in a convoy comprised of a white Cadillac convertible, two small trailers, and the pick-up. "Festivity is required. If anything goes wrong, the party must celebrate life, not mourn death."

A parody of a motorcade, the Dangerous Sports Caravan weaved, skidded, and violated the law at an average of seventy miles per hour across the Great American West, white Cadillac in the lead, packed to the brim with silly-looking weirdos in ties and tails. To the uninitiated, the convoy itself looked like dangerous sport: $1,280 worth of liquor stowed in the trunk, all being pumped with indecent haste into the already saturated livers of Britain's sickest and strangest, who even in England could not be relied on to find the right side of the road.

No one slept, of course, for total party required total commitment. Besides, if the revelers tried to sleep, they might actually pass out, and given the amount of alcohol diluting the blood of those Englishmen, it might be weeks before they would see daylight again. After eighteen hours of continuous merrymaking, the Dangerous Sports Club pulled into the truck stop in Ely, Nevada, at six o'clock in the morning. The boys tightened their bow ties and swaggered in. Forty-five truckers' jaws dropped into sedimented cups of coffee. Warily, the waitress approached. Kirke smiled his evil smile, while all eyes bulged expectantly. Anthony Murphy, part of the supporting cast, stepped diffidently forward. Dressed in a Royal Navy dinner jacket with tails, he peered benevolently at the permanent-waved waitress. "Excuse me, but can you tell me, how *viscous* is your porridge?"

Later that day, as we crossed into Utah, a storm blew in, and how the Brits loved it! Windows rolled up, visibility zero, we fishtailed wildly down the invisible road—forty miles an hour on a skating rink you couldn't even see! This was danger fit for dangerous men, and they reveled in every bit of it. With public school voices jabbering at cocktail-party levels, the drunken caravan roared on into the dark, a meteor of the English upper class burning insanely across the snowdrifts of the American desert.

We arrived in Cañon City, fourteen miles outside Royal Gorge, one day before the jump. Up to that point the club had been a bit worried about how seriously *That's Incredible!* was going to take its sport. One look at producer Alan Landsburg's preparations and all were reassured. In addition to a dozen cameramen, a helicopter had been rented for some aerial shots. Eyeing the chopper wistfully, Kirke said, "There may be some tangible benefits from this television company, after all. Perhaps I could persuade them to let me have a go with their helicopter."

At the site, the boys took a look around—and down. Standing atop the windswept bridge, 1,053 feet above what looked like a pencil line of river, the club looked for the first time just the slightest bit pensive. It was a long way down.

No time for regrets now, thought Kirke, and he took the rest of the Brits off for early-afternoon drinks among the natives of Cañon City, while the two Americans on the team set to work tying on the cords that would be used in the next day's jump.

It was a tricky business. In previous jumps, Kirke had explained, to my horror, they had used seven-millimeter yachting rope and overhand knots to secure the bungee cord to the bridge. With that sort of knot tying, the jumpers would have about a 50 percent chance of dropping directly into the river below. So we spent eight hours constructing a line from two strands of seventeen-millimeter bungee cord, then tying the line into a carefully designed mountaineering-rope anchor that would secure the cords while preventing a fatal, frictive rub between the bungee cord and the bridge. Meanwhile a piano was rented for Gibbs. It began to look as though the event would come off.

Everyone was "quite keen" to be the first off the bridge. Kirke decided to have five jumpers leap simultaneously, on cords spaced evenly along the span. Kirke, in the middle, would be on a 415-foot length. Weston and Hunt would flank him on 240-foot lengths, leaving the outside positions for the novices (Foulon and me) on 120-foot cords.

The biggest risk was Kirke's. Dangling at the end of one thousand feet of line, to within a few feet of the water, he would be subject to immensely widened pendulum swings. The slightest breeze from the wrong direction could blow him off course and slap him into a sheer granite face only thirty feet away at the base. "Strawberry jam spread on rock" was Weston's cheerful description of the probable result of an error in his calculations.

Another problem was the force of gravity, and, again, Kirke was to be most affected. Exactly how much force he would be exposed to if all went well, no one really knew. The Weston-Keeling estimate of five gs seemed plausible, but no one would have been surprised if they'd been off by 200 percent. Astronauts in their specially designed suits pass out with a force of ten gs. No one wanted to think what would happen if any of the jumpers was head-down when the g force built up.

All in all, this was unmistakably a Dangerous Sports Club presentation: No one knew to precisely what length the bungee cords would stretch on a jump from this height. Moreover, no one had really tried to find out. Not knowing, and not wanting to know, was what the club was all about.

Our celebration lasted until three the next morning. The jump was planned for eight o'clock, in order to minimize the breezes that could turn Kirke into a pulp, but it wasn't until nine that the first of the club staggered in. We quickly set up a portable bar right next to the ambulance thoughtfully provided by *That's Incredible!* Missing members of the club were pulled from bed at eleven o'clock but still had to dress for the event.

Overhead the chopper blades chopped ominously, and a crowd started to gather. Five characters dressed as game-show emcees were about to fling themselves off the bridge. This promised to be better than a hanging.

At noon Kirke finally arrived, had a drink, and was promptly approached by the bridge authorities. They wanted him to sign forms relieving them of all responsibility. His hand trembled as he took the pen. He had to steady himself before he signed. No one had ever seen Kirke shake before.

Looking down at the looped bungee cords dangling off the bridge and blowing gently in the wind, the sportsters were beginning to think quite seriously about getting hurt, and to think especially that if anyone were going to get hurt, it would very likely be Kirke. Hearing that Weston and Keeling had estimated that he would come within nine feet of the river, Kirke approached me and said, "Geoff, old man, I realize you have worked hard on the preparations, but is it still possible to extend my rope by four and a half feet? I'm quite keen to just touch the bottom before bouncing up." When it was pointed out to him that he was likely to be unconscious, he decided to reconcile himself to the nine-foot margin. That settled, the club members wanted to enjoy a few leisurely drinks before the jump, but everyone else seemed impatient. The television crew began to worry about whether or not the leap would take place at all. The ambulance crew fretted about the winds whipping up the canyon, which would throw the jumpers off course. And the tourists complained of the cold and began to call for the jumpers to hurry. Kirke was undaunted. Quieter than usual, he requested that his breakfast of eggs Benedict be lowered to him after he jumped. While Gibbs played appropriate bungee music on the piano, Kirke pondered how to keep the eggs warm on the descent.

Finally, after posing for a picture next to the ambulance, the group began to get ready. Beyond having a few more drinks, that involved my tying each of them into a full-body harness and attaching it to the bungee cord. The club has a tradition of never checking its own knots, and only Foulon, who was wearing a cowboy hat with his tuxedo, was gauche enough to inspect his harness. Weston, dressed in a gray morning suit and club tie, seemed worried as he was secured to his bungee, calling for "More drink, please." He lit a large Havana cigar and puffed nervously while the others were readied. Next to be tied in was Hunt, who sported a black tux with tails and a gray top hat secured under his chin.

Now, only minutes before leaping into the unknown, Kirke was moving slowly. Weston impatiently cried out, "*Please* get to your rope, David. I can't wait much longer. I have to jump off soon."

Kirke nodded and solemnly walked to the long cord in the middle. "Have a good one, old boy," he called to Weston. As I tied him to his harness, he tried to light his pipe, but his hands shook too much to strike the match. Dressed in a black morning suit with tails, a black velvet top hat, and the club tie, he allowed one of the cameramen to assist him with a light. He quickly got control of himself and joked that the harness was too tight. "I really must go on a diet!" he exclaimed. With Gibbs at the piano setting the mood, I finished Kirke's knots and headed for my own rope. It was almost three o'clock.

Walking from Kirke to my place at the side, I was struck by the reality of what I was about to do. Until that moment, I had been so absorbed in the partying and preparations that I had not really worried about my own jump. Suddenly, there was nothing more I could do for the others. Now it was my ass out on the line. The sounds of classical piano and helicopter blades were replaced in my ears by the pounding of my heart. I gave a final glance at my comrades, then looked down.

Nearly eleven hundred feet below, the river looked like a thread. The canyon walls seemed only inches apart. I trusted the bungee cords and the knots I had tied. I was the only one using a safety line—a security measure that Kirke considered highly unethical. Rationally, I knew I would be safe; yet I was gradually enveloped by fear. I tried to calmly remind myself that I'd been subjected to more danger than this climbing vertical rock walls. Just as I began to regain control of my trembling body, I was interrupted by a cameraman who said, "Boy, aren't you afraid that there safety rope will wrap around your neck as you bounce up and hang you as you fall back down?"

I hadn't been, but suddenly I was. My testicles quickly receded into the safety of my body. My entire groin tightened. My mind raced incoherently. The others were already over the retaining fence. I clambered after them while my panicked brain screamed, *No!*

For a moment we paused on the farthest supports. It was reassuring, at least, to see how much farther Kirke's cord hung down into space, blowing gently at the limit of my vision. All sound ceased. Time stood still. Kirke raised his hand, signaled "One. Two. Three," then stepped calmly into the air.

I pushed off and my mind immediately signaled, *Error!* Like a cartoon figure, I desperately tried to walk back to the bridge while hanging motionless in the air. Then I fell.

My mind stopped. My heart stopped. The only thing moving was my body, free-falling into the void. My life became calm as I came to a gentle stop four hundred feet down—only to be catapulted violently skyward. Accelerating upward, totally out of control, I was elated. The bungee had held. I slowed to a stop again, now fifty feet below the bridge. Regaining body control, I was able to turn and see the other jumpers. Foulon, at the far side, was at the same height I was. Far below, Weston was beginning his first upward bounce. Kirke was still falling, a dot disappearing in the abyss. I watched them all during my next descent, noting happily that no one had become strawberry jam. I thoroughly enjoyed my last few bounces, trying several somersaults as I rose and fell.

Soon we were all hanging like spiders, suspended between heaven and earth in a giant V. The television helicopter circled us and we waved to it and to one another, thumbs up all around. It was now only a matter of waiting to be hoisted back up. Soon Hunt, Foulon, Weston, and I were safely on the bridge. Foulon appropriately described the feeling for the television audience as "incredible."

Meanwhile, Kirke's cord proved to be impossible to pull up. For nearly three hours he hung nine hundred feet below us, without so much as an overcoat to protect him from the cold. With wind whipping up the canyon and the temperature near freezing, we knew he was in considerable pain. The harness would be cutting off circulation to his legs. The medical crew began to worry. Finally, we found a way to bring him up by pulling the bungee with a tow truck. When he reached the bridge, Kirke's only concern was the whereabouts of his prized top hat and pipe, both of which had been lost in his struggle to remain upright.

Kirke described the jump for the television cameras, saying such an experience "definitely gives one heightened appreciation for life." Privately, he admitted a slight disappointment with the event. The Weston-Keeling estimates had been way off. He hadn't passed out and had stopped a good one hundred feet short of the water.

"Quite the worst of it was, I didn't get a good bounce," he said. "My cords stretched and stopped. The shorter jumps were definitely better sport."

While the television crew disbanded, Gibbs and various of the sportsmen took turns jumping. And, as always, the party went on.

For most of them, the Dangerous Sports Club is only an occasional diversion, so this was a rare event, to be savored and prolonged. Only Kirke has made the club a way of life, moving from one event to the next. In 1981 he made the first motorized hang glider crossing of the English Channel, nonstop from London to Paris. Since the Frenchman Jean Marc Boivin surpassed Kirke's high-altitude hang gliding mark, Kirke has been trying to talk his way onto an expedition to the peak of Mount Everest. "I shall hang glide off Everest," he predicted, "even if I must charter a helicopter to the summit." He is also planning "an extremely festive outing" for his friends in a padded school bus floating over Niagara Falls. His top priority, however, is to set the world free-fall record by parachuting from a helium balloon at 130,000 feet. It will require a pressurized suit to keep his blood from boiling and a temperature-control device to prevent his freezing in space or burning up on reentry to the atmosphere. Weston and Keeling are still working on the designs.

5

JOURNEY
TO THE
STONE AGE

Thrusting from the island of New Guinea's steamy equatorial jungle, a snowcapped mountain pierces its perpetual shroud of mist. Deep in the mountain's shadow live a Stone Age people, the Dani. To them, the peak is Dugundugu, which is also their word for "white" and "ice." They believe the mountain's ice offers strength, like the white meat of their pigs.

To the Indonesians who rule Irian Jaya (the western portion of New Guinea, the world's second largest island after Greenland), the mountain is Puncak Jaya or "Victory Peak." And to the Western world, it's Carstensz Pyramid, after the Dutch explorer Jan Carstensz, who described it from his ship in 1623 during a rare break in the fog. Naming the peak was one thing. Getting there took more than three hundred years. In 1914 a British expedition of 262 people spent fifteen months inching just thirty miles into the jungle. Following the expedition, A. F. R. Wollaston reported to Britain's Alpine Club: "Even if we spent twice that time in the country, I doubt if we should have come as far as the foot of the highest range."

Indeed, the first foreigners to climb 16,023-foot Carstensz were Heinrich Harrer and team in 1962. They made first ascents of the three highest summits while getting to know the Dani people of the surrounding jungle. In his book *I Came from the Stone Age*, Harrer evocatively described the climbs and the year he spent among the people he described as "gentle cannibals." Gentle from his own interactions. Cannibals by reputation.

While cannibalism on the island of New Guinea is a fact, the local evidence is unclear. In the late 1960s a Harvard-Peabody anthropology expedition lived with the

Dani near Wamena, two hundred miles from Carstensz Pyramid. They discovered piles of bones that seemed to imply occasional cannibalism; and the Dani, when pressed, would admit that perhaps such deeds happened. Mostly, though, the team described constant ritual warfare, with men of rival villages gathering on a hillside to fight with sharpened sticks. The fight ends as soon as someone is mortally wounded, with the losers fleeing to their home territory. Before long, however, both groups begin preparing for the next battle—deaths must be avenged to appease the spirits. Such battles have since been stopped by missionaries and government soldiers.

In 1962 the Dutch turned over control of Irian Jaya to Indonesia. For reasons still unclear, the new proprietors closed access to the entire Carstensz Pyramid area. Perhaps the Indonesians didn't want visitors to think their country primitive. Perhaps there was too much truth to rumors of fighting between natives and Indonesian troops.

In any case, the effect was to limit the Dani's contact with the outside world to a few missionaries. Until the late 1970s, those Dani inhabiting remote areas close to the mountain had almost no contact at all. In 1979 Britishers Peter Boardman and Hillary Collins arranged for a missionary pilot to land them illegally near the mountain. They returned with wild stories about the natives—and an alluring photo of an unclimbed two-thousand-foot rock wall leading directly to the summit of Carstensz Pyramid. When I saw their slide show, I had to go.

While the Dangerous Sports Club followed their vision of adventure, Bob Shapiro and I went all-out pursuing our dream of going to Carstensz Pyramid. We secured another A. C. Irvine Grant, sponsorship from the Oxford Exploration Society, and an American Alpine Club Young Mountaineers' fellowship. Unfortunately we were still several thousand dollars short of funding our trip to Irian Jaya. I joked with a friend who worked for *Time* magazine's London bureau, and had previously abused his expense account on my behalf, that he should cover our trip to New Guinea for the magazine. He sent off a letter to his editors in New York who promptly told him to get stuffed; but they did pass the proposal on to *Sports Illustrated*. Two weeks later we received a telex saying that *Sports Illustrated* would pay all of our expenses if they could send a reporter along with us.

Our timing was perfect. Sam Moses, a former football star and professional motorcycle racer, was *Sports Illustrated*'s macho writer covering motor sports and the outdoors. He'd written a couple of pieces on climbing and had been wanting to go on a mountaineering expedition when my friend's letter was passed to him. Before committing he checked a local climbing shop. In front of the information section of *Mountain* magazine, the world's authority on climbing, the headline read, SHAPIRO

AND TABIN MAKE THE COVETED FIRST FREE ASCENT OF MOUNT KENYA'S DIAMOND BUTTRESS.
He assumed we were legitimate and decided to go. Sam was given two months' leave
from the magazine to train full-time with a private guide and climbing instructor.
The magazine gave us our airfare and a carte blanche to purchase any equipment
that was required. Bob and I decided that we needed all-new clothing and gear. The
plan was for Sam to train until the last possible moment. Bob and I would go to
Indonesia and arrange permits and transportation and telex for Sam to come when
everything was set. He would then fly to meet us with the equipment and expense
money.

Bob and I finished our exams at Oxford, celebrated in England and Singapore,
and reached Jakarta to find that it was impossible to obtain permits to go to the
interior of Irian Jaya in 1980. We did succeed in getting fancy endorsements with letterhead and official stamps from the U.S. and British embassies and the head of the
Indonesian Sports Federation. Encouraged, we wired Sam to join us, telling him,
"Everything is perfect, permits no problem, come immediately!" expecting that our
impressive papers would overwhelm the minor officials in Irian Jaya. Once we
reached Jayapura we discovered that the Carstensz area was completely closed. Our
imposing documents made us much too important for any official to risk his career
sanctioning our going into an area where they believed we would certainly be killed
and eaten. The chief of police, Mr. Bimbang, said he would give us a Surat Jalan, or
walking papers, if the governor gave written permission. The governor said we
needed a letter from the head of military intelligence, which is an oxymoron anywhere, but particularly in Indonesia. The director of military intelligence, in turn,
referred us back to the chief of police.

On the day of Sam's arrival in Irian Jaya, Bob went to the airstrip to meet him
while I made a last-ditch effort to find a way into the interior. The police chief
begged me to go just to Wamena, a lowland Dani village in the Baliem Valley, where
there was a military outpost. He assured me that we could see the naked savages
and that he would be able to guarantee our safety. I then met Leroy Kelm, a pilot
who had flown in Vietnam and for Air America in Cambodia and Laos and now
flew for the Missionary Air Fellowship. Leroy had flown Peter Boardman and greeted
me warmly when I came to his office. He said that he didn't need a permit. He had a
landing strip right at his house and he'd happily fly us to the village nearest to
Carstensz Pyramid.

Success! I met Bob and Sam back at our sweltering thatched bamboo room in
Jayapura. Sam had been traveling for thirty-six hours and was in no mood for jokes
or bad news. Bob had judiciously failed to mention that we could not get permits. I

blurted that Leroy would fly us illegally and Sam hit the roof. He accused us of lying to him and lying to *Sports Illustrated*. He said that he represented a very important magazine and the country of America and that he would not under any circumstances break the law.

In the midst of a tirade about how he would break every bone in our bodies and then bring us back to America to face the full fury of the law, he glanced down and saw my feet, clad in sandals. On my last night at Oxford my girlfriend had painted my toenails, saying, "You might remember me a bit longer if I paint your toenails, mightn't you?" I thought it was romantic and let her go ahead. Sam stopped and stared at the lustrous red on my right foot and bright blue polish on the left. This trip was not shaping up as he expected. Suddenly it occurred to me that Sam didn't read Indonesian. I had a solution. Trying not to sound too patronizing, I affected an attitude of great astonishment that he should be so upset, explaining that he had completely misunderstood. What I'd actually meant to say was that we'd have the permits tomorrow.

The next day I went to Chief Bimbang, gave him a hefty bribe, and said we'd take the Surat Jalan to Wamena. I rushed to Leroy Kelm and explained the situation to him; he agreed to back me up. I then proudly showed the permits to Sam. The following morning Bob Shapiro, Sam Moses, and I bounced down a grass runway at Leroy Kelm's home outside of Jayapura, the capital of Irian Jaya. Our Aero Commander lifted off, bound for Ilaga, the closest Dani village to Carstensz Pyramid. We droned inland over an endless expanse of jungle-green hills furrowed with jagged, twisting canyons. The peaks grew larger and more dramatic as we neared the Carstensz Massif; flat land was nowhere to be seen.

—

We wing over a few clusters of round brown huts and terraced fields clinging to the steep green walls. "There's no landing strip," Leroy drawls. "I'll try to put her down in that sweet potato patch." He points to an ominously tiny clearing on a hillside above a group of huts. He noses the plane into a sickening dive, muttering the Lord's Prayer under his breath. My terror mounts as we swoop toward the sloping, muddy field.

We touch down softly enough, but Leroy's wide-eyed look says something is seriously wrong. The plane doesn't slow down; instead it skids on the mud as if it were ice. The end of the clearing looms closer at an alarming rate. We slide diagonally until one tire sticks in the mud, and spin violently to a halt with the left wingtip fifteen feet from the drop-off to an oblivion of jungle.

As Leroy chops the engine and silence washes over us, my heart races with giddy relief. But when I look around, new sights and sounds electrify me with a jolt of adrenaline. From all sides, men and boys come at us, screaming a guttural "oooh-whah, oooh-whah," with their voices cracking to a falsetto on the "whah." Each carries a spear or a stone. All are naked except for a *kebowak*, or penis gourd, which they pound with their palms, drumming a resonant counterpoint to their shrieks. They surround the plane, pounding and screeching.

Leroy steps out, a big grin splitting his silver muttonchop sideburns. He makes eye contact with a couple of Dani in the front. They return bright, toothy smiles. Sam tapes their chanting on a small cassette recorder, and when he plays it back the sounds break the ice completely. Dani boys close in around us, yelling and singing, curiosity filling their eyes.

Below us stretch terraced sweet potato fields, some only fifteen feet wide, linked by footpaths down to a central group of dwellings. Scattered on the surrounding slopes are a smattering of round huts and other fields carved out of the foliage. Farther below and all around, tangled rain forest hems the inhabited land. Here in the high foothills, warm tropical air sweeps up to meet cool mountain breezes, creating a zone of near-constant mist and precipitation.

Leroy's inventive pantomime organizes a group of Dani men to wrestle his plane out of the mud. We unload our packs and he hops aboard, revs the engine, and takes off, leaving the three of us to find our way to the mountain. We have a two-hundred-word Dani vocabulary list from the Harvard anthropologists and ten loads of gear. We hope to enlist ten Dani men as porters to haul it all to the base of Carstensz Pyramid—or Dugundugu, as we understand in the Dani tongue. For payment we've brought ten steel ax heads, ten bags of salt, ten bags of sugar, and ten Boy Scout knives.

We embark on our own wild game of charades trying to explain what we want. Only three of our Dani words seem familiar to these Ilaga villagers, two hundred miles from the tribesmen whom the anthropologists studied. We draw pictures and show photographs of the mountain. One older man, Seppanous, becomes very excited and demands my pen. I hand it to him. He immediately removes the *am whyak*, or boar's tusk, from his nose and proudly inserts the pen.

We sit on the ground amid a cluster of thatched huts, negotiating, gesticulating, laughing. The women go bare breasted, wearing only beads and loose grass skirts. Naked infants and the children play in the mud around us. Pigs, their only domesticated animals, roam freely. Women carrying stone hoes walk past on their way to and from the fields. A few steel axes are the only visible sign that we aren't entirely in the Stone Age.

We are at eight thousand feet, and despite our proximity to the equator, when it clouds over and rains, I feel chilled. The naked Dani seem perfectly comfortable and a bit amused as I search for my rain top.

Eventually we think we've struck an agreement: Ten men will carry our loads and escort us through the jungle to Dugundugu. After a night of singing we hand out ten equally weighted packs. To our horror, the Dani rip the bags open and spread gear all over the ground. Villagers come by, picking from our things. Bob, Sam, and I stare at each other in disbelief, amazed at how quickly our climb is over. As we watch helplessly, dozens of men, women, and children gather up our belongings and file out into the forest, chanting a song.

We're left with no choice. We get up and follow the merry expedition past the farthest cultivated fields and into the cool, dark jungle. We wander under a canopy of dense foliage, sometimes in thick mud, sometimes on rotting logs suspended high above the ground, always on trails that I could never follow on my own. At first the compass says we are traveling north; a few minutes later it reads south. Before long we put the maps away and just walk along, hoping we are hiking toward Dugundugu.

After five hours we stop in a small clearing. The Dani spread out, shouting and laughing, each taking on a task. Some gather firewood while others chop at large trees with stone axes. Yoni, a graceful athletic young man, takes dry moss out of his *kebowak* and strikes two flints together, catching the spark in the moss. He blows gently, puts the glowing pile on the ground, covers it with wet wood, and fans it into roaring flame.

Women take pandanus fronds, break the tips, and pull single strands from the fibrous palm leaf to make instant organic needles with thread. Then they sew the fronds together to make a waterproof covering for their shelter. When a giant oak is about to topple, great debate ensues about where it will fall. As it comes down, much "oooh-whah-ing" and pounding on the *kebowaks* accompanies the descent. By the time we set up our tent, the Dani have built a wooden hut covered with a waterproof layer of pandanus leaves.

Minutes later Martinus, one of the older men, sees me struggling to boil water on my pack stove. He returns with a pot of boiling water. I thank him with a piece of chocolate and watch, amazed, as he takes only a tiny nibble and then brings it around so everyone can have a taste. At night they build a huge fire in their shelter with the flames licking at the wooden roof. Songs and laughter radiate from the smoky hut well into the night.

As I observe the Dani, they observe me. They are fascinated by miracles (like zippers) that I take for granted. But I see no sign of jealousy, either toward us or among themselves. Not a single item of ours will disappear. When the stronger Dani men drop their loads at the top of hills, they go back to help the older and slower members.

Their emotions seem very close to the surface. Displeasure shows quickly, often evoking tears. But moments later, the same two people embrace and laugh. They are constantly amused by my struggles to adapt to the changing environment and care for myself with all my bulky possessions.

Every day I grow more amazed by our companions. We mountaineers are immediately dependent on them for our directions. By the second night they bring us water, fire, and other necessities—treating us like children who have not yet learned to care for themselves. When I try to kindle the sopping wet wood using a lighter and finally fuel from my stove—all without success—Yoni watches knowingly from a distance. Just as my frustration peaks, he walks over, plucks a clump of moss from his *kebowak*, strikes two pieces of flint, blows, piles on soaked wood, blows some more, and stands back, smiling at the blaze.

I come to see that the Dani live in utter harmony with the rugged, hilly rain forest. The forest meets their needs as surely as the malls provide ours at home. Most of their diet consists of fire-roasted *mbee*, or sweet potatoes, which they carry in *yums*, orchid-decorated woven reed bags that hang from their foreheads down their backs. But they also gather roots, grubs, and insects to eat as we walk.

On our third day in the jungle Wanimbo, a tall athletic Dani in his mid-twenties, presents me with a live bat he's holding by the feet. He smiles gently; I flinch away. With a shrug he takes an arrow, pushes it into the bat's anus, and sticks it into the fire. A few minutes later he carefully divides the meat among everyone.

Twenty-four Dani stay with us for the full ten days it takes to reach Dugundugu. In the last days we climb steep, muddy hills to finally emerge from the forest onto the expansive Ngorilong Plateau, a flat, moss-covered bog. At twelve thousand feet our naked escorts stay warm with frequent fires and pandanus-leaf ponchos made on the spot. We cross a snow-covered, sharp-cobbled limestone pass at nearly fifteen thousand feet; they all pad along barefoot.

No one seems surprised to see snow; they have clearly come this way before. I wonder why naked people would climb to a snowy mountain. Perhaps the easiest trade route involves climbing through the high mountain passes rather than fighting thick jungle. Unfortunately, we are still communicating through gestures, and I cannot ask such a complex question.

In the end we succeed in making our planned first ascent on Carstensz and a few other fine climbs besides. And while I came for these routes, the real experience was the privilege of spending time with the Dani. To their mountains we have brought the latest in Gore-Tex rainwear, freeze-dried foods, high-tech everything. Still, we are humbled by our Stone Age companions. With one stitch of a palm-leaf needle, one strike of a flint against *kebowak*-dry moss, I learn how much we have sacrificed in our modern world.

6

KANGSHUNG 1981—EVEREST'S UNCLIMBED EAST FACE

Mount Everest is a three-sided pyramid lying on the border between Nepal and Tibet. Of the mountain's three great faces, the Kangshung, or East Face, is its largest. It spans more than three miles between the two great ridges which form its edges, and rises almost twelve thousand feet from glacier to summit. Buttressed by dark cliffs of rock and capped by vast, broken snowfields, it is an impressive site. But the Kangshung is a face of paradoxes. It is the easiest face to approach, and the most difficult to ascend. It demands the most technical climbing, but offers the most direct line from base to summit. It was the first to be reconnoitered, and the last to be climbed. It was not even attempted until sixty years after the first British Everest expedition saw it in 1921.

Everest treats everyone equally. The Sherpa people and Tibetans, who live in her shadow, call the Goddess Mother of the Earth Chomolungma. They believe she resides in the mountain bearing her name. In 1842 the British survey of India calculated the height of Chomolungma to be 29,002 feet above sea level (it is actually 29,035 by modern measurements), and proclaimed it the highest mountain in the world. In 1863 the English renamed her Mount Everest, after Sir George Everest, a former surveyor general of India, and proposed that she should be climbed. They brought Sherpa people along on their initial foray and were amazed by their strength at altitude and natural mountaineering talent. Moreover, as ardent followers of

Mahayana Buddhism who believe that true nirvana should be delayed until every-one on earth finds happiness, they are a delight to be with. They have accompanied so many expeditions that the name *Sherpa* has become synonymous with the job of high-altitude porter.

One of the principal explorer-climbers on that 1921 reconnaissance was George Leigh Mallory. He made an excellent topographic map of the mountain and was the first Westerner to gaze upon Mount Everest's largest and steepest face. His report was not encouraging. He wrote:

> *We had already by this hour taken the time to observe the great Eastern Face of Mount Everest, and more particularly the lower edge of the hanging glacier: it required but little further gazing to be convinced, to know, that almost everywhere the rocks below must be exposed to ice falling from the glacier; that if, elsewhere, it might prove possible to climb up, the performance would be too arduous, would take too much time, and lead to no convenient platform; that, in short, other men, less wise, might attempt this way if they would, but, emphatically, it was not for us.*

Mallory then moved around to the north where he discovered what he felt to be a feasible route. He returned in 1923 to attempt the northern approach to Mount Everest. After a failed first attempt he made plans to return the next year. When a reporter asked him why he was attempting to climb Mount Everest, Mallory replied, "Because it's there!" In 1924, with Andrew C. Irvine (in whose name whom the A. C. Irvine Grant is endowed), Mallory disappeared high on the slopes of Mount Everest. The mountain remained virginal until May 29, 1953, when Sir Edmund Hillary and Tenzing Norgay Sherpa reached the summit via the mountain's south side from Nepal. In 1960 Wang Fu Chow and his Chinese compatriots, climbing in a large national expedition, made the first ascent of Mallory's route on the north side of Everest. In 1963 the first Americans reached the summit of Mount Everest, with Tom Hornbein and Willi Unsoeld climbing the technically challenging West Ridge, which delineates the border between Nepal and Tibet. In 1975 Chris Bonington's British expedition achieved a breakthrough in climbing difficulty on Everest when they scaled the imposing and sustained Southwest Face. Three years later Peter Habeler and Reinhold Messner succeeded in making the first climb of Mount Everest without supplemental oxygen, and a Polish expedition climbed the moun-tain in winter. By 1979 every face and ridge on two-thirds of the mountain had been climbed. The mountain had also been climbed solo and during the monsoon. But the largest and steepest side of Mount Everest, the massive Kangshung, or East Face, had still not been approached.

Meanwhile the Chinese government was changing its policy toward outsiders. China had annexed Tibet in 1950. The Dalai Lama, the theocratic ruler of the country, fled into exile in India. China kept Tibet a completely restricted area. In 1979 the Chinese gave a permit for a Japanese expedition to enter Tibet to attempt Mount Everest from the north. Rumor was that they were soon to open Tibet to Western climbers. Dick Blum, the husband of Senator Dianne Feinstein (then mayor of San Francisco), was a keen trekker who had walked in the Nepal Himalayas on several occasions. He was about to depart for a friendship trip to China with his wife when American climber Eric Perlman suggested that he request a permit for Americans to attempt the Chinese approaches to Mount Everest. The timing was perfect. Blum was in the right place at the right time. The Chinese government granted the first permit for an American expedition to climb in Tibet.

On the advice of his climbing friends in San Francisco, Blum asked Lou Reichardt, a well-known Himalayan climber, to help plan the climb. Reichardt, a research professor at the University of California, San Francisco, medical school and dean of the American high-altitude climbing community, had both a scientist's interest in the unknown and an adventurer's desire for challenge. The permit would allow an assault on the mountain from any side. Blum was interested in approaching Everest's summit by the easiest route possible, the Northeast Ridge. Reichardt, however, was drawn to the Kangshung Face, with its legend of difficulty and mystery. He had seen a photograph of Everest taken from the top of neighboring Makalu, the world's fifth highest peak, and from the photo thought there might be a feasible route up the mountain from the east. With this in mind, Reichardt set about building a climbing team that could tackle the challenging alpine rock and ice route. He also set about the harder task of persuading Blum and Perlman to consider the East Face instead of the easier Northeast Ridge.

Blum, meanwhile, had enlisted the help of Sir Edmund Hillary, whom he knew from his charitable work with Hillary's Himalayan Foundation. Hillary stated that "if the Americans climb Mount Everest from the north it will just be another ascent of the mountain, but a climb from the east will be history." Reichardt asked his good friend, Andrew Harvard, an experienced expedition mountaineer, to join in his plans for Everest. He also spent time researching rumors and legend to get as accurate a description as possible of the East Face.

To this forbidding summary, the Reichardt's research added some more detail. The rock buttress jutted out just south of the center of the face and rose to form a rough triangle that peaked at around twenty-two thousand feet. The rest of the lower East Face was a series of deep gullies, scoured by avalanches released from an

expansive, jumbled snowfield that seemed to cover the whole east side of the mountain above twenty-four thousand feet. The upper part of that snowfield could be
seen by climbers looking down from the South Col route, and what they saw
appeared to be unstable, and very steep. Between twenty-two thousand feet and the
steep upper section, the snowfield appeared to be a windswept, low-angled maze of
crevasses. Mallory's judgment about the avalanches was undoubtedly correct, but
the question was whether or not the rock buttress could now be safely climbed
using modern technology and equipment. Beyond this, would climbing the buttress
lead to a safe route through the snow above?

In August 1980 Harvard left on a small expedition to Gongga-Shan, another
mountain that the Chinese had just opened to outsiders. When he left, the choice of
routes on Everest was still undecided. Reichardt had enlisted a small core group of
dedicated climbers who were interested in the East Face, but Blum and a few others
were still very reluctant.

Reichardt was supposed to join Harvard on the Gongga-Shan trip in a couple
of weeks, but before he arrived he wired Harvard in Beijing: "Everest Reconnaissance
necessary STOP Can you do this after Gongga-Shan STOP Should take two weeks STOP
Regards Louis STOP."

After returning from Gongga-Shan, Harvard began his first trip to the East
Face of Everest. A Chinese interpreter, Tsao Hong Juen, and a veteran Chinese
climber, Cheng Rong Chan, accompanied him. During Harvard's journey he wandered by jeep and on foot and with yaks through territory that was, for all practical
purposes, a still-unknown corner of the earth. Heading into the valley of Everest, he
entered a world of late-autumn colors: dark red and brown earth and rocks; deep
copper and bright golden fields. In the distance the stark black and white of high
rock and ice offered contrast to the earthy tones of the valley and framed the landscape. Each day Harvard added to the map he was making and to his notes. He photographed the changing scenery. Harvard became the second Westerner to view
Everest's East Face and concluded that, given the improvements in equipment and
techniques since Mallory's time, climbing it would be difficult, "probably the hardest
climb ever attempted," but possible.

With the objective established, the next tasks were fund-raising and team
selection. Blum, a professional financier by trade, remained expedition leader, while
Reichardt was named climbing leader on the mountain. Sir Edmund Hillary joined
the effort as a special expedition adviser who would accompany the team to base
camp. The team that was selected was a who's who of the best American climbers in
1980. In addition to Eric Perlman, Andy Harvard, and Lou Reichardt, the group

included the current hot Himalayan superstar, John Roskelley; the tandem responsible for the hardest alpine ascents in North America, George Lowe and Chris Jones; a top Alaskan guide in Gary Bocarde; and arguably the two top rockjocks, Jim Bridwell and Henry Barber. Also on the initial team were Sue Giller, an excellent Himalayan climber; two experienced climbing doctors, Jim Morrissey and Dan Reid; and Bruce McCubbry, a solid Bay Area mountaineer. The fund-raising went smoothly. Many people and organizations, including ABC Television, were eager to be involved in the historic ascent.

A few months before departure Jim Bridwell decided that he could not go on the expedition. The team began looking for a replacement. Because most of the expedition members were in their thirties or forties it was suggested that they might choose a strong rock climber under twenty-five. This happened at the same time that Sam Moses' two-part article appeared in *Sports Illustrated*. When I'd first heard that Sam's account of our trip to Irian Jaya was going to be published I had some trepidation. I had no idea how he perceived me. We had become friends during the trip and I had led our team up the climb. Still, Sam had never seemed comfortable with my painted toenails. I also had donned a *kebowak* for part of our approach march, ate insects when the Dani did, carried three penis gourds to the top of Carstensz Pyramid, and insisted that Sam and Bob strip naked for a *kebowak* summit photo despite a raging blizzard. In addition, Sam had found out that he'd been deceived about the Surat Jalan when we were arrested upon our return from the mountain.

Although he did describe me as "cheerfully oblivious to society's norms," Sam's articles made me out to be incredibly energetic and enthusiastic: "Geoff was up there on the leading end of the rope, the 'sharp end,' as climbers call it, often unprotected, 800 feet off the ground, standing on tiny edges and clinging to a wall of rock while icy water dribbled down his sleeves to his armpits." Moreover, he mentioned that a Kowloon fortune-teller had said that I was the "luckiest sonofabitch" he had ever seen, which is a good attribute to have on an expedition. Sam's article got me noticed, and no one on the team knew me well enough to say anything negative. Finally, Bruce McCubbry was a friend of my father's and actively supported my candidacy.

I had enrolled in Harvard Medical School in the fall of 1980. My focus was on becoming a doctor; I had no plans for big climbing adventures in the near future. This idea was reinforced six weeks later when I was bouldering without a rope at a small outcrop just outside of Boston called Hammond Pond. A rock broke off while I was climbing an overhanging route. I was only fifteen feet off the ground, but I had my foot hooked up above my head so that when my handhold pulled loose I torpedoed straight down, breaking my left arm and knocking myself unconscious.

Fortunately, I was with a medical school classmate named Hansel Stedman who saved my life when I stopped breathing. Hansel gave me mouth-to-nose resuscitation and kept me breathing while carrying me a few hundred yards to the road, where he flagged down a motorist who took me to Newton-Wellesley Hospital. I remained in a coma for thirty-six hours and spent a week in the hospital. I struggled to catch up with my medical studies while having recurring problems with short-term memory and concentration. By the second semester I was back to doing some rock climbing on the weekends. With the help of the medical school I had nearly caught up with my classes.

In the spring of 1981 I was studying for a pharmacology exam when Lou Reichardt called to ask if I would be interested in joining the team that was going to attempt the last unclimbed face on Mount Everest. Lou would be in Boston the following week and wanted to know if I could meet him for lunch. I was bouncing off the walls with excitement. I would have been overjoyed just to have lunch with Lou Reichardt. The people on the team were the heroes whom I had been reading about. Reichardt was America's best high-altitude mountaineer. I knew of the tragedy on Dhaulagiri when he had been the only person to survive an avalanche that killed seven of his teammates, and of his successful ascent of the mountain two years later. I had read of his exploits on Nanda Devi and how he'd made the first ascent of K2 without supplemental oxygen. And now he wanted to talk to me about joining him to climb Mount Everest. It would probably ruin my medical career. I knew I wasn't experienced enough for that kind of climb: The biggest mountain I had been on was seventeen-thousand-foot Mount Kenya. I was also in the worst shape of my life. I instantly replied, *"Yes!"*

I put on my faded pile jacket, my Peruvian herder's cap, and painter's pants, trying to look like the kind of experienced climber he would want for his expedition, and went to meet Lou Reichardt on the steps of Harvard Medical School. I arrived early and waited. The only other person on the steps was a long, gangly man with checked polyester pants, a striped polyester shirt that was a size too small, and thick glasses that were fogged, filthy, and sitting askew on his nose. With large, open-mouthed bites he was eating a tuna fish submarine. I was looking desperately for the great mountaineer when, with a big tuna fish smile, Lou Reichardt warmly extended his hand and said, "Geoff?"

Lou went back to California telling me that I would be considered for the team. A few weeks later I was told that they had chosen Kim Momb, a top young climber from Spokane, Washington. I was selected as an alternate. The week before the team departed I called Lou and Jim Morrissey, wished them good luck, and thanked them for considering me. Then, several days after the team was supposed to have left, I received a phone call from a man who introduced himself as Scott MacBeth, the team's base camp manager. Scott explained that he'd been delayed in his departure because of a blood infection and hadn't left with the rest of the group. He added that one of the other climbers, Henry Barber, had not gone at the last minute for personal reasons. "Do you still want to go to Everest?" he asked.

"What? *Yes!*" I answered. I was soaring ten feet off the ground. I made a quick phone call to the dean of students and told him that I had just been invited to go to attempt the last unclimbed face of Mount Everest. I'd be leaving medical school, and would be returning in December. Inexplicably, the dean was not as excited as my climbing friends. It was impossible for me to go, he told me. I tried to explain that this was Everest. He replied, "Yes, and other students like to go to the beach on their vacations. What's the difference?"

Now a full two and a half weeks late, Scott and I flew from San Francisco to Beijing, tagging along behind the rest of the team. Everyone else had already flown from Beijing to Chengdu and then on to Lhasa, where they explored the old capital, just waking from its forced decades of silence. From Lhasa the team loaded our gear into three trucks and themselves into a bus for the long ride to Xigase, Xigare, and on to Kharta. They arrived in Kharta with considerable fanfare. Loads were prepared and mounted on a large herd of yaks. The beginning of their trek was leisurely and uneventful. Even given the rainy weather, slippery rocks, and slow pace of the yaks, there was much to admire on the trek, especially when they arrived at the lush forest descending from Shao La into the Kama Valley. Here they were welcomed by a rich scene of wildflowers, rhododendrons, tall grasses, moss, and ferns. The team let the yaks graze for a day at a forest camp they made before heading along the Kangshung Glacier for the three-day climb to base camp. On the team's final day's walk to base camp, they had intermittent views of the face as clouds teased back and forth about the glacier. They could see bits and pieces of Everest's East Face, but never the whole route, top to bottom, that we would be attempting. Arrival at base camp was celebrated in the cook tent. Drinking and singing lasted long into the night. McCubbry had a guitar and a melodious voice, which, together with Momb's, was strong enough to keep the team reasonably in tune. The harmony produced may not have been perfect, but it was very alive.

While the team celebrated their arrival on the mountain, Scott and I followed after them. Scott turned out to be an ideal traveling companion, and our Chinese hosts most hospitable. Unfortunately, the transportation into Tibet was not regular at that time. Moreover, Scott was as interested in seeing the sights of China as in getting to the mountain. The days in Beijing rolled on. We were guests at wonderful banquet after wonderful banquet. The meals lasted for hours with dozens of courses and toasts of Mao Tai liquor between each dish. We took trips out to the Ming tombs and the Great Wall of China, and explored the Forbidden City and other tourist sites of Beijing. We wandered the streets early in the morning watching the city awaken with Tai Chi, felt the bustle of the days, and rode bicycles through the town in the late afternoon, absorbing the sounds and smells before our evening banquet. It was fun, but my mind was on Everest. I was concerned about my role on the team, nervous about meeting my teammates, anxious about climbing in the Himalayas, worried about my own acclimatization, and a bit more impatient than Scott. Finally, after six days, we boarded a plane to Chengdu in Szechuan province. We encountered similar delays in Chengdu before finally being shuttled out to an old Russian turboprop. The flight took us over a seemingly endless array of immense, shimmering rock and ice peaks. I kept my face pressed to the window throughout the spectacular four-hour trip, over hundreds of miles of uncharted Himalayan mountains, to land in Lhasa, Tibet.

Lhasa in 1981 was a place of contrasts. Physically, it was beautiful. Softly colored hills rose on all sides of the city, and golden statues glistened from the rooftops of the temples and monasteries. On a hill above town the traditional home of the Dalai Lama, the Potala Palace, dominated the architecture of the city and projected a feeling of grandeur to everything below. Traditionally clad Tibetans chanted mantras and spun prayer wheels as they went about their business. Yet the tension between the Tibetans and their Chinese conquerors was palpable. All of the main religious buildings were completely shut down, with only Chinese guards outside. The smiles vanished from Tibetan faces as they passed Chinese soldiers. There were no tourist hotels in Lhasa at the time, so we were housed in an army barracks on the edge of town. We spent several days wandering through the city. It felt awkward to be allowed access to the monasteries and temples that the faithful were denied. We visited the deserted Jokang temple, which had previously been the main shrine for the people of Tibet. In the Potala Palace the artwork and ornate golden statues were beautiful beyond my imagination, yet there was an eerie feeling walking alone through the vast 999 rooms with only the occasional glowering Han Chinese soldier sharing the sacred building.

We were delayed another week in Lhasa waiting for transportation. By this time I was fully enjoying Scott's company, his knowledge of the region, and his explanations of Tibetan Buddhism. I learned that Siddhartha believed there to be four essential truths: "Man suffers; suffering comes from unfulfilled desires; one can eliminate suffering by overcoming desire; and to overcome desire one must follow the eightfold path to wisdom." I finally began to adopt a Buddhist attitude of acceptance. Things were the way they were and I couldn't rush the trip. I became absorbed in David Snellgrove's and Hugh Richardson's wonderful text *A Cultural History of Tibet*, in reading about Mahayana Buddhism, and in trying to understand the changes in Tibet since the Chinese invaded.

After a week in Lhasa, Scott and I were given a jeep and a driver and set out along the arid Tibetan plateau. Our first stop was Xigase, the second city of Tibet, with its impressive Drepung Monastery. From there we drove on a heavily rutted dirt road to Xegar, the site of the Xegar Dzong, a hillside fortress that was the last outpost of Tibetan resistance to the Chinese invasion in 1953. The Tibetan landscape unfolded before us with a long, arid, richly textured plateau stretching to the horizon in one direction and the spine of the Himalayan range on the other side of our jeep. Unfortunately, the mountains were socked in with monsoon clouds, and we had no views of the highest peaks. The monsoons sweep north from India and hit the high Himalayan peaks where they drop their precipitation, leaving the Tibetan plateau a harsh thirteen-thousand-foot desert.

From Xegar, Scott and I followed a winding single track that wove into the mountains with precipitous drops at every curve until we finally arrived at the small yak-herding village of Kharta. We were given three yaks and a yak driver to help us with our seven-day trek to Mount Everest, which proved to be one of the greatest hikes of my life. Glimmering twenty-thousand-foot peaks rose up on all sides. I was mesmerized. I was overwhelmed by the scale. The jagged summits floated a vertical mile and a half above us. At every turn in the trail the views changed, becoming even more dramatic. We walked over a high pass adorned with prayer flags and dropped into the lush Kama Valley. We descended to a small wooded camp with beautiful rhododendrons in full bloom from the monsoon storms. The trail then wove back upward into the world of rock, snow, and ice to join the Kangshung Glacier at sixteen thousand feet.

Nothing I had ever seen prepared me for the grandeur of the highest Himalayan peaks. The icy walls of Chomolonzo glistened in the morning sun, and Makalu rose twelve thousand feet vertically above us as we came out onto the glacier. We followed the side of the glacier for one day on our way toward base camp before we were able to see the East Face of Mount Everest and the North Face of Lhotse in the distance. Both rise more than two vertical miles. The sheer mass and beauty would have taken my breath away, had I not already been gasping from the altitude.

Looking up the glacier, we were surprised to see people coming down. It turned out to be Dick Blum and an entourage of porters. Dick had decided he didn't enjoy life in the base camp and was leaving the expedition. I thought it a bit strange that the expedition leader was leaving. I was also a bit worried, as Dick seemed to have no knowledge that Scott had invited me along.

We walked only a few more hours before we ran into the next group of people descending the trail. I instantly recognized Sir Edmund Hillary from his photographs. He was staggering along the path with a bloody bandage wrapped around his head. The man with Hillary warmly greeted Scott and, after being introduced, I too was enthusiastically welcomed by Dr. Jim Morrissey. Sir Edmund Hillary then turned to me and asked, "Are you driving the bus?"

Morrissey explained that Hillary had developed a slight case of cerebral edema and had fallen, struck his head, and then rolled over, contaminating the open wound in fresh yak dung. The gash in his scalp had become infected. Morrissey was terrified that our expedition would be remembered only for killing Sir Edmund Hillary. He was rushing the man down to lower altitude, expecting to take him to Beijing where he would receive additional medical care. Despite a dirty rag wrapped around his head and an altered mental state, Hillary had the carriage of a great man. I had read many books by and about him. Beyond making the first ascent of Everest and his impressive climbing résumé, Hillary had traversed Antarctica, been to both the North and South Poles, built schools and hospitals for the Sherpa people, started his own foundation to help the indigenous populations of the Himalayas, and served as New Zealand high commissioner to India and Nepal. He was one of my heroes. Yet despite his illness, I was even more impressed than I expected to be by Hillary the man. A quiet warmth emanated from his dazed eyes. I asked him to pose for a picture. He smiled gamely and wished me luck on the climb before stumbling on down the trail.

Two days later we walked into base camp. It was obviously not a happy place. I tented my first night with John Roskelley, who had distinguished himself with the hardest climbs of any American over the past several years and had recently been hailed by the media and the top European climber, Reinhold Messner, as the greatest mountaineer in the world. I knew of his bold climbs in the Himalayas, including the first ascents of several technically difficult peaks as well as the first American climb of K2, and I was eager to learn from him. As I crawled into our tent, slightly in awe, John Roskelley's only words to me were, "This face is suicide. If you climb on this route, Geoff, you are going to die." Then he rolled over and went to sleep.

I lay awake all night. This was not turning out like I had expected. The expedition leader had left, Sir Edmund Hillary had high-altitude sickness, and our route was too dangerous for John Roskelley. Before morning I was aware of what a great adventure I had already had and how privileged I was to be in Tibet and seeing these mountains. I attempted to push my preconceptions out of my conscious thoughts, keep an open mind, and flow with the adventure.

The East Face of Everest is enormous. There was no consensus over what was a feasible or safe route. One faction, spearheaded by Chris Jones, wanted to follow the ridge that makes up the north side of the buttress. Jones felt that this would be much easier climbing and afford a feasible route to the upper snow slopes. A second group felt that Jones's line was suicidal because of avalanche danger. This team, led by George Lowe, was trying to push a very difficult direct route up the sheer initial five-thousand-vertical-foot rock and ice buttress.

Roskelley felt that Lowe's route was impossibly hard. The vertical mile of technical difficulties was insurmountable. And even if it proved possible to climb the buttress, he was certain the slopes above were suicidal, with unreasonable avalanche danger. Roskelley strongly advocated going around to the easier and safer north side to simply make a successful climb on Mount Everest. Andy Harvard told me to ignore Roskelley: John, as a professional climber, needed to reach the top of the mountain for his reputation, and wanted to do what was easiest and best for himself. While the arguments raged, Lou Reichardt, our climbing leader, avoided the controversy and led by simply carrying heavy loads, often making double carries in a single day, to support whatever activity was going on up on the mountain.

I was shocked to see my heroes bickering and confused about what to do. Adding to my discomfort was a feeling that I was in over my head, even if the route were climbable. Base camp sat at an altitude of seventeen thousand feet, the same as my previous high point. I felt the pulse pounding in my temples and became short of breath with moderate exertion. I was worried that my physical skills were not in the same league as those of any of the team superstars. I rested a week before moving seven miles across the Kangshung Glacier to our advanced base camp. I decided that I should at least check things out for myself before making any decision. On the day that I moved to advanced base camp, Roskelley made an impassioned plea on the radio for Kim Momb to come down. He said, "I brought you on this trip, Kim. I owe it to your family. Don't let me down. You must come home alive. Come off the mountain at once if you want to live. I'm getting out of here tomorrow. Walk out with me. Please!" I met Kim Momb for the first time as he was retreating off the mountain. We briefly shook hands before he, Bruce McCubbry, and Roskelley left.

Meanwhile the climbing team pushed along Lowe's route toward the top of the initial vertical buttress. The climbing was hard, at a level of technical difficulty never before attempted on a peak the scale of Mount Everest. There were pitches of vertical ice, arduous free climbing, and very strenuous overhanging aid climbing on crumbly schist where the only way to make progress was to pound pitons into the friable rock and pull yourself up on these insecure anchors. George Lowe was doing the majority of the leading on the hardest sections. Also working on the route were Eric Perlman, Gary Bocarde, Sue Giller, Dan Reid, and ABC cameraman David Breashears. An enormous avalanche had swept over the ridge that Jones had suggested. Fortunately no one was in its path. All climbing efforts were now concentrated on the "Lowe Buttress" route.

I rested a few days at advanced base camp, listening eagerly to stories of what had happened on the mountain. I was particularly fascinated by the tales of Dan Reid. He was supposed to be a team physician, but when they needed help on the route he headed right up. I heard about how he had attempted to solo climb a vertical icicle, taken several long falls, and self-belayed on a single knife-blade piton before finally giving up on a stormy day when no one else was willing to climb. This pitch later became known as Reid's Nemesis.

When I started up the fixed ropes, I was amazed by the difficulty of the climbing that the team had accomplished. The leaders installed permanent ropes that I followed using mechanical ascenders that slide up the rope but catch and lock when weighted downward. I spent a night at Snow Camp, the first camp on the mountain, which was located below a snow ridge leading up to the ice gully where much of the debris from the upper face funneled down. Unfortunately, the gully was the only line of weakness in a series of impassable mushroomed snow ridges, and our only possible route to the upper headwall. The worst time to be on this part of the buttress was in the afternoon, when the sun warmed the upper face. The heat melted the ice into water, which seeped into cracks. At night the water froze and expanded. The next day the warming loosened adhesions, and rock eroded down the mountain into the gully. They called the chute the "Bowling Alley": Bowling-ball-sized pieces of rock and ice ricocheted through every day as soon as the upper face was touched by the sun. I left very early in the morning and then raced as quickly as possible, like a scared rabbit, up the seven-hundred-foot, sixty-degree ice chasm to reach the camp on top of the chute, aptly named Pinsetter Camp.

At Pinsetter Camp I met Dan Reid for the first time. This slightly built man projected an incredible energy. He had a wide grin and scraggly beard; through his granny glasses his eyes focused intensely on anyone he was speaking to. He spoke matter-of-factly, saying that he thought the Bowling Alley was overrated and that I shouldn't be scared because "when it's your time to go, it's your time to go and there's nothing you can do about it."

Meanwhile Eric Perlman and Gary Bocarde had just reached the Helmet Camp, on top of the buttress at 21,500 feet. Gary, a veteran mountain guide on Mount McKinley, observed the crevasses stretching out above and declared the upper face to be unclimbable. He and Eric then retreated off the mountain, saying they were not going to climb anymore. Similarly, Sue Giller decided the risks were too great to venture higher. Chris Jones had broken some ribs with a high-altitude coughing fit and was unable to climb, Andy Harvard was sick, and the film crew had pulled back. Thus there were only four of us still on the mountain willing to move upward: Lou Reichardt, George Lowe, Dan Reid, and me. We discussed our options. George, who had done most of the difficult leading to that point and had been breaking through psychological barriers in the climbing world for fifteen years, felt that we should at least give it a try. Lou argued that it was not worth the risk. He pointed out that of the four of us, he was the only one who had been above twenty-three thousand feet previously without oxygen, while I was still poorly acclimatized. Moreover, we had no support and only twelve days' worth of supplies. Dan Reid then said that the only thing to do was to sign a death pact. If we all agreed that we should make a headlong dash for the summit, then one of us would most likely reach the top and get down alive, and we'd succeed on the first ascent on the East Face of Mount Everest. The death pact would state that if any one of us became sick or injured we wanted our partners to leave us to die so that they could make the top. As long as we signed a death pact he felt it would be legal. The other three of us looked at each other and realized that this expedition was over.

The next morning we began rappelling down the ropes. "Death-Pact" Dan said he wanted to take one last look, and remained high on the mountain. George, Lou, and I descended through the Bowling Alley in the dark and waited at Snow Camp for Dan. We began to worry when the sun crept up onto the upper face, and were relieved when we heard Dan yodel as he approached the camp. Then we saw that his right leg was completely red. His boot and lower leg were soaked through with blood. With a cheerful grin he said, "A couple of big ones came through while I was rappelling. I dodged most of 'em but one sucker got me." We pulled up his wind pant leg and found that he had an implosion injury, exposing five inches of his tibia. We helped him down to advanced base camp, where we learned that Jim Morrissey had returned from successfully evacuating Sir Edmund Hillary back to Beijing. Jim looked at Dan's leg and decided it would not be possible to move him back to base camp. He would remain with Dan in advanced base camp after sewing Dan's leg closed in three layers with thirty-eight stitches.

The rest of the team began carrying loads back across the glacier from advanced base camp to base camp while we sent a messenger out for yaks to evacuate camp. While waiting for the yaks, George Lowe asked me if I would like to make a first ascent on a peak called Kartse, which dominates the vista behind base camp. George and I had a perfect day, climbing a beautiful, steep ridge in perfect sunshine and calm air to the 21,390-foot summit of Kartse. I was still floating on the summits as we walked back to base camp. I felt great on top of Kartse, had learned that George was not only a great climber but also a great guy to climb with, and realized that with acclimatization I could climb with him.

We returned to find base camp in an uproar. Jim Morrissey had called on the radio to say that Dan Reid, after his week of resting at advanced base camp, had popped a handful of his own medications—thus earning a new nickname, "PercoDan"—and solo climbed up the fixed ropes. Jim tried to catch him but did not have the technical climbing skill, and because he'd gone down with Sir Edmund Hillary, he lacked Dan's acclimatization. Dan brought an unusual assortment of gear for his solo bid—including a stove but no fuel, so he was unable to melt water, and a considerable amount of food that all needed cooking. He also brought with him a tent but no sleeping bag. I had images in my mind of Dan limping into the clouds to disappear like George Leigh Mallory. He eventually returned, having climbed for thirty-six straight hours, saying he had gone up to retrieve the Explorers' Club flag that he'd left up at the high point, and to check out snow conditions for future years. It was the consensus of everyone that Dan Reid, one of the most wonderful and warmest people we had ever met, was completely nuts.

On the trek out our liaison officer, Wang Fu Chow, who had been the first Chinese man to summit Mount Everest, expressed sympathy that we had not made the summit. Wang Fu Chow had also made the first ascent of Mount Xixibangma, the only one of the world's fourteen highest mountains that is completely in Tibet. He told us matter-of-factly that it would be possible for us to attempt to climb Mount Xixibangma. George Lowe, Eric Perlman, Lou Reichardt, Jim Morrissey, and I instantly took him up on the offer. We said good-bye to the rest of the team at Kharta.

Xixibangma rises abruptly from the Tibetan plateau at fourteen thousand feet and climbs to just over twenty-six thousand feet with no intervening foothills. It is probably the most dramatic relief in the world. The route we tried is technically quite easy, following a low-angle ridgeline to a steep ice slope that allows one to gain the final ridge. Unfortunately, the winter jet stream winds lowered to twenty-two thousand feet. George, Eric, and Lou were poised to go for the top when our high camp tent was ravaged by one-hundred-mile-an-hour gusts. It was impossible for our team to reach the summit. Still, the team experience was absolutely perfect. We were perfectly together, shared a common attitude toward the climb, and had a lot of fun. On our way back to Lhasa we all decided that with the right team and knowing the route up the initial buttress, the East Face of Mount Everest could be climbed. Jim Morrissey decided to apply for a permit to return in two years to make the first ascent of the Kangshung Face. We reached Beijing and went to the Chinese mountaineering office, where Jim gave a strong presentation: We had figured out the feasible route, he said, and had done all the hard work; the Chinese should keep the route virginal until we were able to return to try it. The man smiled broadly and through an interpreter said, "No problem, Dr. Reid already have permit."

7

EVEREST 1983— THE FIRST ASCENT OF THE KANGSHUNG FACE

I returned from Tibet to find that I was out of medical school. I reapplied and was reaccepted with the understanding that I would not leave again. Meanwhile, Dan Reid turned over the permit for the return to the Kangshung Face to Jim Morrissey, who assumed expedition leadership under the condition that Dan remain part of the next team. Dan agreed to just be a base camp doctor and assured Jim that he would not do anything dangerous. Jim was the perfect leader for this type of trip. He had a vast amount of expedition experience, lots of common sense, and strong leadership skills; in addition, because he was primarily a doctor rather than a climber, he did not have a climbing ego that would clash with his team. He was thus able to listen and weigh all options and then make a decision. Tall and powerful, Jim had a commanding personality and a strong sense of self-confidence that persuaded people to follow. Jim selected a team that he felt gave the best chance for success, blending top climbers who would work well together. The common attribute was a shared belief that the Kangshung Face could be climbed.

From the 1981 team he asked Dan Reid, Andy Harvard, Lou Reichardt, Kim Momb, George Lowe, and me to return to Everest with him in 1983. Adding to this nucleus of seven, Jim invited Carlos Buhler, Carl Tobin, David Coombs, Jay Cassell, David Cheesmond, and Chris Kopczynski. The result was not necessarily the best thirteen climbers in America in 1983, but very likely the best team America could have produced. A final addition was John Boyle, a banker, engineer, and yachtsman, to serve as base camp manager. The trip again was well funded, with *National Geographic* magazine as a principal sponsor.

Climbing the last unclimbed face on Everest had become a consuming romantic quest for me. I desperately wanted to go on the trip, but there was no chance of Harvard Medical School giving me leave to go climbing again. Then Michael Wiedman, the professor of eye surgery, approached me and proposed that we do a research project on the physiology of high altitude. In particular, Dr. Wiedman was interested in retinal hemorrhaging at high altitude and whether an ocular exam could be used as a prognosticator of high-altitude cerebral or pulmonary edema. I was thus able to schedule a research elective and did not have to apply for a leave of absence. Beyond learning to perform ophthalmoscopy, I trained for the trip by running the five miles to and from my apartment to school every day, sprinting the steps of the Harvard football stadium, and traversing a rock wall and climbing rock and ice every weekend. I easily completed the Boston Marathon in the spring and ran a complete traverse of the Presidential Mountains in New Hampshire in less than four hours, normally a three-day hike. When I flew to San Francisco in August 1983 I felt prepared and confident.

An optimistic group had gathered in San Francisco. The mood at the airport was one of frantic excitement. Kopczynski distributed stylish Eddie Bauer team jackets; I brought along a double shipment of boots and Gore-Tex running suits from New Balance. Someone supplied a cake covered in mounds of sticky icing, but there were no forks, so we all grabbed a handful. A strip-o-gram, sent by anonymous admirers of Morrissey, waltzed onto the scene and danced through the happy confusion of climbers and their luggage, friends, and family.

We were going to climb the last unclimbed face on Mount Everest—the hardest mountaineering route that had ever been attempted—and we were going to do it with minimal supplemental oxygen and no native support on the mountain. We traveled through China, each day becoming a more and more cohesive team. We spent three days in Beijing where, between visits to the Great Wall and the Forbidden City, we built up endurance by running through the streets in our bright and scanty shorts. Tobin tried to find some rock walls but discovered that the climbing of ornate walls encrusted with the statues of demons long dead is one of the forbidden things in the Forbidden City. As a team, our collective mentality was similar to what I have read about the psychology of people going off to war. A macabre sense of humor prevailed, with lots of "jokes" about climbers who have perished. We all knew that sixty-two lives had already been lost on the slopes of Mount Everest, that no new route had been opened on the mountain without the loss of life, that none had been climbed without native load carriers on the mountain, and that ours was the hardest and most dangerous path. Still, none of us broached the subject of whether an accident could happen to us. Interestingly, there was also a prevalent hypersexuality and much flirtation with flight attendants and other Western sojourners, perhaps our bodies' way of telling us to propagate our genes before embarking on the dangerous mission. I personally adopted an attitude that I had trained well enough and was with such a great team that I would be safe. I had no conscious thoughts of the risk. My mind remained completely immersed in the present, with little talk of the past or future, as we again enjoyed banquets and sight-seeing.

Arriving in Lhasa, I found that Tibet had changed dramatically in two years. The Chinese had eased many of their restrictions. The Potala and Jokang were now crowded with chanting pilgrims, and the streets were bustling with activity. Chinese soldiers were still present, but less obvious. We stayed in a comfortable guest house and ate well. There was little time for tourism, though. We were a team with a mission! We packed our gear on trucks and began the drive to Mount Everest after one day. A monsoon had washed out the main road, so we took an alternate dirt track that was so bumpy you couldn't even pick your nose. The ride was more beautiful than I remembered. We passed alongside rolling hills with layers of brown, yellow, and green banks woven into the sand. The monsoon gave a constant, unpleasant drizzle; still, the swirling clouds made the landscape all the more impressive. We arrived in Xigase late in the evening and left for Xegar early the next morning. Despite the hectic pace we were beginning to get to know each other.

It soon became clear to me that my three-hour-per-day training regimen left me one of the weakest members of our team. Three people stood apart as being in a different physical realm. Kim Momb looked like a shorter version of the Incredible Hulk. He had been high on the West Ridge of Everest the previous spring and trained full-time during the intervening two months. Prior to his becoming a professional climber, Kim was a top-ranked skier, motorcross racer, and black belt kickboxer with an undefeated professional record. He had a ready smile and firm handshake. Carl Tobin's income was derived solely from competing as the mountaineer in a made-for-television event called "Survival of the Fittest." One look at his rippled, muscular physique and it was easy to see why. He had been living in Fairbanks and consistently pushing the limits of what had been considered possible in the mountains of Alaska. Carl was quiet with a piercing sense of humor that left you slightly off balance. For instance, when the group discussed romantic movies, Carl mumbled earnestly, "Yeah, I always get teary at that love scene in *Deliverance*." When Tibetans stared at Carl, he stared back with a look of such profound and—at the same time—

simple curiosity that they turned away. Carl would then follow them, continuing his study. The third powerhouse was Dave Cheesmond, a South African living in Canada. Dave had been Carl's partner on many of his hardest climbs and had distinguished himself as one of the most prolific and accomplished mountaineers in the world during the past two years. "Cheese" was gregarious and helpful and always willing to tip a beer or join in a bawdy song.

A second contingent were the older masters: George Lowe, Lou Reichardt, Andy Harvard, and Chris Kopczynski. George had already established himself as a legendary climber with a will, tenacity, and determination second to none. He had been the driving force on the route in 1981 and exuded a quiet confidence about this trip. Lou, a professor of neurophysiology, had climbed more twenty-six-thousand-foot peaks than any American. He shared George's work ethic. What Lou lacked in technical skills he more than made up for with a physiology that did not seem to be affected by altitude. Andy had been on a phenomenal number of expeditions and was a master of logistics. A lawyer by trade, he was thoughtful and articulate. Chris Kopczynski also knew about expeditions. He had reached the top of Everest, via the South Col Route, in 1981 as well as making the first American ascent of the North Face of the Eiger. "Kop" was a building contractor from Spokane, Washington, who had a straightforward western friendliness and a button with a picture of his wife and kids that he wore over his heart throughout the climb.

I thought of myself as being similar in strength to the other three climbers until we went out for a training run in Beijing. Carlos Buhler, Jay Cassell, and Dave Coombs left me in the dust. Buhler, a mountain guide from Bellingham, Washington, was a full-time climber with wider interests than just mountains. Carlos was multilingual with deep thoughts about international and interpersonal relations. He was warm but intense, and very sensitive to "feelings" on expeditions. I found Coombs to be an upbeat man who was one of the hardest workers I have ever met. His climbing résumé and background were similar to mine. He was a Harvard graduate with an MBA who trained intensively for this trip. Similar in many ways to Coombs was Jay Cassell, an MBA and ex-marine who had the least big-mountain experience on the team. Still, he had finished strongly in the Iron Man Triathlon and Western States 100 endurance run, and was, perhaps, our most aerobically fit member. Jay had a personality that was mentally as solid as a rock; he was a man who would break before he bent.

The final two climbers, Morrissey and Dan Reid, were both busy cardiothoracic surgeons in California. Neither was able to spend much time training. In fact, Dan had not climbed since his drug-addled solo ascent of the ropes on Everest in 1981. This time he came prepared, though. Dan had THE LITTLE ENGINE THAT COULD embroidered on all of his climbing clothes as well as a formal kilt to wear into base camp. The final member of the team was our "Mister Organization," base camp manager John Boyle. Boyle handled the detail work before the trip and developed a winch system that we hoped would save us considerable time and effort on the mountain. To reach the top of Everest we had a three-part task: We first had to reclimb the sheer initial forty-five-hundred-foot rock and ice buttress. Next, we had to carry enough supplies up the route to support a summit climb. Then we still had to climb a vertical mile and a half up a steep snow ridge to the top of the world. Boyle's plan was to launch a rocket attached to a cord from the top of the buttress. Next, he planned to rig up a continuous nine-thousand-foot loop with high-tech yachting pulleys at the top and bottom. He had a Honda engine to power our loads quickly over the difficult climbing. Most of the team was a bit dubious, but we all hoped it would work.

The trek to base camp again started from Kharta. Our gear was loaded onto yaks for the journey. It was a festive march with the colorfully robed Tibetan yak herders whistling, singing, and chanting mantras as we walked. With us on the trek were a group of seven doctor friends of Morrissey's who had donated to the cause and Jack Alustiza, the owner of a Basque restaurant whom Jim had asked to be the expedition base camp chef, our Chinese liaison officer who was again Wang Fu Chow, and our official interpreter, Mr. Tsao. Boyle, Alustiza, and the scientists were all a bit slower than the climbers, and we adopted a leisurely pace. The views were again stunning with bright red rhododendrons flowering in the monsoon wetness. The mornings were glorious with shimmering peaks dancing above us. By late morning clouds rolled in and covered the sky. Precipitation started before noon every day and lasted until late in the evening. As we gained altitude the rain turned to snow. Dan Reid never wore more than his kilt and stripped naked to bathe in every glacial pond.

It was encouraging to see how close the team grew as our trek in continued. On some evenings the large dome tent we used for cooking and dinner became a climbers' tavern, fraternity house, stage, or minstrel show. On one night bawdy songs replaced more gentle and harmonious melodies as the banquet continued long into the night. Cheesmond led our band of ill-matched voices while Hank played his harmonica. We later switched to limerick song and I improvised, developing a caustic profile for each of my fellow teammates.

An eccentric doc named Reid
Follows a bizarre old Scottish creed
He roams the hills in a dress
Attempting to impress
The yaks who still pay him no heed

The last days of the trek passed quickly, with the weather remaining sunny and the rhythm of travel becoming comfortable. We reached base camp at an altitude of seventeen thousand feet at the edge of the Kangshung Glacier on August 26. The area was welcoming. The base camp was large and open, on flat ground with grass and moss and wildflowers and running water nearby. Everyone, including the scientists, pitched in to get things set up. Base camp was a busy place. Between the cutting and coiling of rope, the building of stone walls, and the incessant sorting of food boxes, gear, and equipment, there was always work to be done.

The first task we faced in beginning the climb was to find and mark the route across the Kangshung Glacier so that we could carry gear to the base of the buttress. I, meanwhile, was feeling the effects of altitude. My resting pulse raced at more than one hundred beats per minute, double my normal rate at sea level. With exertion, my pulse pounded in my temples at over two hundred beats per minute. The fourteen-mile-round-trip carry across the glacier to advanced base camp with a heavy pack made for a long, exhausting day. An average of about five hundred pounds a day of food, fuel, tentage, hardware, ropes, personal equipment, and winch gear had to be selected from the two hundred yak loads delivered at base camp and moved across the glacier to advanced base camp by our ten porters and the climbers. Advanced base, in contrast to base camp, was stark and rocky and felt like part of the mountain. It was close enough to the face to feel the blast of avalanches. More so than stocking advanced base, the carries were necessary for acclimatization. The entire team left early in the morning to make the carry, except for Dan Reid. We passed Dan in the afternoon. He was still a long way from the end of the glacier. We suggested that he dump his load and return with us, but he refused. An hour after dark we were organizing a search party to go out onto the heavily crevassed glacier to look for Dan when we heard him yodel. With a big grin Dr. Reid raved about how beautiful it was to be alone on a glacier at night. Jim and Dan had a talk about risk and danger, and Dan agreed to stay in base camp and be good.

On September 1 the actual climb began. Lou, Carl, and I started fixing ropes up the buttress. As the climbing leader from the 1981 trip, Lou had the honor of leading the first pitch of the 1983 effort. The climbing went quickly—we knew exactly where the route should go. We were also helped by several ropes and anchors that were still in place from 1981. We regained seven hundred feet of sheer rock before noon. Dan Reid caught up to us late in the afternoon, carrying more rope. We asked him what he was doing on the route. Reid grinned. "Well, you need more rope, don't you?" Dan soon insinuated himself into the climbing rotation, carrying heavy loads in support of the leaders and helping out everywhere. Once again the crazy doc was a full climbing member of the team.

The lower part of the route climbed up steep rock that had lots of small, sharp, incut holds. We made fast progress, reaching our first campsite on the mountain on the second day. We again called it Snow Camp, as it sat perched on a magnificent snow ridge at the top of the first rock step. The next obstacle was a difficult ridge of enormous snow mushrooms and steep ice. Dave Cheesmond, Kop, and Coombs moved into the front. I joined Dan in the group carrying equipment up to support the leaders. The first ones up climbed the rock and ice that the mountain offered and fixed a permanent rope in place. The rest of the team used the fixed rope to safeguard themselves and climb with heavy loads. As in 1981, we used mechanical ascenders, which slide up the rope but lock when weighted, to move up, and rappelled back down using figure-eight friction rings that slowed our slide down the ropes.

After five days we reached the Bowling Alley, the dangerous ice chute that gives access to the upper face. This gully was still a funnel for debris that melts out of the upper rock headwall and was again one of the scariest sections on the climb. At the top of the Bowling Alley we reestablished Pinsetter Camp beneath the rock headwall that was the technically most difficult section of the route. In 1981 it had taken three weeks to surmount the crumbly, overhanging barrier. Climbing this section required laborious and strenuous aid climbing, where the leader pounds a piton into the rock and uses this aid point to advance. Looking up at the path, we saw a tattered rope swaying in the breeze, a remnant from the 1981 effort. Kim volunteered to "jug" up the weather-beaten cord. He clipped his mechanical ascenders onto the old rope and methodically began climbing like a spider on a thread. We watched with horror as Kim, a couple hundred feet above us, hastily detached first one, then the other ascender, and quickly clipped them back onto the rope a few feet higher. In four hours he regained the entire headwall. When I came up, I saw that where Kim detached his ascenders, the old rope was worn 95 percent of the way through; only one strand of frayed nylon, less than an eighth of an inch in diameter, remained.

I was now supposed to rotate back to advanced base camp for a couple of days of rest while Jay, Andy, Carlos, George, and Cheese moved to the front to push the route up the next section. Above the rock we had to surmount a nine-hundred-foot ice slope angled at seventy degrees that was protected by fifty-foot-high icicles at its top in order to reach the top of the buttress, a place we named the Helmet. Starting down, I met Cheese. He told me that he was not feeling well; he had to turn around and descend to base camp. Carlos and Andy were also ill. We were short of load carriers. I knew that I was very tired, but I decided that the team needed me to stay up and work. I was still insecure about my being on this team of great climbers and believed that this was a chance for me to prove my worth. The next morning I carried a fifty-pound load of ropes and ice screws to the top of the rock. Back in the tent at Pinsetter Camp, I was too tired to help Kim with the laborious tasks of melting snow into water and preparing dinner. I crawled into my sleeping bag and began shivering uncontrollably. Kim gave me tea and helped me throughout the night. In the morning I had not slept a minute and was very lethargic. Kim and George helped me pack up and I headed down.

As I started to rappel down the rock below Snow Camp I heard a roar. Looking up, I saw that a house-sized block of rock had broken off directly above me. It hit and shattered one hundred feet overhead. Car-sized chunks rained down on me. I curled up as small as possible and realized, *I am going to die.* I was calm; my mind was blank as I faced my doom. Three large boulders smashed within five feet of me, but I escaped unscathed. The air was heavy with the acrid, gunpowderlike smell of the rock dust. The sound of the avalanche resonated down the valley. After a moment of calm, my heart began to race. My pulse rose to more than two hundred beats per minute and my whole body shook uncontrollably. It was several minutes before the trembling stopped and I was able to stand and continue my descent.

Jim Morrissey had heard about my shivering and lethargy. He was concerned that I had cerebral edema and insisted that I return to base camp for a rest. High-altitude cerebral edema, a swelling of the brain, can quickly become fatal. Falling rock can end a climber's life in an instant. Walking dejectedly back across the glacier to base camp, I wondered if climbing any route on any mountain is worth dying for. At the same time I thought about my teammates, realizing that I had never been with a group so full of life. There was an intense prevailing appreciation for both the immense beauty surrounding us and the small joys of existence. I came to help this team climb the Kangshung Face and would return to the cause, if I could. I felt awful that I might have hurt our team's chances for reaching the top, not to mention ruined my own summit aspirations, by pushing myself too hard when I knew that I was not feeling well. I vowed to listen to my body from now on.

The rest of the team quickly succeeded in fixing ropes up to the Helmet. The climbing of the buttress has been accomplished in only twelve days. Now we needed to carry our gear up the wall. We all focused on Boyle's winch system. Carlos and Jay carefully uncoiled the polypropylene trail line and aimed the rocket launcher. The first effort dribbled off into an avalanche cone and was lost in the debris. The second firing was also a dud. We only had three rockets. Jim, Lou, and Boyle discussed the options. We could hazard another firing from the top station. If it failed, we would have no winch support. They decided on a second option, which was to fire a rocket from Snow Camp.

The route below was sheer to the glacier. They thought the rocket would surely work from there, and it did. We would get some support from the motorized winch.

The second part of the plan was to install a gravity hauling system on the over-hanging rock headwall above Pinsetter Camp. Dave Cheesmond and George Lowe engineered a two-thousand-foot continuous line with pulleys at the top and bottom. Haul bags were filled with rock and snow at the top station and clipped onto the rope, while the haul bags filled with our food and equipment were tied on the bottom. The upper haul bags were released and pulled up our gear. Both the gravity system and Boyle's engine-powered winch worked perfectly. We still had to man-carry the loads from Snow Camp up through the Bowling Alley to Pinsetter and from the top of the rock up the steep Helmet ice field. We needed all the manpower we could muster. So after five days of rest at base camp, I returned to the task. I was feeling much better and hoped that I had a virus and not cerebral edema or any other high-altitude illness.

With everyone putting in 110 percent every day, progress moving our gear up the mountain was steady. I again carried as heavy a load as I possibly could, plus ten pounds more every day. The monsoon continued to linger, with wet snow falling every afternoon. Still, every one of us pushed hard, working with no rest days. We all, of course, had our own summit aspirations, and no one wanted to burn himself out. Yet we were in a desperate race against the winter winds and storms. Once the jet stream lowered its one-hundred-mile-per-hour wrath down on the mountain and the winter Himalayan storms unleashed their fury, it would be impossible for anyone to reach the top. So despite having already pushed too hard once on the trip, and feeling exhausted at the end of every day, I continued to work with every ounce of my strength. The rest of the team put in an equal effort, which inspired each of us to do more. Lou, Carl, Carlos, Andy, Dan, Jim, and I were based at Snow Camp, bringing loads up to the gravity winch at Pinsetter Camp, with Lou often making two impossibly heavy carries per day. Jay and Dave Coombs were working the bottom of the gravity winch while George, Cheese, Kim, and Kop dropped down from the Helmet to work the top of the winch and ferry loads back up to the Helmet Camp. Kim put in a herculean effort—two carries every day for a week. We slowly moved more people up as more loads accumulated at the upper winch station. Finally, on September 29, our entire team of thirteen climbers and all of the necessary gear was on top of the buttress.

After a solid month of work we were only at 21,500 feet. This is the same altitude that yaks can walk to on the north side of Everest and where advanced base camp sits in Nepal. We still had a vertical mile and a half to climb on an unknown route and lit-tle time before the weather changed for the winter. Statistically, the jet stream was due to lower during the first two weeks of October. Jim and Lou began to work out a tentative strategy. Everyone had to continue to push as hard and fast as he could. We would establish three higher camps: Camp One at 23,500 feet, Camp Two at 25,500 feet, and Camp Three—High Camp—nearly 27,000 feet. We had a total of thirteen bottles of supplemental oxygen. So each person would carry his own one bottle of gas up to High Camp, sleep without extra oxygen, and use the bottle for the summit climb.

A typical day for us began several hours before sunrise when someone awoke to light the hanging stove suspended inside the tent. We melted pile after pile of snow carried to the stove with a stuff sack. High altitude amplifies the difficulty of melting snow into water. Even at its best, the procedure is like melting cotton candy to get a sugary syrup. A full pot of snow yields less than an eighth of an inch of water. Each morning we fed the pot until we had enough water for tea and soupy oatmeal. After breakfast we geared up and either climbed in a traditional manner—one person is belayed as he climbs upward while his partner plays out the rope for safety—or we carried ropes and equipment to support the upper climb. In addition to working twelve hours per day every day with no rest days, we had to take care of ourselves on the mountain. We had no native cook staff, so after an exhausting day climbing, we collapsed in our tents, still faced with the daunting task of melting snow into water to rehydrate and to prepare our meals.

At 21,500 feet I could feel my pulse beating in my temples, even at rest. Every step upward was a new altitude record for me. On October 1, I wrote in my diary:

> I realize that I am among the weakest of the thirteen of us. I also know the risks involved, even for the strongest. Consciously, I do not think that it makes sense to jeopardize my life to climb a mountain. But I am beginning to understand what Mallory must have meant when he said he was climbing Everest "because it is there." It is not just that the mountain is "there" externally, but it is because it is "there" internally, within me. It has become a personal quest. Yes, the beauty of the high mountains, the camaraderie, the teamwork, and the joy of movement are all reasons to be climbing here. But in these really high mountains there is a definite element of self-realization, and of learning exactly where my limits are, driving me upward. I do not want to die. But this is my shot at the top of the world, and I'm going for it, savoring every moment of life!

The weather turned perfect, and the massive team effort continued unabated. By October 5 everyone had been to twenty-five thousand feet without supplemental oxygen. Jim decided that the first summit team would be Kop, George, and Cheese. Along with Lou and Kim they headed up to establish High Camp. The group had to break trail through knee-deep snow angled upward at thirty degrees. With their loads they moved at a pace of four breaths per step with many rests. Digging out a tent platform from the steepening ice at over twenty-seven thousand feet was exhausting. They took turns working until they were gasping, then passed the shovel on to the next climber. It required three hours to chop out space for a single two-man tent. All were too exhausted to stay at High Camp. Cheese, who had been the strongest and the hardest worker on the team, developed a wet cough at the end of the day. He worried that he might be developing high-altitude pulmonary edema and elected to drop back all the way down to Helmet Camp. Kop had a bad headache and decided to descend to Camp One. George felt exhausted and realized that he also could not continue without a rest.

Jim hastily reorganized summit plans. He moved Lou, Kim, and Carlos into the first try. George, Jay, Dan, Kop, and Andy were the new second team. Dave Coombs, Carl, Jim, and I would be the third summit team. It sounded great to me. I could use the extra day of rest that being on the third team would afford. Moreover, with two parties ahead of us we wouldn't have to break trail through deep snow, making it much easier for us. Finally, it was exactly the team I wanted. I liked the concept of a Tabin-Tobin summit team. Carl's razor-sharp wit, laid-back personality, and incredible strength made him a joy to climb with. Dave Coombs was as mentally tough as anyone I've ever met and the most safety-conscious member of our team, which is a great asset for an Everest summit partner. Jim was a person I admired greatly and with whom I would be honored to share the big day.

The plan was to rotate the three teams to the top in three days. We had two tents at twenty-five thousand feet and a two-man tent at High Camp. You can descend quickly from the High Camp to Camp Two by sliding on your butt in the snow, braking with an ice ax. The first team would go to High Camp, sleep without supplemental oxygen, and use their bottles to go for the top. They would then descend to the second camp, where the third team would have hot drinks waiting for them. Meanwhile, the second team would have moved to High Camp. The next day, team two would summit and descend to Camp Two, where the first team would take care of them. Meanwhile, the final team would move into position for a summit bid. On the third day my group would climb to the top of Mount Everest and descend as far as possible. An air of excitement engulfed us. In three days we would have either made it or failed.

—

On October 8 Carlos, Kim, and Lou set out for the summit of Mount Everest at two o'clock in the morning. George, Dan, Andy, Kop, and Jay headed for High Camp. Jim,

Carl, Dave Coombs, and I set off for Camp Two. The first big news was that Andy had a sharp pain in his chest and a deep cough. Jim's diagnosis was an inflammation of the lining of the lungs. Andy headed down to base camp. Jim decided that as a doctor he had to stay with Andy and turned around. Next, Carl found that his toes were freezing and he could not warm them. He had developed frostbite in Alaska the previous winter and decided that the summit of Everest was not worth the risk for him, as he would surely lose his toes—and the frozen foot would add to the danger of a fall. Next, Coombs developed a terrible headache and was unable to hold down food. Worried that he was developing cerebral edema, he turned back.

My entire summit team had disintegrated on me. We all returned to Camp One. I was very upset and confused as to what to do. I felt good enough to go for the summit, but was afraid to try it alone. Then Cheese called on the radio to say that he was feeling healthy again and was keen to make a bid. Dave Cheesmond and I thus became the new third team. We planned to move to Camp Two, at twenty-five thousand feet, the next day. Meanwhile the weather remained perfect with a cloudless calm sky. Jay, Dan, and George reached High Camp feeling strong. We all eagerly awaited word from the first summit team. The second team reported that the snow was deep above camp. Trail breaking must have been exhausting for Kim, Carlos, and Lou.

At noon we got an excited radio call from our Chinese interpreter, Mr. Tsao, who was watching the progress from base camp via a high-powered telescope. "I see climbers on ridge! Climbers are on ridge!" he reported. This was at twenty-eight thousand feet where our route merged with the Southeast Ridge. The East Face had been climbed! Now we only needed to follow the ridge to the top. In the background on the radio we heard Tibetans chanting mantras for our success. The next message we heard was bizarre. "Seven climbers, seven climbers going to get them!" We had no idea what Tsao was talking about. We later learned that a Japanese team climbing the South Col route from Nepal met up with our team just below the South Summit at 28,500 feet. The Japanese were climbing without supplemental oxygen and soon fell behind our climbers.

The final climb to the South Summit was steeper and scarier than expected. The angle was more than forty-five degrees with a hard crust over sugar snow. It would have been impossible to self-arrest a fall. To save time and weight they were climbing unroped. Any slip would be fatal. Above the South Summit a heavily corniced knife-edged ridge led to the short vertical obstacle known as the Hillary Step. This thirty-foot wall was passed by strenuously bridging one foot on rock while kicking the other foot's crampon points into the ice. Finally, at two-thirty in the afternoon, twelve hours after starting out from High Camp, Kim's voice crackled on the radio, "We're on top of this fucker!"

Back at Camp One we whooped with joy and hugged all around. Kim, Carlos, and Lou walked the final steps to the top together. Kim was openly weeping on the top of the world. The three spent forty-five minutes in perfect sunshine and air calm enough to light a candle, enjoying the view and taking photographs. All three were out of supplemental oxygen when they cautiously headed down. They encountered the Japanese, still stumbling upward, at the South Summit. None of them had a pack. This meant that they did not have any extra clothing, sleeping bags, water, or stoves for a bivouac. It was past four o'clock in the afternoon. Our team suggested that it was too late and that the Japanese should turn around. They shook their noticeably blue faces and continued upward. A Sherpa climbing with the Japanese then fell and started sliding ten feet above them. Lou looked directly into the terrified man's eyes as he tumbled past, missing Lou by only a few inches, before accelerating into a seven-thousand-foot drop into the Western Cwm. A few minutes later one of Lou's footholds gave way and he flipped upside down, suspended by only one foot punched through the hard crust in the snow. He hung, unable to right himself, with just a couple of toes keeping him from falling off the mountain. If his foot had let go, he would have torpedoed seven thousand feet, headfirst, following the path of the Sherpa to certain death. Carlos climbed fifteen feet back up to help him. Badly shaken by the near fall and having watched the Sherpa perish, Lou and Carlos faced into the slope and backed slowly down the steep ice.

Kim continued descending alone, unaware of Lou's slip, and reached High Camp at six o'clock. He came down all the way to Camp One, joining me in my tent at 23,500 feet at eight o'clock. I had never seen a human being who looked so exhausted. His eyes were sunk back into his face and he was barely able to whisper. Meanwhile Carlos and Lou still had not returned to High Camp. Our team became progressively more anxious. Kim postulated that they may have opted to descend the easier route down to the South Col in Nepal and stay with the Japanese. We worried that they had fallen. Finally, at nine o'clock, George reported that they had staggered into High Camp. Six people were crammed into the tiny two-person tent; any movement by one person affected everyone else. Lou had terrible nightmares and coughed incessantly. Carlos had full-body muscle cramps and convulsions. No one got any sleep. Dan later said that, physically, the hardest part of his summit day was holding Carlos's arms and legs during the night.

At two o'clock in the morning, on October 9, George started brewing up, melting snow into water. At three-thirty he was set to go. Kopczynski had had a bad headache all night and felt it was getting worse. He was also concerned about Lou and Carlos going down alone. Kop volunteered to help them. Dan and Jay wavered a bit, then decided to go for the summit. Since the track had partially blown in, they decided that George should start out breaking trail; they would catch up. The wind picked up toward morning. After an hour George stopped and looked back. He saw no one behind him. He later wrote in his diary:

> Wind whips snow across my face. Can't even tell if I'm standing up straight. Complete vertigo! So alone! Have never felt such an alien environment, clearly a place where man was not meant to be. Why haven't Jay and Dan started? Storm is increasing—will just continue 'til it seems unreasonable.

Dan and Jay discussed what to do for a long time. When they finally decided to go for it, Dan found that the oxygen fogged his glasses, and they were delayed further as Dan struggled to clear his vision. Meanwhile, down at Camp One, I brewed up for Kim and enjoyed a celebratory breakfast of tinned cake and pudding. Jim Morrissey came over to our tent. He was elated at the team's success and said he now just wanted to see everyone safely off the mountain. Cheese joined us in great spirits, totally optimistic about our summit bid. "The track will be in, so we'll just walk up the steps. We'll have a perfect summit day, Geoff," he said. I was feeling great and very happy to have Dave as my summit partner. We headed up to the next camp carrying our oxygen bottles and personal gear. At Camp Two we had a great reunion with Lou and Carlos coming down. Both were wasted, but healthy. Kop was also feeling better. His headache was gone and he opted to join me and Cheese and go back up. This increased my confidence. Not only was Kop strong and safe, but he'd been to the top before. I only wished that Jim, who had also been powerful and fit, had decided to join us.

The wind increased in intensity as the morning wore on. Clouds began to build down in the valley and move up the mountain. Up high, George was continuing to climb solo and was finding very hard snow and a steeper slope than he expected. He climbed cautiously, because he knew that he could not self-arrest a fall. Then he saw a figure above. In his diary he wrote:

> He moves incredibly slowly, taking a few steps, then collapsing on his ice ax to rest. I am going up and he is coming down. Yet we are covering ground at about the same rate. I ask the Japanese climber if he is okay. He replies, "bivy," and points up. He is very blue and his motions uncoordinated. I have no rope to help him, so just pat him on the shoulder and continue.

Dan and Jay were now struggling up the lower slopes, finding that George's steps had already disappeared with the wind. Cheese, Kop, and I watched the weather carefully. Dave reassured me that the clouds were just down in the valley and conditions should hold for a few more days. I still worried about my own summit chances as I watched the mist slowly creep up the mountain.

The climbing steepened for George. Just below the South Summit he turned up the rate of his oxygen flow. At the South Summit he found a movie camera left by a Japanese climber the day before and wondered how many had had to bivouac. George moved onto the dramatic upper ridge and over the Hillary Step. He continued in his diary:

> Above the Hillary section is a steep bulge of snow. It feels awkward moving over it, especially since I can't see well with the mask and goggles. Immediately above is an ice ax sticking in the snow. Looking down I see scrape marks in the snow until they end at steep rock a few meters below. The realization hits that one of the Japanese died here yesterday. I push on, now just wanting to be finished.

George reached the summit just before ten o'clock in the morning. He spent half an hour surveying the view, turned up his oxygen, and started the descent. He picked up the Japanese ice ax for added security on the steep sections. At noon he met Jay and Dan just below the dangerous part. George told them about the Japanese and urged them to set a turnaround time. He recalled, "Dan says they will turn around by one-thirty. Knowing Dan does not give me any confidence in that prediction."

George stopped briefly at our top tent and left his extra oxygen. He also turned on his headlamp and left it suspended from the top of the tent in case Dan and Jay returned after dark. He then zipped down, stopping for a quick congratulatory hug and a brew at our camp, and reached Helmet Camp by four o'clock in the afternoon. I was very psyched by George's fast ascent. Our team had already achieved great success, and I began to believe that I would reach the top of Everest. Then, over the next two hours, the clouds continued to surge up the mountain and the wind began to whip the tent. I began to worry again about my summit chances.

George's footprints were already invisible outside our tent. Then the realization hit: Dan and Jay were still out there! The storm intensified into a whiteout blizzard as the sun set. "Death-Pact PercoDan" had not been on a mountain in two years. This was Jay's first trip to the Himalayas. Worry gave way to panic, made all the worse because there was nothing we could do. It would be impossible for anyone to survive a night out at this altitude, in this storm. Then, at nine o'clock, Dan and Jay came on the radio to say they had just returned to the High Camp tent.

They, of course, had ignored the turnaround time. Jay and Dan reached the summit at three-fifteen, out of supplemental oxygen. They stayed on top until four o'clock and started to descend, just as the storm hit them. For psychological support they took a small length of rope that Dan had carried and tied themselves together so that if one fell they both would die. Both were totally exhausted and disoriented in the blizzard. It was completely dark. Both were freezing. At eight o'clock they argued about where to go. Dan felt that they must have passed the tent and advocated going back up. Jay was too tired to ascend and insisted they must have lost the ridge and that they should move laterally. Then the storm abated for an instant and they saw a glimmer of a light beneath them. An hour of desperate struggle later they found the High Camp tent and crawled inside. George's headlamp battery had gone dead, but it lasted just long enough to help Jay and Dan survive.

Dawn on October 10 revealed the full fury of the mountain. The blizzard still raged. High winds and two feet of new, windblown snow made it difficult to move, and the avalanche danger was extreme. There was no question. We had to go down. Kop, Cheese, and I waited for Dan and Jay, then began breaking trail down to Helmet Camp. Jay's right hand had fingers black with frostbite, but he never complained. Dan was having trouble seeing because his glasses were becoming covered with snow, but he kept on smiling, even after he wandered off the trail and tumbled twenty feet, stopping only a few inches from a fatal drop. I descended the avalanche chute, tied Dan to a rope, and helped him out. We crawled, wet and miserable, into Helmet Camp after seven hours of hard work. The next day we rappelled down into the swirling tempest, having to dig out icy ropes that had frozen into the buttress. Forty scary times we slid down the slick ropes with freezing hands barely able to work the braking device. We were trying to bring all our gear and garbage off of the mountain with us, and it was difficult to balance the enormous loads. At the top of the Bowling Alley I slipped, and my pack flipped me upside down. Spindrift avalanches swept over me. I couldn't breathe and couldn't untangle myself. Just as I started to drown, Dr. Dan returned my favor of the previous day and came back up a rope to save my life.

Eight hours later our entire team was reunited at advanced base camp. Everyone was safe. With the exception of Jay, who would lose a couple of fingertips to frostbite, all of us were healthy. Six Americans had reached the top of Mount Everest via the first ascent of the largest, steepest, and most difficult face on the mountain. The route we pioneered remains the most difficult on Mount Everest and has not been repeated in nearly twenty years. Many of the cognoscenti felt our route was too dangerous and too difficult, and that we had no chance for success. Doubts among our peers helped develop the cohesive bonds among us. We did it with a minimum of supplemental oxygen and no native support or porters on the climb. More importantly, we did it as a team of brothers who were all leaving the mountain as friends, bonded for life.

8

PUSHING
THE
EDGE

For me, the ascent of the East Face of Mount Everest was an experience of maximum intensity, and totally fulfilling. I didn't make the top, but I felt good about my effort toward the team's success. Still, I couldn't help but wonder whether, if the weather had cooperated, I would have been able to make it to the summit. I wasn't as strong as several of my teammates who'd nearly died going to the top. I had pushed hard, but not to the very edge of my limits. I wanted to know exactly what I was capable of. During the next two years I continued to expand my limits on technically difficult rock and ice climbs. Reaching the top of a climb wasn't the issue; I wanted to maximize my efforts during every moment. This philosophy also extended into my academic efforts.

I graduated from Harvard Medical School in the spring of 1985 and immediately went to Nepal. With me were Steve Ruoss, my main climbing partner in Boston during the past year; Jim Traverso, a climbing guide who was living in Kathmandu; and Dave Dossetter, an old friend who was new to climbing and would trek with us. We were joined by a young Sherpa named Dawa Tsering whom Jim arranged to have as our trekking guide. Dawa Tsering and I quickly became good friends despite having no language in common. He told me that he wanted to be a climber. We joked about climbing Mount Everest together. Little did either of us suspect that three years later we would embrace on top of the world.

Our plan for the pre-monsoon season of 1985 was to walk through the Khumbu region near Mount Everest to acclimatize, and then climb two twenty-one-thousand-foot peaks by technically difficult routes. Trekking through the Nepal Himalayas in the spring is one of the most pleasurable activities I know. There are no roads, only hiking paths, connecting the villages. The native people maintain these routes of transportation and commerce such that the walking surface is usually perfect. Yaks carry all the heavy gear. We walked unencumbered, with only a light day pack on our backs. The spring days were long and sunny with green budding in the forests, alpine flowers blooming bright orange, violet, pink, and red near our feet, and the snow-covered peaks dancing in the deep blue sky above. The pungent smell of rhododendron, juniper, and pine tickled our noses in the crisp, clear air. Our Sherpa cook boy started every day with a smile and "Chai Sahib, Geoff," bringing sweet Sherpa milk tea to my tent. Next came a four-course breakfast. We walked leisurely, taking in the views, for several hours each morning and afternoon with a long break for a sumptuous lunch in a scenic location every afternoon. The trail was dotted with Sherpa teahouses. These smoky wooden structures were the source of lots of laughter, chai, and home-brewed *chang*. Being part of a small group with an equal number of Americans and Sherpas, we were welcomed into many homes and parties. We spent two weeks wandering and adapting to the altitude.

All five of us then walked up to the easily accessible eighteen-thousand-foot summit of Gokyo Ri, from where many of the best pictures of Mount Everest have been taken. From the top we could survey five of the world's eight highest mountains. Next, Jim and I climbed a beautiful, steep snow ridge to the twenty-one-thousand-foot summit of Parcharmo. It was impossible to set anchors in the ridge, so we moved together with the knowledge that if one of us fell, the other would have to immediately jump off the other side of the ridge. Parcharmo bridges the Rawaling region and the Khumbu. The 360-degree panorama from its top spans the seemingly endless Tibetan plateau on one side and the lush terraced rice paddy fields glowing green beneath us in Nepal. Still, our main goal was for Steve, Jim, and I to climb the sheer seven-thousand-foot North Face of Kusum Kangruru. This would be the first ascent of the steepest line on one of the most difficult mountains in Nepal.

A storm blasted us and the mountain while we were on the final approach walk to the peak, coating everything with wet snow. From our base camp at fourteen thousand feet we surveyed the vertical mile-and-a-half wall above us. The North Face proper was too dangerous from the threat of avalanches, so we switched our objective to an unexplored rock buttress on the Northeast Ridge of Kusum Kangruru. We estimated that the climb would take five days up and down. With this in mind we brought food for four days and fuel to melt snow into water for six days. The trek and previous ascents allowed us to become well acclimatized. Our plan was to climb the route "alpine style"—starting at the bottom and climbing to the top with no fixed ropes or permanent camps on the mountain. The climbing started on steep rock that was continually challenging, but never desperate. We anchored to tiny ledges to spend the nights. We had to carry food, fuel, climbing gear, and clothes for the ascent, and our packs weighed more than fifty pounds. I attempted to reduce the size of my load by leaving my sleeping bag behind. I tried to sleep in a down suit and bivouac sack, but found I was too cold. I shivered and watched the stars until dawn every night. We made steady progress up the cliff, although rime ice coated the stone and every move was tenuous. The difficulty required removing our gloves to hang on tiny edges, but then our fingers would quickly go numb. It took us six days to surmount the five thousand vertical feet of rock climbing. By this time we had been out of food for more than a day and had no more fuel to melt snow into water. Above us a snow ridge led to the summit, only seven hundred feet higher in altitude. We chopped sleeping platforms out of the ice for our seventh night on the mountain. My mouth felt like I had swallowed glue. The next day I could barely swallow and my throat felt like a herd of yaks had stampeded through during the long night. Still, we started for the peak at first light. The ridge had a double cornice, and we had to anchor and belay each rope length of progress. At one o'clock in the afternoon we were still a few hours from the top. We were past all the difficulties. The summit looked close enough to touch. But we had been climbing above twenty thousand feet for twenty-four hours without water and nearly three days without food. Any exertion caused panting, and we lost more moisture with every breath. It was now a struggle just to remain standing. Steve looked at me and asked, "What do you think, man?"

"I'm wasted," I whispered. Jim stood behind me and nodded.

"It's down or die!" Steve concluded.

With no further discussion we belayed back down the corniced ridge and started retreating down the wall. The rock was too difficult to climb down, so we placed anchors and rappelled. We tied our two ropes together with the knot near the anchor, slid down the doubled rope, then pulled one end to retrieve the ropes. On our third rappel a rock was dislodged and cut one rope near its middle. Now, instead of dropping 165 feet each time, we were only able to descend less than 100 feet from each anchor. Two rappels later a second rock cut our other rope. Now we were reduced to seventy-five-foot rappels. This meant we were both descending more slowly *and* running out of equipment to secure our ropes. Moreover, the rock was loose, and it was difficult to find safe anchors. We continued our desperate retreat through the night. Loose rocks pelted down around us, whistling past, sounding like missiles in the dark. We were all beyond exhaustion and moving purely by instinct. I had no conscious thoughts; there was no conversation; all energy was focused on the task. Still, we worked perfectly as a team, communicating silently. If any of us made a mistake in placing an anchor, all three would die. Our bodies screamed for us to stop, sit, and rest, but we knew that if we did we would never get up. Thirty-six hours of maximum concentration later we safely reached the glacier. Steve's fingers were swollen like sausages, and his face was puffed up like a blowfish. My tongue had expanded to the point where it completely filled my mouth; I was unable to swallow or talk. But we were alive! I had learned how much reserve strength I could muster when all bridges were out behind me and there was nowhere to go but on.

This experience put me in good shape for an every-other-night-on-call surgical internship at the University of Colorado. I actually enjoyed the year. My learning curve was very steep, and there was great satisfaction for me in gaining competence as a physician. It was also a wonderful climbing year for me. Henry Lester was living in Boulder and specializing in short, severe, overhanging rock test pieces requiring maximum gymnastics, and we renewed our partnership. In addition, George Lowe was living in Denver. George pushed me to maximize my time off, accepting no excuses. During a period when I worked twelve-hour shifts in the emergency ward, George helped me take advantage of a rare twenty-four hours of freedom to climb a route on the Diamond Wall of Longs Peak in Rocky Mountain National Park. I worked until midnight and had to be back in the emergency room at midnight the next day. George picked me up at the hospital. I slept in the car until we arrived at the parking lot at the base of Longs Peak at three o'clock in the morning. We hiked to the base of the climb at eight, finished twelve pitches of rock climbing by four in the afternoon, scrambled to the top of the mountain, and descended to George's car by nine. I napped in the car and returned to work at midnight, surviving my shift without a mistake or mishap.

A thirty-two-hour break was enough to climb a six-hundred-foot sandstone spire called Moses Tower in Canyonlands National Park with George and Neal Beidleman thanks to George's pilot's license. A week's vacation allowed me to climb a five-day route up the overhanging three-thousand-foot granite face of El Capitan in Yosemite Valley with Tom Dickey. I particularly enjoy the sensation of big-wall life, hanging progressively higher each night and watching the everyday world below, and its problems, becoming smaller and smaller.

In 1986 I began a residency in orthopedic surgery in Chicago. I enjoyed the work and the city, but missed the mountains. With Matthew Childs, Rob Slater, Arturo Perez-Reyes, Mike McCarron, and Brad Werntz, I lived the life of a climber in exile. The six of us "buildered" together, climbing on the walls of buildings, and made the long drive to climb at Devil's Lake, Wisconsin. My girlfriend, Beth Peterson, was in Denver, and for the first time in my life I found myself wishing I were someplace else. In December 1987 Jim Frush, a climber I'd spent time with in Nepal in 1985, called from Seattle and invited me to come as a doctor on his Mount Everest expedition the next year. Everyone whom I mentioned the trip to said the same thing: "Impossible! You cannot quit a residency in orthopedic surgery!" I did not hesitate. I told Jim, "Yes!"

It was five years since the ascent of the East Face of Everest. The mountain was still "there" inside of me. In addition to the expeditions to Tibet and the Nepal trip in 1985, I had been climbing in the Andes three times. I knew my body and what I needed to do to climb Mount Everest. I returned to sprinting stadium steps while I was in Chicago. When I finished my commitment to my residency in June, I moved to Colorado to train full-time for six weeks. I was going on the expedition as a doctor with a first priority of keeping everyone on my team healthy. But in the spirit of Dr. Dan Reid, I was ready to take the risks to reach the top of the world. What I was not prepared for, however, was the craziness I encountered on Mount Everest in 1988.

9

HEAVY TRAFFIC ON THE EVEREST HIGHWAY 1988

The ridge I am climbing is barely two feet wide. To the east is a sheer drop of twelve thousand feet into Tibet. Westward it is eight thousand feet down to the next landing, in Nepal. The angle increases from seventy degrees to vertical at the Hillary Step. Climbing unroped, I delicately balance the crampon points on my right foot on an edge of rock. I swing my left foot, with all my remaining strength, into the adjoining ice. Precariously balanced on quarter-inch spikes attached to my boots, I gasp for breath. Forty feet higher the angle eases. Adrenaline mixed with joy surges through me. After eight hours of intense concentration, I know I will make it. The seventy-mile-an-hour wind threatens to blow me off the ridge; the ambient temperature is far below zero. Yet I feel flushed with warmth. Ahead stretches a five-foot-wide walkway angled upward at less than ten degrees. Thirty minutes later, just after ten o'clock in the morning, the path ends in a platform of ice the size of a small desk. Everything is below me. I am the 209th person to stand on the summit of Mount Everest.

The sky is deep blue and cloudless. The cliché is true, the vistas *do* seem to stretch infinitely in all directions. I look down over Lhotse, the world's fourth highest peak, upon the endless chain of mountains in Nepal. The Tibetan plateau on the other side extends to the horizon, where I can see the curve of the world dropping away. For fifteen minutes I savor the view as the highest person on earth. Then the crowds start to arrive.

Within an hour climbers from three countries are taking turns being photographed on the summit of Mount Everest. An American woman arrives on top. A Korean makes the climb solo to commemorate the October 2 closing ceremony of the Seoul Olympics. On the way down the woman, Peggy Luce, becomes snow blind and then takes a near-fatal fall before being rescued by the heroism of Dawa Tsering Sherpa. And this is one of the dullest days of the season.

Thirteen teams from ten countries made at least one attempt on every face and ridge on Mount Everest during the post-monsoon season of 1988. It was the first time that the Nepalese and Chinese gave out multiple permits for a mountain. Climbing styles ranged from siege tactics utilizing fixed camps, Sherpa porters, and supplemental oxygen to a solo, oxygenless, nonstop attempt from base camp. Everyone was out to set a record or do something new. Without a "first" it is nearly impossible to obtain sponsorship.

I was with the Northwest American Everest Expedition. Accompanied by thirty Sherpas, our team of eleven climbers, led by Seattle attorney Jim Frush, included three women bidding to become the first American woman to climb Mount Everest. The media played up this angle, as did our sponsors. Having been there before gave me a realistic perspective on the task ahead. Any success would have to be a team effort. Diana Dailey, Peggy Luce, and Stacy Allison had all been selected for their climbing ability, strength, and personal qualities. They just happened to be women. On the mountain we would all be equal.

On August 1 we left Kathmandu for the twenty-day approach march to the mountain. Trekking in the Himalayas can be inspiring—but the only poem to result from our muddy monsoon walk through the torrential rain was titled "Leech on My Dingus":

Leech on my dingus
Leech on my dingus
You gave me quite a scare
This morning before breakfast when I found you there
I even wore nylons to keep you away
But they ran at the crotch hiking yesterday

Leech on my dingus
Leech on my dingus
You crawled in through that hole
And made a beeline, straight for my pole
Why is it I who must suffer the hex
Of an engorged leech feeding at my sex

Leech on my dingus
Leech on my dingus
I don't wish to be intimate anymore
To me you are nothing but a cocksucking whore
And no matter how much you suck my dingus
I will never reciprocate with leechalingus.

There are two windows of less terrible weather in the Himalayas: one immediately before and one just after the monsoon. During the long winter the one-hundred-mile-an-hour jet stream winds lower to twenty-three thousand feet. Daily monsoon snows limit visibility and create prohibitive avalanche danger during the summer. We were suffering now, hoping to take advantage of a post-monsoon window of good weather on the mountain.

The Sherpas know the suffering Chomolungma can cause. One hundred seventy-two have died on her slopes. Before going to Everest we had to go to the Tengboche Monastery for a Pujah, or blessing ceremony, for safety on the climb. Set on a ridge crest directly below the spectacular summit of Ama Dablam and ringed by Everest, Nuptse, Lhotse, and Thamserku, Tengboche is a place where prayers will reach the gods. Twenty monks chanted continuously for twenty-four hours while the pungent smell of rancid yak butter mixed with the aroma of incense and burning juniper branches. Six monks worked for five days creating an intricate sand painting beseeching Chomolungma to be kind, and we had personal blessings from the Rimpoche Lama.

The Rimpoche Lama of Tengboche is the highest reincarnation in the region. The Sherpas believe that he founded the monastery four reincarnations ago and has mystical powers. When the Rimpoche dies they search the countryside for his reborn form. The current Rimpoche Lama is a wizened man of about sixty with laughing eyes shining from an otherwise impassive calm face. He personally said prayers for my safety and tied a blessed red "protection cord" around my neck. I hoped they had picked the right guy.

Three nights later I had my doubts. At four-thirty in the morning the world began to shake and vibrate. It was impossible to stand up on the moving Tilt-A-Whirl that had been the ground. Then, as the shaking stopped, the thunderous roar of avalanches filled the pitch-black air. We later learned that the earthquake registered 6.9 on the Richter scale and killed more than two thousand people. Geologically we were in an unstable area. The Himalayas are being formed from the movement of tectonic plates. The Indian subcontinent crashed into Eurasia twenty million years ago, causing a subduction zone of uplift, the highest point of which is Mount Everest. India is still moving at a speed of three centimeters per year relative to Eurasia, so the Himalayas are still being uplifted. We were lucky the earthquake struck when it did. Had it come two weeks later, when we were climbing, we would have been killed. Instead it shook down most of the unstable snow and ice that accumulated during the monsoon, making the mountain safer.

Finally, on August 24, we walked out of the rain into the snow of base camp at 17,500 feet on the Khumbu Glacier. The setting was on jumbled glacial moraine at the end of a long valley with the majestic peaks of Nuptse, Pumori, and the West Shoulder of Everest towering over us. The only gaps in the boxed-in canyon were back down the glacier or up the Khumbu Icefall ahead. The Nepalese call the Khumbu Icefall the "jaws of death." We would have to pass this obstacle to gain the upper slopes of the mountain. First we had to turn the glacier into our home for two months. Garbage from past expeditions was strewn about and had to be cleaned up. Ironically, much of the debris had EVEREST CLEANUP EXPEDITION stamped on it. It took a week to flatten platforms for tents, build shelters of stone walls covered with tarps for cooking and communal dining, and unpack equipment. I felt fine when I arrived at base camp, but panted for breath after chopping at the ice for one minute. The seven days spent preparing camp were good for acclimatization, and I felt ready to go.

First we had to have one more Pujah to consecrate the stone altar our Sherpas built in the center of camp. They erected a flagpole with hundreds of colorful prayer flags extending in a triangle out over the glacier from the top, believing that the wind would carry their prayers to the gods. Offerings of food and liquor were made. The High Lama of the Pangboche Monastery and three other monks came up to chant, juniper was burned, and blessed rice and *tsampa*, a barley flour that is a staple of the Sherpa diet, were tossed into the air. Next, all the alcohol was consumed and a drunken food fight erupted. Sherpas and sahibs covered in *tsampa* were staggering around the glacier. We decided to acclimatize for one more day.

At three o'clock in the morning on September 1, I started into the Khumbu Icefall. A river of ice flows from the upper slopes of Everest and Lhotse down through a flat valley known as the Western Cwm. The angle changes abruptly with the ice tumbling steeply for two thousand vertical feet to the Khumbu Glacier, forming the icefall. It is an area where unstable ice formations the size of apartment buildings frequently and unpredictably crash down amid ever-changing crevasses. Dozens of climbers have been crushed to death attempting to negotiate its jaws. In addition, five-thousand-foot walls of ice rise on either side, threatening to erase any path that we attempted. *If it weren't Everest I would not risk the objective danger, but it is and I will.*

A large Korean team moved in next to us at base camp. They had a permit for the South Pillar route, which also starts with the icefall. We worked together to fix the route. This involved finding the least dangerous path and then placing a safety rope, anchored into the ice, to use when climbing with a heavy load. There were numerous crevasses, or cracks, in the ice. Looking down into the gaping holes, I could see for hundreds of feet without discerning a bottom. But the scary ones are those you can't see because their openings are covered with fresh snow. To protect ourselves while establishing the route, one person was always anchored into the ice playing out the rope, ready to catch the leader should he fall. After climbing the pitch (about 150 feet) the leader secured himself and belayed up the second. This is standard technique unless you are climbing with the mighty and dangerous Om.

The "most dangerous man in Korea" stands five feet five inches tall, with enormous hydraulic pistons for legs and a never-ending mischievous grin. Hong Gil Om has a fifth-degree black belt in Tae Kwon Do, a second-degree black belt in Ju Jitsu, and is a member of Korea's elite antiterrorist squad specializing in underwater demolition. In 1987 he reached twenty-eight thousand feet on Everest during the winter. We were paired together leading in the icefall. I went one rope length, anchored myself to the ice, and belayed Om up to me. He led the next section, disappearing over an ice cliff. A few minutes later the rope tugged at my harness. Assuming Om was anchored, I began to climb. The rope pulled a substantial portion of my weight as I balanced upward on the front points of the metal crampons attached to my boots. Climbing vertical ice is strenuous, particularly at twenty thousand feet, and I appreciated the tight rope from above. Surmounting the final overhanging bulge, I stepped into deep snow angled upward at forty degrees. I was promptly pulled over, planting my face in the snow. Standing up, I struggled to where the rope went up another ice serac. On top of this obstacle, gasping for breath, I realized I had been following this "pitch" for three hundred feet. Then the rope yanked me over again. Ahead was Om, his legs churning madly in the thigh-deep snow, with an ice ax in one hand and an upside-down ski pole in the other. I yelled for him to stop, but he just laughed and continued to tow me, like a water-skier, up the mountain.

Om led 80 percent of the route we shared with the Koreans. He was not a safe climber by American standards, but in the Himalayas speed can mean safety and success. With his help we reached Camp Two on September 5, six days ahead of schedule. A few of us had been affectionately referring to the Koreans as "the dogeaters" behind their backs. I decided to find out if Om was powered by dog meat. Sharing a mug of ginseng tea on hard blue ice angled at seven degrees at 21,600 feet, I asked Om if he ate dog. He spoke little English, but after three minutes of pantomime and barking, Om understood the question. He shook his head, saying, "No like, no like." I then raised the question of whether he had sex with animals. Whirling through the air, his left leg rocketed out, propelling my teacup fifty feet, his right boot tapped my nose, and Om landed gently on the ice without spilling a drop of his own tea. I assume he meant no.

A greater danger than teasing Om remained the Khumbu Icefall. After establishing the route we still had to carry food and equipment up the mountain. Nearly two hundred loads needed to be carried through the icefall. The glacier shifts constantly, necessitating daily repairs to keep the path open. Worse, the threat of an ice cliff toppling over on us was always present. We climbed during the dark, as fast as possible, because the warmth of the sunlight makes unstable areas more likely to break off. At five-thirty on the morning of September 3, I was in the area where four climbers were killed during the 1982 Canadian Everest expedition, crossing the detritus from a previous avalanche, when I heard a loud crack. A massive ice cliff broke loose from the West Shoulder of Everest, four thousand feet above me, scraping the rock clean for a horizontal quarter mile.

I was next to Mr. Chung, a powerful Korean climber. Don Goodman, the rock-solid deputy leader of my expedition, and Kami Phurba Sherpa were just above us. We desperately looked for somewhere to go as the white death increased in size and in its seeming intent to bear down directly upon us. Alas, as Joe Louis said, there was "no place to run, no place to hide." Feeling as secure as if I were locked in a rolling boxcar with a starved three-hundred-pound sewer rat, I squeezed into a crevasse, secured myself to the fixed line, drove my ice ax in to the hilt, and waited. I glanced over at Mr. Chung, who was similarly anchored, and said, trying to reassure myself, "I think it will stop."

He returned a weak smile and said, "I hope!"

The avalanche floated down in slow motion as if Sam Peckinpah were directing it to maximize my anxiety. Don Goodman recalls thinking, *So this is what it is like to die in the Khumbu Icefall.* My terror lessened slightly upon seeing a large cloud of snow billowing up and out toward me. Generally the avalanche itself moves much faster than the cloud of snow and wind that follows. I was waiting to feel the wind-blast that would indicate survival when a wall of ice slammed into me. I heard a cry from my right side, but I was blasted about the head and shoulders and could not see Mr. Chung being swept away. It felt like twenty lightweight contenders were using my body as a speedbag, simultaneously, without gloves. I pressed down, trying to cover my head with my pack and arms and my mind went blank. The pummeling gave way to a swirling gale-force wind with crystals of ice choking my lungs. Then all was quiet. I was surprised that I could move all four limbs. I lifted my head. Everything was white. Mr. Chung, Don, and Kami Phurba had vanished.

I ran down the avalanche's path, screaming, "Hello! Don! Chung! I'm here to dig you out! Hello!" Thirty seconds later Mr. Chung, looking like a dazed snowman, emerged slowly from a crevasse. He had been swept three hundred feet and, like me, escaped with only bruises. A minute later we found Don Goodman tending to a stunned Kami Phurba. They had been pushed over a thirty-foot ice cliff and miraculously escaped being buried. We were lucky. Had the avalanche been 1 percent bigger or had we been fifty feet higher, we'd be dead. It was typical of Don Goodman to be more concerned with everyone else when he had the most severe injuries. Don's right hand was deformed by a broken bone. He barely flinched when I reset it for him. We limped back to base camp to find another kind of tempest building.

Czechoslovakian, New Zealand, and French Mount Everest expeditions had arrived at base camp and were told that they would have to pay to use our path through the icefall. Jim Frush and the Korean leader, Mr. Nam, worked out the equipment and transportation costs of establishing the route. They decided that this cost should be shared equally by all teams using the ropes. Frush, a successful attorney, had a compelling case. Our route was clearly the safest, and none of the other teams had brought enough equipment to fix a new route. So, the muscular six-foot-four-inch Frush argued, either they paid or did not climb.

Josef Just, a scowling Czechoslovakian with fiery black eyes, a thick black beard, and a chiseled body that would scare a bear expressed the sentiments of the newcomers, growling, "Zis iss bullsheeet! You climber, we climber, must share, no pay! Zis iss bullsheeet!"

The New Zealand leader, tall and affable Rob Hall, was the diplomat of base camp. He agreed that, perhaps, some compensation should be given. However, since his group and the Czechs planned to climb alpine style, or in a continuous push without fixed camps, and would thus only be using the ropes a couple of times, they felt that they should pay a smaller percentage of the cost. The French arrived, splintered into three groups who were barely speaking to each other. One faction was funded by a French insurance company and French television. Antennae 2 and U.A.P. had already paid nearly forty million francs preparing for a live broadcast from the summit. Their producer, Guy Garibaldi, a man of action not words, decided that it was silly to risk his program for a few thousand dollars and agreed to pay. But he specified that he was not paying for Marc Batard. This set a difficult precedent for the other, less endowed groups. Rob Hall tried to strike up a deal with Garibaldi whereby French television could film the Kiwis if they paid their icefall fee. Hall assured him that the film could be sold for a profit in New Zealand. The second French contingent, which sported the festive, phosphorescent glow of pink and yellow "Jean Marc Boivin Extreme Dream" attire was caught in the middle. They agreed, in theory, to pay, but said that they did not have the money with them. The Czechs remained adamant that they would never give in to capitalism on a mountain: "Iss bullsheeet!"

In the midst of the debate, a diminutive Frenchman approached the crowd. "I am Marc!" his voice boomed, like a tiny terrier with the bark of a Great Dane. He had come up from Pheriche that day, normally a three-day trek away. After listening to the problem he announced, "The weather changes, I go tonight." While those negotiating with him were still in midsentence, he turned and walked quickly away with his "Marc Batard 24 Hour Everest" support team scurrying after him.

Marc Batard always walks fast. The week before, to acclimatize, the wiry thirty-seven-year-old speedster from Megeve, France, climbed the world's sixth highest mountain, Cho Oyu, in eighteen hours from base camp. Now he was going to race up Everest, solo and without supplemental oxygen, in less than twenty-four hours, broadcasting live on radio back to France. His sponsorship depended on it. He also was rushing to get up before his countrymen, Michel Parmentier and Benoit Chamoux, performed a similar feat from the north side. Donning his custom-made, ultralight, bright orange climbing suit with its two-liter bladder for black coffee connected to a straw running up his collar to his mouth and a built-in radio microphone, he signed an IOU without looking at the two pages of legal jargon and, at eight o'clock at night, turned on his headlamp and began dashing up the mountain. Cries of "Allez Marc!" rang out into the darkness until his light bobbed out of sight. At least the icefall access controversy was settled. The "Extreme Dream" French, the Czechs, and the New Zealanders quickly signed IOUs with varying intentions of paying. Batard stumbled back to camp at six the next evening. He claimed to have reached twenty-six thousand feet before he was stopped by bad snow conditions and exhaustion. Sounding remarkably like Inspector Clousseau, he told me in his heavily accented English, "I don't eat two days, I come Pheriche, I anger and think bad, is no good. Now I eat, then summit maybe."

He rested six days before learning via the radio that Chamoux and Parmentier were making their bid. Batard suited up, poured in the black coffee, and sprinted again, this time leaving at six o'clock in the evening. He passed Camp Two in full stride at ten-thirty and disappeared up the Lhotse Face. Late the next afternoon I met Marc descending to Camp Three. The skin was drawn tight over his prominent cheekbones. Only his bulging eyes differentiated Batard's thin face from a skull. He seemed to have aged ten years. I gave Marc tea as he muttered, "I make one hundred vertical below top. I can make summit, but I die. I am so sick, every breath vomit, vomit; so I think maybe I go down now or else I die."

Marc was not only dealing with an endurance problem. He was also running his supermarathon with a quarter of the oxygen pressure that exists at sea level. In 1978 Tyrolean climbers Peter Habeler and Reinhold Messner were the first to reach the summit of Everest without supplemental oxygen, a feat physiologists had predicted would be fatal. It was later shown that variances in barometric pressure and in the atmospheric pressure near the equator make it possible, but only barely. Any altitude above eight thousand meters, or twenty-six thousand feet, is still considered to be in the "death zone" where there is not enough oxygen to sustain life.

Batard's decision was a wise one. We later learned that Michel Parmentier died at twenty-seven thousand feet on his attempt. He became exhausted and collapsed; Chamoux was unable to bring him down. On the same day a small avalanche hit one of the Spanish tents on the West Ridge, killing Narayan Shresta, a high-altitude porter.

Shresta was one of the most experienced people on the mountain, having summited Everest in 1985. Although not a Sherpa, he shared their Buddhist faith and deserved a proper cremation. It took two days for the Spanish team to lower his body back to base camp. Then they carried him down to a magnificent hillside under the majestic summits of Taweche and Cholatse. Amid three dozen *chortens,* rock memorials, commemorating the lives of Sherpas who died on Everest, Narayan Shresta's soul was released to the wind and a new *chorten* built. Meanwhile Chomolungma revealed a gentler side to her personality. The daily monsoon storms stopped. Her flanks basked in the glow of bright sunshine. But even in perfect weather the lack of oxygen makes movement above twenty-four thousand feet difficult and dangerous. My lungs burned as I climbed the vertical mile of ice to our high camp on the South Col, the saddle between Everest and Lhotse at 26,200 feet. Three or four gasping breaths between steps did little to ease the pain. My mind, dulled by a lack of oxygen, continually urged me to "go ahead, sit down and rest for a while." But I knew that if I stopped, I wouldn't go on. I developed a rhythm. Swing the ice ax, take three breaths, move the left foot up and sink the crampon points into the ice, take three breaths, move the right foot up and take four breaths. I continually tricked myself, saying, *After fifty steps you can take a rest, Geoff,* to be followed by *Just kidding, sucker, do fifty more.* My mind felt as clear and light as the morning after drinking a fifth of Jack Daniel's, six shots of tequila, and a bottle of red wine. I reached the col at two-thirty in the afternoon. All things considered, I was moving pretty well.

I reflected on the craziness of risking my life for an endeavor so reliant on luck. Five years ago I had been at this altitude ready to try for the top when a storm nearly took my life. Now I was again within striking distance. Looking down through the cloudless sky on the tiny mountains that had seemed so enormous from below, I dared to think I might make it, while silently beseeching Chomolungma to remain kind for a few more days. I thought about my karma and fingered the red string around my neck as I directed my gaze toward the summit ridge.

I traced our route. Above loomed fifteen hundred feet of steep ice leading to the Southeast Ridge. From there we follow the jagged, knife-edged crest to the South Summit, the highest point visible to me. On summit day I would climb solo. There is not enough time to stop and belay and still reach the peak. A rope means two people die instead of one if there is a slip. Regaining my breath on the South Col, I was actually pleased by how strong I felt. I wished that I could continue on up. But we still had to establish our assault camp and stock it with food, fuel, and oxygen before attempting the summit. Securing the ropes in place, I slowly turned to descend.

The weather remained perfect. Every team, except the Spanish who were delayed by the funeral, made rapid progress up the mountain. The first success of the year was claimed by the Czechs. Josef Just and Duson Becik powered to the 27,890-foot summit of Lhotse via a new route after an all-night push from Camp Three on Everest. They climbed unroped and without supplemental oxygen. A technically difficult first ascent done on the world's fourth highest mountain without supplemental oxygen is a mountaineering coup equivalent to pitching a no-hitter and slugging a home run in the ninth inning to win the game 1–0. But, for them, it was merely a training and acclimatization exercise. Along with teammates Peter Bozik and Jaraslov Jasko, they were preparing to attack the most difficult climb ever attempted: an alpine-style ascent, without oxygen, of Everest's Southwest Face.

The Czechs were not the only ones with outrageous plans. Jean Marc Boivin lives extreme dreams. The thirty-seven-year-old mountain guide with dancing eyes from Chamonix, France, has been on the forefront of climbing, hang gliding, and extreme skiing for most of his life. Feats like solo climbing the North Face of the Matterhorn, then skiing down its sixty-degree West Face only to climb another route on the North Face and descend by hang glider, all in one day, are routine for him. He came to Everest with his newest toy, a light steerable parachute called a parapente. Boivin was also going to carry skis to the top. Depending on wind and snow conditions he would ski or fly, whichever was more fun.

Marc Batard no longer saw Everest as fun. He wanted to go home. Frozen vocal chords reduced his formerly commanding voice to a barely audible raspy whisper as he lamented, "I must make top, you know. I no want to go up more but, is not possible to make sponsors if no success here." So the exhausted man prepared to endure a little discomfort now to ensure financial backing for the pleasure of walking to the North Pole, and then the South Pole, in the future.

Meanwhile my team and the Koreans continued our methodical approach to the mountain. We both prepared high camps and carried up bottled oxygen to support our summit bids. With all of the incredible plans around us, it seemed boring to be just climbing Mount Everest. Johnny "Rotten" Petroske, a deadpan humorist from Seattle who had SUMMIT OR DIE embroidered on his jacket, told the other teams, with a straight face, that he was going to roll down from the summit in a barrel. He calmly explained that his new lightweight barrel had been tested on Niagara Falls and was ready for Everest. I was proud to be introduced as his "pusher." After every explanation of his plans he would thunder, "It is my *destiny!*" In the midst of Marc, the Czechs, and other assorted "extreme dreams," no one batted an eye.

A more controversial issue for my group was the selection of summit teams. Nine of us were strong enough. Frush selected himself, lean and bearded Steve Ruoss, and the small but powerful Stacy Allison for the first try. They retreated back to base camp to rest while the camp at the South Col was being stocked. I told Jim that I felt this slowed our progress and created tension among several team members, particularly the women in our group. Everyone realized that the first American woman to reach the summit of Mount Everest would reap huge material rewards, and all three of our female climbers seemed strong and able to make the top. One suggestion was to have an all-female team. Since we had received enormous sponsorship predicated on the idea that we would get the first American woman to the top of Everest, however, Jim felt it best to hedge our bets and have our female climbers spread out across three summit teams in case of unpredictable weather. If the first team could not make the top, the second team would also contain a woman. I thought that we should all be equals, with everyone working as hard as possible to get us into a position to go for the summit. Then, like our expedition to the East Face in 1983, the strongest should head to the top. Unfortunately, Frush held to his decision.

We were delayed at least three days by a reduced work staff on the mountain and could not participate in the biggest party Chomolungma had ever had. At six o'clock in the evening on September 25, Marc left base camp for his third and final charge. Five hours later the mighty Om left his tent, at twenty-seven thousand feet on the South Pillar, along with another Korean and two Sherpas. At midnight the "Extreme Dream" team set out from the South Col. Boivin was accompanied by the "Big Swiss," André George (who resembles a slimmed-down André the Giant), three other French guides, and three Sherpas. The two groups met at the South Summit, continuing the last hour up the final ridge together. At three-thirty in the afternoon eleven climbers from four different countries embraced on the summit of Mount Everest. An hour later, twenty-two and a half hours after leaving base camp, a "very much exhausted" Marc Batard joined the celebration. His phenomenal speed ascent was soon to be matched by an equally prodigious speed descent.

I was at Camp Two at 21,600 feet when I heard the news from the French radio. Boivin was going to jump. It is true that the day was calm with the jet stream in a rare pause. But seriously, the last idiot to try to use a chute up this high was the crazy Japanese man who found out too late that the air was too thin to slow his ski descent from the South Col. Now Boivin was going to jump from three thousand feet higher? Taking off from the absolute summit, he plummeted like a stone. Then the parapente caught air and he began to soar. He was still just a dot, a mile above me, as he slowly began to lap the cirque of Everest, Lhotse, and Nuptse. Five hundred feet overhead he swung above his canopy. My heart dropped. But he continued on around, completing a perfect flip. He added one more loop for good measure before touching down at Camp

Two as lightly as a feather, on his feet, with Everest in the background, the sun at a forty-five-degree angle on his face and his hat and glasses off, six feet from his crew of cameramen. The crowd of twenty Sherpas, climbers, and cameramen who witnessed the landing began screaming and applauding. Boivin's youthful face responded with a shy, *what's the big deal?* smile. He had descended eight thousand feet in eleven minutes.

Three days later Stacy, Steve, and Jim left the South Col going for the summit. They expected three Sherpas to come with them, each carrying an extra cylinder of oxygen. Only one, Pasang Gyalzen, arrived. None of them was willing to risk going to the top without extra oxygen. So Frush decided they should have a lottery. He told Pasang to pick a number between one and ten. Then the three Americans would guess. Whoever was closest would get the gas. Steve picked "six." Stacy said "four." Jim chose "eight." Then they all turned to Pasang.

The slightly built, five-foot-three-inch Sherpa was terrified. He later confided to me, "I think, *Why they ask me this? Why they make me choose? How to choose?* Then I think, *Who is nice to give big tip?* I think maybe Stacy give best bonus. So, I say, 'Stacy most close, my number must be three.' " Cursing their bad "luck," Jim and Steve turned back while Stacy climbed into history as the first American woman to reach the summit of Mount Everest. Pasang continued to the top with her, pausing to set the high-altitude cigarette record with a quick smoke on the South Summit. At the peak they met my friend from the icefall, Mr. Chung, and two other Koreans for a photo session before descending.

Two days later, on October 1, I returned to the South Col along with Peggy Luce and three Sherpas, Dawa Tsering, Nima Tashi, and Phu Dorje. I had originally been on a third summit team with Johnny Petroske and Don Goodman and was supposed to have been at base camp resting for our attempt. I argued, however, that as a doctor I should stay high in case one of the people in the first team had a problem. I knew my body and its reaction to altitude and felt confident that I would be able to go for the top without a rest. Moreover, I was concerned that the spell of good weather would not last, and thought that it was likely that a spot would open on an earlier attempt. Sure enough, both Diana Dailey and Jean Ellis from the designated second team became ill and turned back from Camp Three. I was at Camp Two. Jim Frush called on the radio and asked if I could go up and join Peggy and the three Sherpas. I left immediately. By staying high I made my own luck. I ascended the Lhotse Face to the South Col, knowing that this was my shot at the top of the world.

The Lhotse Face is an undulating cliff of ice with an average angle of fifty or fifty-five degrees that flows down from the high slopes of Everest and her sister peak Lhotse. We had a fixed rope to help with carrying loads and to safeguard our descent. The surface varied from a Styrofoam texture to brittle ice. I took my time climbing the forty-five-hundred-foot vertical rise and arrived at the South Col after six and a half hours of effort, feeling great but slightly thirsty. I sat down in Nima Tashi Sherpa's tent at two o'clock in the afternoon. He handed me a liter of hot noodle soup with fresh chilies, which I quickly drank. I washed this down with a second liter of hot soup and a bowl of ramen noodles. By three o'clock in the afternoon, I felt well fed and well hydrated, but quite tired. I told Nima Tashi we'd plan to leave for the summit at one o'clock in the morning. My suggestion was that he melt snow for the next few hours while I took a short nap. I asked him to wake me at seven-thirty, when I would take over the task of melting snow while he slept. He smiled and nodded. I then turned on the oxygen tank in our tent and plugged into the regulator. I was instantly engulfed by warmth and drifted off into a sound sleep. I awoke later when I badly had to pee. I asked Nima Tashi for the time. When he handed me my watch, I was shocked to see that it was already eleven o'clock at night. Thanks to Nima, I had enjoyed seven hours of blissful sleep and woke feeling energized and ready to go. Nima Tashi then handed me a liter of hot tea, which I quickly gulped down. This was followed by a second liter of hot tea and a full liter of hot energy drink as well as a bowl of oatmeal. I asked Nima Tashi why he had not wakened me; he simply smiled and said, "It's okay."

By midnight, I was ready to go. Unfortunately, the wind had picked up during the night; it was impossible to stand outside the tents. At one o'clock it was no better. We finally left at two, leaning into the eighty-mile-per-hour gusts. Carrying an eighteen-pound oxygen tank, an extra pair of mittens, a little water, and no bivouac gear, I was committed to making the top and descending back to camp.

Climbing by moonlight, we made good progress up the icy slopes. *One slip and you are dead; concentrate!* I kept commanding myself. Focusing on my breathing, I tried to ignore the rapid pounding in my chest. The powerful winds had scoured the trail clear and the initial slopes held the consistency of Styrofoam. Nima Tashi, Phu Dorje, Dawa Tsering, Peggy Luce, and I climbed side by side unroped. As we moved higher, we became hidden in gullies, which sheltered us from the wind. Around three in the morning my headlamp began to fade. I worried that I would have to stop until dawn. But just as my headlamp went out, the full moon rose over the horizon, illuminating Everest's snowy slopes with a warm glow. We continued quickly by moonlight and reached the Southeast Ridge well before the first glowing embers of sunlight began to touch the tips of neighboring Lhotse and Makalu, the world's fourth highest mountain. The heavens smiled down with radiance as, one by one, the high peaks of the Himalayas caught the fiery tip of the new day's sun. By seven o'clock, I was sitting just below the South Summit, enjoying a few sips of hot energy drink from a leather bota bag I carried against my chest.

From here the angle steepened and the friendly Styrofoam consistency changed to black brittle ice. I carried only a single ice ax, and climbing the short section of steep ice made me nervous. I turned the regulator on my oxygen cylinder up from one and a half liters to three liters per minute and negotiated this obstacle. Surmounting the short ice bulge landed me on the South Summit. Here I met the Korean leader, Mr. Nam, who had timed his ascent to coincide with the closing ceremony of the Seoul Olympiad. Bracing ourselves against the wind, we continued up the steep and narrow ridge leading to the peak of the world. Above the forty-foot rock obstacle known as the Hillary Step, unadulterated joy welled up inside of me. I knew that I was going to reach the summit of Mount Everest. The peak seemed to be just ahead. But when I reached the ridge crest, another, higher point rose above me. Chomolungma teased me with several more false summits before the ridge dropped sharply away. The world spread out beneath me. I spent fifteen minutes savoring life as the highest person on earth, alone on the six-foot-by-three-foot platform of ice that is the top of the world.

The summit of Mount Everest was everything I had fantasized it to be and more. Mr. Nam, Dawa Tsering Sherpa, Nima Tashi Sherpa, Phu Dorje Sherpa, and Peggy Luce also made it. I placed a pink plastic lawn flamingo on top and tied an American flag around its neck. I also left pictures of my family and a girlfriend and chopped out some stones. After forty-five minutes at the summit, I renewed my concentration and started down. I contemplated taking Boivin's skis and boots, which were stashed in the snow glowing with their "Extreme Dream" logo. I decided that it was not worth the increased chance of a fall and continued descending as fast as I could. Like Boivin I returned to Camp Two before dark. I did not learn until later that Peggy fell on the descent. By luck she arrested inches from an eight-thousand-foot plunge. She lost her sunglasses and quickly became snow blind. Fortunately, Dawa Tsering stayed behind and guided her down safely. They spent the night at the South Col and returned to Camp Two, in deteriorating weather, the next day.

Chomolungma had now allowed a record twenty-three of us on her crest, but a two-day storm signaled that her mood had changed. Back at base camp I celebrated success with Om and Duson Becik. Having no language in common mattered little. Our communication was perfect. We gesticulated about life and made plans to climb together next year. Duson showed pictures of his two children and we teased Om about sheep. We exchanged summit stones from Lhotse and Everest and drank slivovitz until we all passed out.

Not everyone was celebrating. Three groups had not been able to capitalize on the good weather. The Spanish failed on the West Ridge. French television could not begin their live broadcasts until October 4 because their satellite was being used for the Olympics. And the New Zealanders could not find a route to climb. The Kiwis shared a permit with the Czechs but were not willing to try either the route on Lhotse or the Southwest Face of Everest because of the difficulty and danger. Rob Hall tried, without success, to get his four-person team permission for the Korean route.

Lydia Brady, a smiling, sleek, twenty-five-year-old free spirit with long blond dreadlocks from Christchurch, New Zealand, was not happy with the situation. Lydia was one of the most experienced female mountaineers in the world. Her sights were firmly fixed on Everest. She was already banned from climbing in Pakistan for scaling twenty-six-thousand-foot Gasherbrum 2 without a permit. Dancing by herself on the glacier, with heavy metal blasting from her boom box, she told me she was going to be the first woman to climb Everest without oxygen even if she had to go solo and on the sly. Lydia also lays claim to the unofficial high-altitude sex record. When confronted with the possibility that her achievement may have been surpassed in 1987, she retorted, "But we both had orgasms, mate." If she got there with a willing and capable partner Lydia hoped to set an unbeatable high-altitude sex record on top of Everest. She had it all planned out, with a summit suit that featured resealable Velcro and rip-stop nylon flaps in her wind suit that provided easy access to a series of slits in her inner layers of clothing that became perfectly aligned when she bent over.

When the skies cleared, a large plume of snow was blowing off of Everest from the north, indicating that the jet stream had lowered. Undaunted, several teams continued the assault. My teammates Don Goodman, Johnny Petroske, Dave Hambly, and Diana Dailey, as well as Ruoss and Frush, still had summit aspirations. French television was now broadcasting live and needed to reach the top with their camera. To increase the odds they invited four of the strongest Spanish and two Sherpas to join them. Lydia and two other Kiwis prepared to climb while Hall continued to negotiate for an easier route. Meanwhile, Josef Just readied himself for the Southwest Face. As his final detail he asked, "You have drug for all or nussing?" After obtaining eight tablets of dextroamphet-amine, he headed up the mountain with Duson, Jaraslov Jasko, and Peter Bozik. Bozik had recently made the first ascent of the "magic line" on K2, the world's second highest mountain. That climb, also done without supplemental oxygen, was the hardest big-mountain route yet done. But, he said, "Ziss iss most more diffeecult!"

The crowd gathered at Camp Two to wait for a break in the wind. Every day saw the annihilation of two or three tents. Travel between tents was often impossible. Radio communication to base camp was difficult to understand over the howling wind. Its roar was slightly less on October 12. Five Chamonix guides acting as cameramen, along with four Spaniards and five Sherpas rushed to the South Col. Most of the tents had been blown apart, and they spent a sleepless night crammed seven to a tent. The next day the wind picked up again. French cameraman Serge Koenig persevered with Sherpas Pasang Temba and Lhakpa Sonam. Everyone else retreated back to the col.

Koenig and Lhakpa Sonam made the top. The cable connecting the camera to the transmitter broke and there was no live broadcast. I was in the French television control tent. The director was on the radio swearing at Koenig, demanding that he fix it. Koenig replied in a cracking voice, "Impossible!" adding that he was cold and exhausted and must come down. Amid further swearing the commentator sent the excited message of *"Serge Koenig au sommet!"* along with views from base camp back to France. The director walked in circles declaring, *"C'est une tragedie!"*

Chomolungma quickly reminded everyone what is really tragic. Neither Sherpa returned to the South Col. A frostbitten Koenig surmised that they had fallen descending behind him. Then, as if to mock the efforts of the day, the winds suddenly abated. At midnight the four Spanish and two Sherpas prepared to leave for a summit try. Leaving the tent, they encountered a blond woman with dreadlocks. "D'ya mind if I tag along, mate?" Lydia asked.

She had started early the previous evening from Camp Three. The Spanish shrugged and headed up. Lydia stopped to melt snow for a drink, falling far behind. An hour from camp the Spanish came upon what, at first, looked like a large rock in the snow. It was the twisted and frozen body of Pasang Temba. A little higher they found his brother's body. They continued up to the South Summit, where Sergei Martinez became very weak. Giving Martinez all of their remaining oxygen to use while waiting, Jeronimo Lopez, Nil Bohigas, Luis Giver, Nima Rita, and Ang Rita pushed on to the top. It was Ang Rita Sherpa's record fifth time to the summit of Mount Everest without supplemental oxygen.

Meanwhile, in an effort to take advantage of the lull in the wind, Steve Ruoss and Johnny Petroske headed for the South Col. The four Czechs also prepared to leave. The first ascent of the Southwest Face required six camps, 180 bottles of oxygen, 160 Sherpas, thirty-five climbers, six thousand feet of fixed rope, and more than a month of climbing. The Czechs brought two sleeping bags for four people, two days' worth of food, and a small stove with fuel to melt snow for three days. Even if they completed the ascent in three days, they would be climbing without supplemental oxygen in the "death zone," above twenty-six thousand feet, where there is barely enough oxygen to sustain life, longer than anyone had ever survived at that height.

Steve and Johnny's climb did not last very long. Halfway up the Lhotse ice face a body went hurtling past them. They immediately turned back to see if the climber was alive and needed help. When they reached the body, they found it was the now mutilated remains of Lhakpa Sonam Sherpa. The French had thrown the two dead bodies down the mile-high ice cliff without telling any of the other teams via the radio. The other body hung up on rocks and never made it down.

The Spanish summit team returned to find Sergei lapsing in and out of consciousness. They used rope to make a basket to drag and lower him in. Leaving the South Summit they met Lydia crawling upward on all fours. It was already four-thirty in the afternoon. They told her to descend. She refused. Already overextended and fearing that Sergei would die, they did not argue. Ang Rita looked her in the eye and said, "You are going to die!" before she crawled out of sight.

Down at base camp Lydia's teammates were informed by the French radio that she was making her solo bid to be the first woman up Everest without oxygen. They discussed the situation and decided to leave for Kathmandu. Rob Hall explained that she was told that they did not have a permit; he was concerned that her illegal ascent would result in a climbing ban on other New Zealand climbers. So he was off to the capital to negotiate with the Nepalese Ministry of Tourism, not knowing if his teammate was alive or dead.

The exhausted Spaniards dragged Sergei back to camp at eight-thirty that evening. My team gave permission to use our oxygen. When they went to get the mask they found Lydia crawling around outside the tent. She said she had made the summit, but couldn't find her tent. They pointed her in the right direction and watched her crawl away. Even with the oxygen, Sergei was worse in the morning. At his best he was blind and unable to walk. They began lowering him down the Lhotse Face. Steve and Johnny tried to go up again, but when they saw the condition of the Spanish, they turned around to help. It took twelve hours to retreat as far as Camp Three. Ruoss, a physician, examined Sergei and decided that he had severe cerebral edema and almost no chance for survival. The next day Sergei was lowered to Camp Two, where Ruoss gave intravenous medicines and put him in an experimental "Gamow Bag" that increases atmospheric pressure to simulate a descent of six thousand feet. Finally twenty climbers, representing every team, carried him down through the Khumbu Icefall to base camp. The French television helicopter then evacuated Sergei, along with Luis Giver, who had severe frostbite, to Kathmandu. Both were safe in a hospital in Spain two days later. Although temporarily lost during the confusion, Lydia reappeared at base camp, walking upright but still having to face the Nepalese authorities. In order to lessen her fine, Lydia told authorities in

Kathmandu that she had climbed on the mountain without a proper permit, but that she did not make the summit. This cast considerable doubt on her later claims to be the first woman to climb Mount Everest without supplemental oxygen. Personally, I am absolutely certain that she made it. I write this based on knowing Lydia as a person, having spoken to her immediately upon her descent, and because the conditions on the mountain were such that it was much more difficult and dangerous to descend from the South Summit than to continue over the Hillary Step, where there was a fixed rope, and on up to the top. If Lydia had really been so exhausted that she could not make the peak, she would have died on the descent.

As the drama of the Spanish and Lydia resolved, a more intense one started. The Czechs called on the radio to say that they had completed their ascent of the Southwest Face, reaching the South Summit at eight-thirty on the evening of October 17. Having taken one day longer than expected, they were out of food and fuel. This night at twenty-nine thousand feet was their third above twenty-six thousand feet without oxygen or a tent. They said that they were tired and dehydrated but otherwise fine. They planned to summit the next morning and descend via the South Col. On October 18 Josef Just pushed on to the top alone.

He joined his companions on the descent. In their last radio transmission, at four o'clock, they said that three of the four were blind and all were exhausted, but they were on their way down to the South Col. At base camp I paced back and forth thinking about Duson fighting for his life up above, but there was nothing I could do. Don Goodman, Diana Dailey, and Dave Hambly went to the South Col. No one was visible. The next morning the jet stream winds returned with a vengeance. No further trace of the Czechs was found.

In all, an amazing thirty-one people reached the summit of Mount Everest during the post-monsoon season of 1988. Nine died trying. Leaving the mountain in the wake of tragedy, it was hard to find meaning in my accomplishment. On the other side of the planet Bobby McFerrin was rising to the top of the popular music charts preaching "Don't worry, be happy." The Sherpas have a similar philosophy: "*Kay guarnay.*" Literally, this translates into, "What to do when there is nothing to do?" Practically, they don't worry about what they can't control, and are very happy. Here I was, and there was nothing more that I could do. Touching the red string around my neck, I repeated, "*Kay guarnay*" and began the long walk back to Kathmandu.

10

THE
SUMMIT IS
SECONDARY

There is a big difference between climbing a mountain in the company of a guide and having a trip organized to simply get a client to the top of a mountain. With fixed ropes, plenty of supplemental oxygen, and Sherpas carrying all the supplies for clients, the guided passengers on Everest are simply moving through a dangerous endurance test. They are not climbing the mountain for themselves. Given the type of guiding occurring these days on Everest, the goal has shifted from enjoying a climbing experience to procuring the right to say, "I stood on top of the world." A guide should function as both a teacher and a facilitator, allowing his clients to safely do things for themselves and enjoy the process of a climb. Guides should not be the baby-sitters of the mountains, helping inexperienced adventurers stumble every step of the way.

One of my heroes is the famous French guide Gaston Rebuffat. Rebuffat pioneered many of the hardest routes in the Alps and was a part of the first ascent of an eight-thousand-meter (twenty-six-thousand-foot) peak, Annapurna. More importantly, his poetic writing not only describes his delight in high mountains and scaling vertiginous faces, but also speaks of the joy of sharing this experience. His wonderful book *Starlight and Storm* describes guiding clients on ascents of the seven great north faces of the Alps. As a guide he helped his clients safely succeed on many of the hardest rock and ice summits in the Alps. But he didn't merely drag his charges; he was their partner, and shared all aspects of the climb as a teacher, mentor, and friend. He helped his clients learn to savor the process, not the goal. A great guide places safety as the absolute top priority. After that comes enjoying the experience and allowing clients to expand their own abilities. Finally, and least important, is reaching a specific summit. Surprisingly—or perhaps not—the people I consider the best guides are also usually the ones who have the most success getting to the top with their clients.

By this definition Rick Schweitzer, a tall, fit, affable man in his mid-forties, is the consummate guide. With a perfect safety record, he has helped his clients achieve dreams from skiing to the North Pole to kayaking amid whales off Hawaii. Rick is good at almost every adventure sport, but great at none. He is, however, magnificent at organizing perfect trips. Like a top-notch mountain guide who stays one step ahead of any problem to assure safety, Rick stays ahead of any potential travel problem to maximize his clients' pleasure.

Rick's company, the Northwest Passage, asked me to help guide their "Ultimate Alpine Holiday." Our plan was to climb the Matterhorn, Mount Blanc, and the Eiger in a nine-day trip. On days when we were not climbing, we would stay in the finest small Alpine hotels and dine like royalty.

In addition to Rick and myself, we would have two Swiss mountaineers and my friend Neal Beidleman, one of America's finest climbers, acting as guides. Neal is the ultimate fun-hog. He lives in Aspen, Colorado, and is a master of virtually every mountain sport as well as a top ultramarathon runner. Whatever the situation, Neal manages to keep the fun-o-meter dangerously in the red zone. He had recently become a minor celebrity as the guide who struggled to save the lives of his clients on Mount Everest and emerged as one of the heroes of the 1996 disaster, getting all of his inexperienced charges safely down the mountain and saving several from another expedition.

To ensure safety on our climbs, we would have a ratio of one client per guide on the technical ascents. Two of the clients were endurance hardmen. Dave Ladd and Rich Martin had skied to the North Pole with Rick on a previous trip. They were only moderately experienced climbers. Dave, a forty-year-old pediatric anesthesiologist from Denver, had been on a few guided climbs in the Rockies. Rich, a thirty-something software executive from Boston, was just a strong hiker. The other two clients, Scott Minick and George Waring III, were experienced technical climbers. Both had busy jobs that prevented them from keeping their mountaineering skills at a level where they could safely attempt these peaks on their own. Scott, the president of biotechnology company and in his mid-forties, was a keen rock climber in his younger days. George, the oldest member of our group at fifty and a professor at Emory Medical School in Atlanta, had to his credit the first ascent of a twenty-thousand-foot giant in Nepal and had worked on his rock climbing with a son who was spending a year climbing full-time. The challenge for Scott and George would be speed and endurance. For Rich and Dave it would be the steep rock and ice and the exposure.

Rick met us in the Zurich airport with a Mercedes van and whisked the group off to Murren, an idyllic picture-postcard village nestled on a hillside beneath the Eiger, Jungfrau, and Mönch. The Swiss have the hospitality concept perfected, and for two nights we savored the luxury of a four-star hotel and perfectly matched wines and foods. Between feasts we hiked up a straightforward walking trail to the beautiful summit of the Shilthorn and adapted to the altitude. The plan was to attempt the Eiger as our first major peak requiring roped climbing. Unfortunately, the conditions were not good on our chosen route. We quickly changed our plan and spent two nights at a high-mountain hut between the neighboring Mönch and Jungfrau, climbing both peaks. I had the pleasure of roping with George on the Mönch and Scott on the Jungfrau. Both mountains offered delightful steep ice ridges, moderate rock climbing, and spectacular summit panoramas.

After a perfect dinner under the North Face of the Eiger we moved on to Zermatt and the Matterhorn. The weather was stormy when we arrived and we had to endure another night of four-star living. The forecast was grim for the next several days, with the weather map suggesting two fronts moving in one after the other. The local guides said we had "bad luck" and told us they were not going up on the Matterhorn for several days. I've always found that you can make your own luck by being ready for any chance. Neal and I decided that we should go up to the hut just in case. The Hornli hut was nearly empty. We had a hearty meal and turned in early. At midnight the sky was clear. At three o'clock in the morning we tied into the ropes inside the hut and headed for the rock spire that towered four thousand feet straight above us.

The climb was fantastic. The Matterhorn offers continuously steep and fun rock climbing that is never boring, and never overly difficult. The mountain has several possible routes that lead to dead ends, loose rocks, or other dangers, but we were able to stay on the best line and found all solid rock, firm holds, and straightforward climbing. By late morning Rick, Neal, Rich, Dave, and I were on the sharp summit. The sky was still clear and the views stretched for the length of the Alps.

On our descent we caught up with Scott and George and the two Swiss guides. They had been moving a bit too slowly and, with a storm approaching, turned back after completing the most difficult rock climbing. We all made it back to Zermatt just as the second storm system moved in to obliterate all chances at climbing the

Matterhorn for the next several weeks. After a final fondue, Jacuzzi, sauna, and several final bottles of wine we moved across the border to Chamonix, and French cuisine and wines.

The Mont Blanc Massif is one of the most spectacular mountain landscapes on earth. Sharp rock spires, called Aiguilles, hold counterpoint to the rhythmic swells of giant snow summits. Rich, Rick, and I climbed one of the Aiguilles on our first day, and then the entire party headed for Mount Blanc. After a cable car ride and five-hour hike we arrived at our hut. The next morning we followed a well-worn trail up undulating snow slopes, weaving in and out of crevasses. The climb is not technically difficult, but it is long and high. Just as we approached the very top, a huge windstorm moved in. Gusts neared a hundred miles per hour and threatened to blow us off the mountain, while sharp crystals of ice stung our faces. We turned back less than thirty feet from the very top. After a final celebratory dinner and the requisite fine French wines and champagne, we headed for home.

Was this a successful guided trip? In nine days we climbed three major Alpine peaks and one rock Aiguille, as well as coming within thirty feet of the highest mountain in the Alps. Still, of our three objectives, we'd stood on only one summit, the Matterhorn. But for me, which summits are reached is secondary. Everyone came home safely. Dave and Rich expanded their mountaineering skills and climbed steep rock and ice that they'd initially thought to be impossible. Scott and George pushed their endurance to their limits, three times. And Rick made certain that Neal kept his fun-o-meter flush in the red zone. A friend of mine, Alex Lowe, was once asked to name the best mountaineer in the world. Without any hesitation he replied, "The one who is having the most fun." By that definition, we were the best guided expedition in the world.

11

THE
GUIDE'S
DILEMMA

My clients keep trying to murder me! Coming down the steep summit ridge from the top of the Jungfrau, the spectacular mountain that dominates the Bernese Alps of Switzerland, my ropemate Scott Minick began to tire, his usually firm foot placements wobbling from exhaustion. Beneath us stretched a near-vertical slide to the glacier four thousand feet below. The old guide's adage "My client is trying to kill both me and himself" moved scarily toward reality. It had happened to guides before, more times than I cared to count. During the course of twenty-five years of climbing and eighteen years teaching and working as a professional mountain guide, I have seen many variations on this theme. From the fifty-five-year-old lawyer who collapsed at the top of a twenty-one-thousand-foot mountain in the Andes, to the doctor who fell multiple times without warning on the steep ice slope of a twenty-thousand-foot peak in Nepal, to the stockbroker who panicked and developed hysterical vertigo halfway up a five-hundred-foot rock cliff, I have encountered, and safely dealt with everything that clients have thrown at me. Now here I was, courting disaster with Scott. I tightened the rope connecting me to Scott so I would be able to hold him should he fall. When the slope steepened to the point where I could not be certain of holding him, I changed our strategy. No longer would we move together, where a slip by Scott could kill us both. Instead I anchored into the ice and belayed Scott with the rope to a point where he could secure himself. Then, when he was safely tied to the mountain, I carefully descended to him. We repeated this process until we passed all danger. That night our small group of four clients and four guides celebrated our successful ascents of two great peaks, the Mönch and the Jungfrau. Ahead loomed the two jewels of the Alps, the Matterhorn and Mont Blanc.

The Matterhorn is often called the most beautiful mountain on earth. It is also one of the most difficult summits to reach in the Alps. The so-called golden age of mountaineering, when the goal was to climb untrodden peaks, ended on July 14, 1865, when this last unattained summit was reached by four British climbers, Edward Whymper, Lord Francis Douglas, the Reverend Charles Hudson, and D. R. Hadow. With them were three Swiss guides—Michael Croz and the father-son combination of old and young Peter Taugwalder. The climbers succeeded in scaling a peak that had long been believed to be unclimbable. Alas, the joy of their success was short lived. Whymper concludes his classic climbing account, *Scrambles Amongst the Alps*, with the warning, "Climb if you will, but remember that courage and strength are naught without prudence, and that a momentary lapse may destroy the happiness of a lifetime."

On the descent, Hadow slipped and fell into Croz and Hudson. The rope connecting the climbers quickly yanked Douglas from his stance. The Taugwalders and Whymper braced themselves in their holds to arrest the fall. Inexplicably, the rope snapped between the falling climbers and young Peter Taugwalder. Whymper watched helplessly as his four companions fell five thousand vertical feet down toward Zermatt. In the years after the tragedy, the Matterhorn continued to expand its deadly reputation as an increasing number of aspiring mountaineers attempted to scale its icy rock pyramid.

Meanwhile an industry developed catering to mountain sojourners. Small family-run hotels flourished and a cadre of skilled Zermatt climbers acted as guides, helping visitors scale the Matterhorn and other peaks. What began as a sideline for chamois hunters who were familiar with local mountain passes became a respected profession. After World War II both the French and Swiss guides' associations went from meeting local standards to offering national and then international certification of professional mountain guides. To qualify, you must be more than just an outstanding climber with a solid résumé of difficult rock, ice, and mountain ascents. It is also necessary to be an expert in first aid, rescue, weather patterns, avalanche prediction, and the history and lore of the mountains. After passing a grueling series of exams, you must work for two years under supervision before a final winter and summer guiding test. In the United States we have a similar certification process through the American Mountain Guides Association. In theory, with a certified guide you should be safe.

The concept that having a guide ensures safety lost credibility, however, when guided climbs moved to the Himalayas. In the spring of 1996 multiple guided teams converged on Mount Everest. The theory was that with unlimited supplemental oxygen, fixed safety lines from the bottom to the top of the peak, and an army of local Sherpa climbers to carry the loads, a very fit person could be guided to the top of the world. In practice, however, problems arose because at extreme altitude the decrease in oxygen to the brain impairs the judgment of both guides and clients. Moreover, in the "death zone," above twenty-six thousand feet, it is difficult for top climbers to take care of themselves, let alone shepherd an overextended, inexperienced customer. A second difficulty is that with clients paying upward of sixty-five thousand dollars it is difficult for the guide to make and then enforce the hard decision to turn a customer around close to the summit when the weather seems fine and the only problem is reaching a previously chosen turn-around time for a safe return. When clients pay that much money and sacrifice so much time, it is difficult to say no when their only chance at the summit seems close.

On a fateful day in May 1996, two of the half a dozen guided teams that were present set out for the summit of Mount Everest. Prior to guided ascents, no fixed ropes were ever used high on Everest. No climber would have contemplated an ascent without being competent enough to negotiate the terrain safely. The guided climbers in the 1996 tragedy progressed slowly, unable to move without fixed safety lines. They became delayed on the way down by a traffic jam on the fixed ropes. Since they couldn't climb unaided, the clients were all forced to descend at the rate of the weakest. They were engulfed by a vicious storm at around five o'clock in the evening. Guides and clients alike perished in the squall.

When I went to Everest in 1988, there were still only seventeen Americans who had been on the top of the world, and I knew all of them by name. Over the next few years, though, several large changes occurred that changed the way people approached climbing Mount Everest. First, the Nepali government changed its permit policy. Our permit in 1988 cost a thousand dollars for the entire team. The government of Nepal had treated Everest permits as a goodwill gesture that promoted a positive image of Nepal for climbers to carry back to their respective countries. They had issued one permit per year per nation to teams nominated and sponsored by their national climbing organization. By 1989 people from many countries had climbed to the summit of Mount Everest, and it was becoming much more difficult to raise funds for national expeditions. In that year, a Frenchman who had obtained a permit at a nominal cost from the government of Nepal offered climbers a place on his team for twenty thousand dollars apiece. No one made the summit, but the Frenchman made a lot of money.

Soon after, the government of Nepal changed its permit policy. More permits began to be offered, and the number of people at base camp swelled. The Nepali government jacked up the price of each permit to fifty thousand dollars in 1990.

The fee soon rose to seventy thousand dollars for the first seven people on an expedition plus ten thousand dollars per additional climber.

The second, and probably greater, change that affected the way people approach Mount Everest was a modernization of the oxygen delivery system. Titanium and Kevlar canisters were developed for high-altitude mountaineering. These included a more efficient and lighter oxygen delivery system based on state-of-the-art jet technology. Oxygen canisters were reduced in weight and increased in carrying capacity: Whereas from 1963 to 1988 a twenty-five-pound system offered forty-five hundred pounds per square inch of oxygen, now it was possible to deliver six thousand PSI of oxygen from a system weighing less than twelve pounds. Now strong Sherpa climbers could carry additional oxygen canisters, effectively supplying their clients with unlimited oxygen. People could spend much more time higher on the mountain and could begin using oxygen much lower on the climb. With the added help of ultralight fixed ropes, less experienced and weaker climbers had a realistic chance of climbing Mount Everest.

An Austrian guide from Innsbruck organized the first attempt at guiding clients to the top of Everest. No one on his team made the summit, but the trip opened the door to commercialism on the mountain.

Some people have said that Dick Bass, the millionaire entrepreneur owner of Snowbird Ski Resort in Utah, was guided to the summit of Everest by Dave Breashears. Breashears, however, did not fix any rope high on the mountain for Bass and, because of the impossibility of holding a fall, did not rope together with him. He did give up his oxygen just below the summit for Bass to use. Still, Bass, like everyone in the era of heavier oxygen bottles, climbed to the South Col without supplemental oxygen and then proceeded to the summit unroped. Although he was arguably the least experienced mountaineer and the oldest person at the time to reach the summit of Mount Everest, Dick Bass climbed every step of the way himself and in excellent style.

Bass's trip is a sharp contrast to those of the people who now pay for everything to be done for them on an Everest expedition. Such clients are given fixed ropes on every tricky section from the bottom of the mountain to the top, and they receive virtually unlimited supplies of oxygen. Everest thus becomes simply an endurance test. All decision making is relinquished to the judgment of guides.

As far as I'm concerned, such clients are not really climbing the mountain. Their style of reaching the top of Mount Everest is analogous to going on a guided rock climb in which the guide actually climbs and the client follows on a Jumar clamp. The client simply climbs the rope, not the rock, and then says that he has been up the climb. There may be situations where it is nice to have a guide lead a difficult or dangerous rock climb to give clients a secure belay. The client struggles on the rock, works out the moves, and actually climbs, learning from the guide's advice. Similarly, a guide can facilitate moving quickly and safely in the mountains, providing advice on avalanche conditions and leading a client on a great mountaineering route. But the most important component in such an operation is that the clients are actually using their own skill and strength. The guide acts only as a mentor and teacher, not a baby-sitter and bodyguard.

You may wonder how the 1996 tragedy could have occurred if having fixed ropes and unlimited oxygen theoretically creates a safe mountain playground. First, Everest is an enormous mountain. The ability to take care of yourself is impaired at the roof of the world; certainly it is difficult to care for a dependent. When guiding on Mount Everest, if anything in the organizational system breaks down or goes wrong, serious consequences may result. When I worked as a mountain guide, I liked to feel in control and slightly ahead of any possible problem that may have developed. Above twenty-six thousand feet, this is not always possible.

In 1996, for a number of reasons, there was a delay in fixing the ropes high on the mountain to safeguard incompetent clients. When you have only a single fixed rope and a group of inexperienced people, this can lead to terrible traffic jams that precede disaster. In addition, if you are unable to climb down or away quickly, or are unable to make a proper decision when weather changes, any separation of the client from the guide can have dire consequences. I was not present for the 1996 Everest disaster, but have spoken at length with Neal Beidleman, Scott Fischer's assistant guide. Neal agrees that both the inability of the clients to quickly descend on their own and the slow pace caused by the reliance on fixed ropes were factors in the tragedy.

But the most obvious and most dangerous component of the 1996 disaster was the overall inexperience of the clients. People attempting Mount Everest should, in my mind, have a higher level of climbing skill than what they have accumulated simply from having been guided to the top of Aconcagua or Mount McKinley. They should master technical climbing to the point where moving smoothly and efficiently on steep ground can be accomplished with little expenditure of energy. As an absolute minimum requirement, people attempting the mountain should be able to climb easily without a fixed rope in the kind of conditions that might be encountered high on Everest. They must be able to take care for themselves in virtually any environment. If such a person wished to increase his chances of success by having a personal guide to help, it should be a one-on-one proposition. Swiss guides on the Matterhorn are restricted to a one-to-one guide-to-client ratio. That there should be two to three guides for nine clients on the much more dangerous upper slopes of Mount Everest seems an invitation to disaster, especially when many of the clients are so inexperienced that they do not fully understand the dangers of the mountain.

Many clients assume that guides can totally assure their safety. They fail to understand that on a mountain like Everest, when the going gets tough, a guide cannot always prevent disaster. At the same time, however, there is no excuse for a guide not giving 100 percent of his energy and attention to protecting clients. Several people have asked my opinion about the guide Anatoli Boukreev's quick descent in 1996 to regain his strength so that he could perform a heroic rescue when there was a break in the weather. While Boukreev performed valiantly after the climbers were caught in a dire predicament, had he remained with the group or helped a few of the clients down in the first place, the situation might never have occurred. What Boukreev did may be analogous to my hiking with my wife and two small children on Mount Washington in New Hampshire and, when a sudden squall engulfs us, saying, "Okay, I'm going to run down the trail now and start the car in case you need a warm car when you get down. I'll get hot drinks and come back up when you're almost done. Good luck. See you later." Boukreev left clients—who were unable to climb down on their own—high on the mountain to go prepare camp. Of course, I was not there and because of Boukreev's death a year later on Annapurna, I will never be able to get his opinion. The role of a mountain guide should, however, unquestionably center on protecting clients.

Mount Everest still continues to hold a fascination for the general public, particularly after the popularity of Jon Krakauer's book *Into Thin Air*. The 1996 disaster received worldwide media attention and spawned three best-selling books. When I hear an account of the trip, I always shudder. Ironically, instead of people becoming more hesitant about being guided up Everest, the demand for guided trips to the mountain has only increased since 1996. People look to Everest as an ultimate struggle. Climbing a mountain, however, should always be a joyous, exhilarating experience. For me, that's what Everest was.

Part of what made my trips to Everest so different from a guided expedition is the fact that I was not only physically climbing the mountain but also had certain responsibilities and roles to play in planning and decision making. The joy and satisfaction of climbing a mountain comes in part from making decisions on your own. The organization, planning of routes, and day-to-day decisions on where to go and what to do are exciting aspects of any trip. Especially on a big mountain, the joy of a climb comes from accomplishing a combination of mental and physical tasks.

My experience on the 1988 Everest expedition was not the painful, arduous task described in *Into Thin Air*. I was able to experience the mountain as part of a team—a tight-knit group of friends working together for a common goal. My experience was one of joy.

12

FOLLOWING
THE
HEART

"You are such a romantic man. Surely, I must save all my love for you!" This was the message waiting for me when I returned from Everest, thanks to satellite communication and French television. On my way in to the mountain I had met a woman, and became infatuated with her. She was beautiful, with shining dark hair and sparkling blue eyes. Athletic and funny, she had a fantastically quick mind that was readily apparent despite our not knowing each other's language. I sat next to her in a small café in the Thamel district of Kathmandu. She said her name was Ariane and that she had just graduated from the conservatory in Lyon, France, where she had trained as a classical pianist. That afternoon we rode bicycles out through the lush paddy fields along the ring road that surrounds the city. For the next two days we explored together, visiting Hindu and Buddhist holy places and walking hand in hand through the narrow streets of the city. On the last evening before I started trekking into Mount Everest, I suggested that we spend the night together. Ariane said, "No! I do not even know you three days. I cannot sleep with you!" With that, she kissed me on both cheeks and vanished into the night.

Two months later I returned to base camp, having just reached the top of the world. French television was broadcasting live back to France from base camp every day. They asked to interview me. At the conclusion of our discussion about climbing to the summit I asked if I could say hello to my friend Ariane, a pianist in Lyon. The announcer became very excited and began babbling in French, "Blah blah blah blah, AMOUR! Blah blah blah blah blah AMERICAN blah blah blah SUMMIT blah blah

blah blah AMOUR!" He then turned to me and said, "I have say that you make the summit of the world for the love of your French girlfriend, Ariane, and that you dedicate the climbing of Mount Everest to her. This is true, no?"

A few months later I met up with Ariane again and we spent enough time together to get to know each other and share some wonderful moments. Ultimately, however, her life was music, and mine led elsewhere.

After Everest I followed my heart and became a full-time professional climber. My medical career would have to wait for a while. I have found that it is best to flow with life's opportunities rather than fight the current trying to follow a preconceived plan. I worked as a mountain guide, finding great joy in sharing my love of the high places. I found a niche creating international custom dream trips that included technical climbs. These adventures brought me to all seven continents, allowing me to get to know many interesting people and to climb many of my fantasy mountains and routes. Between paid trips I continued attempting routes that stretched my limits. These were now a level below the hardest climbs that were being done on a world scale. I have come to appreciate that my climbs and my dreams need only be significant to myself. I never set out to "conquer" a mountain, which to me sounds as ridiculous as trying to "conquer" a woman. The great French climber Lionel Terray described mountaineers as "Conquistadores of the Useless." As in any meaningful love relationship, the only purpose served by climbing a mountain is the happiness and enlightenment gained by the person who does it; if you approach it looking only toward what you can expect to "get," you will most likely come away with nothing.

13

ANTARCTIC
SOLITUDE

"Another steak, Geoffrey?" my host asks, refilling my cup with fresh coffee. My stomach is already expanded from polishing off sixteen ounces of fine Argentine filet and a baked potato. But the taste of the salsa is still dancing on my tongue.

"*Gracias,*" I reply, stretching my bare feet near the gas heater. Colonel Campos, the host, nods to Juanco, the burly mechanic at the stove. Juanco peels a ripe avocado into the hot sauce and in one motion spears a sizzling steak from the grill and fries an egg to put on top. The aroma is magnificent. All in all, the rescue seems to be progressing well.

Then into the cozy Weatherhaven hut stomp three snow-encrusted figures, icicles dropping from their mustaches and beards. Mugs Stump is the first to speak. "We couldn't get to them. The ridge is too steep for the snowmobiles. We'll have to carry him down."

"Steak?" I mumble while chewing. I hand my plate to Paul and reach for my parka, wind suit, and overboots.

"No thanks, mate. I'm still stuffed from the lobster tails I had at brekkie," Paul replies.

Four thousand vertical feet above us, in a tiny tent pitched in the center of a topless igloo, Peter waits. His right forefoot is black, swollen, and puffed with fluid-filled blisters the size of golf balls. Severe frostbite causes intense pain. All of our narcotics are in my medical kit at base camp. With Peter are the rest of my team: Klaus, a professional mountaineer from Munich who is Peter's partner; Ken, the novice from New York who is now so exhausted he can barely walk; and Rob, the mountain guide from Canada who climbed the wrong mountain. Three hours ago I spoke to them on our walkie-talkie. I happily reported that I had made it over the col, then climbed down the ice face and through the whiteout ground blizzard to the Chilean air force camp. I explained how my private radio transmission was intercepted and expanded into a full-blown crisis by the bored radio operators at bases throughout the continent before I finally reached the National Science Foundation geology expedition, stranded twelve and a half miles away. They cheerfully agreed to disregard their orders and evacuate Peter and Ken with their snowmobiles. Now my partners are expecting help any moment. But we are again learning that down here nothing comes as expected. As Hugh Culver, the managing partner of Adventure Network, is fond of saying, "Hey, this is Antarctica."

On March 5, 1908, six members of Shackleton's Nimrod Expedition left Cape Royds man-hauling a ten-foot sledge laden with 1,230 pounds of supplies. Their goal was to ascend twelve-thousand-foot Mount Erebus. Five days later they proved it possible to climb a mountain on the Antarctic continent. Douglass Mawson uncorked a bottle of champagne when the climbing party returned to the boat, but chloroform was also required for the amputation of Sir Philip Brocklehurst's frostbitten big toe.

The highest mountain in Antarctica is 16,863-foot Mount Vinson in the Sentinel Range. Located seventy-eight degrees south, its summit is arguably the coldest and most remote place on earth. Mount Vinson was first contacted by a living animal in 1967 when the ten-man American Antarctic Mountaineering Expedition, led by Nick Clinch and supported by U.S. military planes, succeeded in making the first ascents of the three highest peaks on the continent. The next people to visit the Sentinel Range came in 1983. Dick Bass's and Frank Wells's "Seven Summits" expedition hired Giles Kershaw, the world's most experienced polar pilot, and a modified tri turbo airplane to make the second ascent of Mount Vinson. Kershaw returned a year later to climb the mountain with Canadian mountaineer Pat Morrow, and the pair began contemplating a commercial airline for adventurers in Antarctica.

Punta Arenas, Chile, is a port town at the southern tip of Patagonia. It is the last stop for ships passing from the Atlantic to the Pacific and home of Mary Teresa's, the world's oldest continuously active brothel. Punta Arenas is also the base for Adventure Network's Antarctic Airways, specializing in flying support for all manner of adventures in Antarctica. This year they are supplying a multinational crossing of the continent with dogsleds led by Will Steger and Jean-Louis Etienne and simultaneously a crossing of Antarctica on skis by Reinhold Messner and Arved Fuchs.

They are also running tourist flights to the South Pole, and will fly me to the base of Mount Vinson. Being both a doctor and mountain guide, I was hired by Adventure Network to come to Vinson and lead their four commercial clients to its summit.

At the time I wondered who would pay more than twenty thousand dollars to vacation at the world's coldest and most remote big mountain. The only one of my clients I'd heard of before the trip was Ken Kammler, a forty-six-year-old surgeon from New York. Soft spoken and hard of hearing from a diving accident that had damaged both eardrums, Ken has the quiet confidence of a man who has succeeded in many endeavors. Unfortunately, climbing mountains isn't one of them. He had taken introductory rock and ice climbing courses in New Hampshire, but had never attempted a big mountain or been winter camping. As for the remaining expedition members, all I knew was that one resided in Germany, one in Canada, and one in the Netherlands.

—

In December 1989 I rendezvoused with my other climbing partners at the Cabo Des Hornos Hotel, a six-story red Georgian building abutting Punta Arenas's town square and dominating the skyline from the harbor. Peter Kinchen is a white-haired and bearded Dutch businessman who looks like Santa Claus after completing a Charles Atlas course, and he wants to climb Mount Vinson, badly. In the last two years he has scaled Mount McKinley and twenty-three-thousand foot Aconcagua in Argentina. Still, he knows the limitations of being fifty-two years old. To acclimatize for Antarctica he spent the previous ten days in the mountains of Ecuador. As a final assurance, he paid full fare for his own personal guide, Klaus Wagner, to join us. Wagner is a German mountain guide who has taken Peter to the top of many mountains. Dark-set and serious, he is focused on the task at hand. "It is a big mountain and I am sure very cold. To guide these people to the top will not be easy," he cautions in perfect but heavily accented English.

Still, the trip may be easier than I expect. The final "client" is Rob Mitchell, a mountain guide and naturalist from Calgary, Canada. An upscale Canadian adventure travel company sent Rob to investigate Antarctica; they were thinking of offering a Vinson climb in 1991 and wanted their guide to be familiar with the mountain. Wiry and energetic with a mischievous grin, Rob is a professional adventurer. He has his own travel company whose custom offerings have included everything from the Paris–Dakar road rally to climbing in the Ruwenzori Mountains. He talks softly but gives the impression of always having something important to say. When Rob speaks, we listen. Lighting a cigarette, he tells us, "I leave every environment a bit better than I find it." Our group vows not only to leave no garbage in Antarctica, where any refuse is preserved forever, but to clean up any trash we encounter while there.

"Americano, dance?" a smiling teenage girl in a blue satin negligee shyly asks, her perfumed hand grazing my shoulder. The pulsating beat of Latin music fills the room, while a silver reflecting ball sends patterns of light across the darkened hardwood floor onto Chilean business executives, Japanese sailors, and an international assortment of scientists and adventurers dancing with the girls of the house. Three days after arriving in Chile I am standing at the bar of Mary Teresa's, straining to hear what Hugh Culver is telling me. "The big problem is the fuel," he says. "The start of the season was delayed by bad weather. We couldn't get our fuel flights in. And we lost a fuel drop that we paid the Chilean air force to make."

The bottom line is that we are delayed at least another week. A full flight of fuel has to go in before any people can go. Ordering another bottle of fine Chilean Cabernet Sauvignon, Culver talks of the difficulties Adventure Network is having keeping the twelve-million-dollar transantarctic dogsled expedition supplied and how Reinhold Messner's and Arved Fuchs's attempt to ski across the continent was delayed so long they were forced to abandon their goal of traversing the ice and now are just crossing the continental landmass. Adventure Network is flying logistical support for both big-budget trips as well as having organized my trip. With a wry smile Culver keeps repeating one phrase like a mantra, "Hey, this is Antarctica!"

At the outskirts of town Rob Mitchell, naturalist, points out the dorsal fin of an orca cutting the azure waters of the Straits of Magellan. "Watch now, there'll be another one. Orcas always travel in pairs. This time of year they come up on the beach to take seal cubs. They'll grab a few cubs and bring 'em out to deep water to share. Killer whales are playful. They toss 'em around a bit before eating them," he lectures.

An hour later we arrive at a penguin rookery. "These are Magellanic penguins," Rob tells us. "Penguins don't have any natural predators on land, but several animals and birds will go for their eggs. The Magellanics dig nesting holes to protect the eggs." He shows us how to approach large groups, downwind, without disturbing them and leads us to a nesting hole where a mother penguin watches a solitary egg. Carefully distracting the mother, Rob gently removes the egg to point out salient features. Then, with a slow hand, he replaces the egg in the nest. The mother whirls and sharply pecks her beak deep into the egg. Yellow-white ooze drips from her perplexed face and seeps from the myriad of cracks in the egg. Rob Mitchell, naturalist, suggests we head for Patagonia.

The Towers of Paine rise abruptly for a vertical half mile from the Patagonian plain. At the base of the spectacular gray and black formation is a clear blue reflecting pond punctuated by gnarled icebergs that break away from the glacier at the base of the peaks. At the far end of the lake the water drops off to a cascade of white water. On an island in the center of the lake, accessible by a long footbridge, is the Hosteria Pehoe, serving fresh fish and Chilean wines that do justice to the views. The hiking is phenomenal, with plenty of guanacos and giant rheas to keep Rob talking. But the longer we stay in Patagonia, the more I see the life of our climb in Antarctica seeping away like a cracked egg. Klaus has to guide in India in a month, Ken has surgery scheduled, and Peter is worried about spending so much time away from his new wife. When we call the Adventure Network office they tell us to stay a few more days. Only Rob Mitchell seems to be having fun.

With time to kill back in Punta Arenas, dinners become prolonged affairs of fresh king crab, giant mussels the size of biceps, and thick Argentine steaks served by sloe-eyed waiters who reinforce the fact that we are in a land where *mañana* doesn't mean "tomorrow" but simply "not today." Also awaiting a flight to Antarctica are French and American film teams that are supposed to record the transantarctic dogsled expedition reaching the South Pole, two Saudi Arabian scientists who hope to be the first Arabs at the Pole, and "Cricket," a mathematician from Chamonix who is the logistical coordinator for Will Steger's and Jean-Louis Etienne's trip across the continent. Radio reports update the dogsledders' progress three times a day. They are already past the last resupply point before reaching the Pole. Meanwhile the press covering Reinhold Messner is in a near panic, as he has not been heard from in nearly two weeks. Then Giles Kershaw arrives and things start to happen.

Despite being a founding partner of Adventure Network, Kershaw works most of the year flying jumbo jets out of Hong Kong for Cathay Pacific Airlines. It is now his vacation. He will fly a single-engine Cessna 185 across the Drake Passage and then buzz around Antarctica on holiday with fellow pilot Max Wendon. Mild mannered and youthful appearing, despite a few gray hairs in his neatly trimmed beard, Kershaw was the driving force behind the British Antarctic Survey and was also the hero of several well-publicized Arctic and Antarctic rescues. His diplomatic skills and clipped British public school accent ease everyone's tension. As if on cue, Messner radios in to say he is fine and had just turned his radio off. Then the good news continues as it is announced that our flight is set to go.

Looking at the ancient DC-6 brings the cracked egg back to mind. Duct tape is ubiquitous. A couple dozen temporary seats are fastened along one side. The majority of cargo space is taken up by fuel drums. We load our gear onto the plane and move our vigil to the airport. The stories we hear from the journalists do not help my confidence. The previous ABC crew had been similarly delayed along with Messner and Fuchs. The first time the group got airborne they turned back from sixty-nine degrees south because of headwinds. The next attempt reached the Antarctic Peninsula before a generator and engine caught fire, forcing them to limp back to Punta Arenas with three propellers. During that flight Messner turned to Rick Ridgeway, who was covering the Steger expedition for ABC, and said, "Rick, I have survived more fucking things than you can imagine, and now I am going to die on this airplane, I know it," before turning to stare out at the swirling seas of the Drake Passage. On the next attempt the plane broke down on its way to the gas pump. The passengers were sent back to the bar for a "short delay." Ridgeway looked out the window, saw the engine in pieces on the tarmac, and decided to go home. The rest of the group finally made it to the Patriot Hills camp, Adventure Network's base camp in Antarctica, which consists of half a dozen Weatherhaven shelters. Then the journalists were stranded at Patriot Hills awaiting a flight out for seventeen days, renaming the camp "the White Coffin" as they watched their supplies dwindle.

Back in the bar at "Aeropuerto PPTE Carlos," Giles tries to reassure everyone, saying, "I've inspected the engines myself. The plane is in excellent repair. As soon as the weather clears, you're off." I am more soothed by Peter Henning, a dangerous-assignment specialist for ABC and a former fighter pilot. He is buying drinks at the bar. Finally the weather report clears, and we put on full Antarctic clothing and climb the aluminum painter's ladder into the unheated, nonpressurized cargo plane to settle into the canvas frame seats. With us are a couple of reluctant replacement sled dogs, the two Saudis whose religion prevents drinking alcoholic beverages and who seem more nervous than everyone but the dogs, the French and American film crews, and Cricket, the field coordinator for the dogsled expedition, who assists with everything. At two-thirty in the afternoon Rick, a laid-back, long-haired flight engineer, locks the hatch, points out the can in the back, and wishes us a good flight. Upon takeoff, cameraman Gordon Wiltsie pulls out his sleeping bag and pad, spreads them on the floor, and goes to sleep. Peter Henning and the French film crew keep the party going for the entire eight-hour flight.

Out the window the white wilderness stretches to the horizon. Endless white, punctuated by giant crevasses and a few rock mountains, extends on and on. After eight hours of flying over glimmering white desert, the plane lowers and banks steeply to land on the blue ice runway at the base of the Patriot Hills Mountains. It is eleven o'clock at night. We step out into bright sunshine and a sharp, cold wind. Snowmobiles drag sleds with our gear while we walk thirty minutes across the ice to

Adventure Network's base in Antarctica. Five semipermanent Weatherhaven tents are secured to the ice. Eight sled dogs eye us from a chain adjacent to the camp. Inside the cook tent a gas heater continually melts ice blocks into water, and the smell of steaming fresh chicken soup with homemade black bread greets our arrival. Peter cracks a new bottle, dons a penguin hat, and the party continues into the night.

It is good company, but having come this far we are anxious to reach the solitude of Mount Vinson. We are informed that we will be stuck at the White Coffin for "several days." The Steger group is three days from the South Pole, and Adventure Network's Twin Otter will be busy shuttling the journalists and Saudis to the Pole to meet them. Then Messner and Fuchs are desperate for a resupply, so they are the next priority. After that, "weather permitting," we can fly.

Klaus is shaking mad. "I must be in India by the end of the month!" he shouts. "This is not possible. We cannot wait," he berates me as we use a woodcutter's saw to cut blocks of ice to build a windbreak to protect our tents.

At six in the morning we lie down to sleep. But with the bright sunlight and tension, I barely close my eyes. I am just starting to doze when I hear the hum of an engine.

I crawl out of my sleeping bag and peer from the tent to see a tiny orange single-engine aircraft circling above camp before landing gently on skis a few hundred feet from our tent. Giles Kershaw and fellow pilot Max Wendon have smiles as bright as the sun reflecting on the snow. They made the first single-engine crossing of the Drake Passage by putting a fuel drum on the backseat and using a homemade pump apparatus leading to the fuel tanks. For the past twenty-four hours they alternated pumping fuel and flying. Giles steps from the plane, hatless and gloveless, wearing a leather flier's jacket and tennis shoes amid down coats, oversized mittens, and muk luks. He strolls over and says, "I'll just have a nap, then I'll fly you over to Vinson. Can you be packed in, say, three hours?"

In three flights of one and a half hours each, Giles and Max take us over the most spectacular rib of mountains I have ever seen. The Sentinel Range is of Himalayan grandeur. Although Vinson tops out at 16,864 feet, the mountains rise 8,000 feet from the Antarctic plateau with no foothills. Behind them a seemingly infinite sea of whiteness extends forever. We set down, smoothly, in a snowy valley under the massive, vertical West Buttress of Mount Tyree. Mount Shinn and Mount Epperly also rise impressively in the foreground, blocking our view of Mount Vinson.

Before they leave, Max and Giles help us build an igloo of snow blocks around our base camp tents, and then we all settle in for a long sleep. With the constant high sun the days blend into one. We adopt a schedule of working and climbing for roughly twenty hours followed by ten to twelve hours of rest. One sleep later, we melt a couple of pots of snow on our MSR stoves, give Giles and Max a final brew of warm tea, and watch the orange Cessna rise from the snow, wave its wing, and leave us to climb our mountain. We have a radio, which is set to a frequency that Patriot Hills will begin monitoring in eight days. Until then, we have a mountain to climb.

The first task is to secure our base camp against the Antarctic winds and to create an area in which to cook and melt ice to drink. The two weeks of delays in Chile bonded us as a team. We spend a long day preparing camp. It is difficult work, as our bodies must adjust to the eight-thousand-foot altitude and minus-twenty-five-degree temperatures.

While sawing the ice into building blocks we hit buried refuse from previous expeditions. The cracked penguin egg comes back to mind as a metaphor for man in Antarctica. The world's fifth largest continent is dotted with twenty-five major research stations. Three thousand tourists visit its coast every year on cruise ships, and adventurers such as ourselves and the transantarctic teams are starting to invade the interior. Although none plans to cause any harm, litter from an American scientific survey in 1967 is preserved in the ice as fresh as the garbage left by climbers a year ago. Two-thirds of the world's fresh water is preserved in the ice of Antarctica. Despite the chill and the well-publicized ozone hole, the air here is the freshest on earth. Gazing down the crest of the range and out onto the Antarctic plateau where no traces of life are visible to the horizon, I can only think of how lucky I am to be here, now.

After another sleep we set out to make an acclimatization ascent of a small peak west of base camp. The climb is straightforward, and a few hours later we arrive on top. Back at Mary Teresa's, a girl had asked Rob, "Who is the most popular singer in North America?" He instantly replied, "Sonny Bono!" Klaus and the girl both expressed surprise. They hadn't heard of him. Ken and I assured them that Sonny Bono is the greatest entertainer in history. We decide to name the hill "Point Sonny Bono." We are about to join hands and sing "I Got You Babe" when we look down and see two planes and a cluster of tents on the other side of the mountain.

Thirty minutes later we arrive at a Chilean air force camp. Colonel Campos is in charge. He welcomes us with lots of orange juice, hot coffee, and fresh apples. He tells us that a month ago a Chilean plane had a hard landing here, damaging its nose. Another plane flew in with mechanics, welders, and engineers to repair the damaged aircraft. He estimates that they will be around for another ten days. "We have plenty of food and fuel. Come back anytime," he says before we leave for the short walk back to our camp.

One sleep later we carry heavy packs to the site of our first camp on the mountain, at the base of a steep ice face. It is just a long walk, but once we top a knoll, the Chileans are far below. We think we are finally alone with our climb. After building a snow wall, we cache our loads and return to base. We crawl into our base camp igloo complex and sleep for twelve hours, then bring the rest of the gear up to Camp One. Ken, Peter, and Rob complete the igloo around the tents while Klaus and I fix a rope on the ice wall. We cook a good pasta dinner and melt lots of ice to drink. Just as I finish the ritual of stripping off four layers of clothing and wiggling into my tight, overstuffed down and Gore-Tex sleeping bag, I hear a strange roar approach and suddenly die.

"Howdy, mate," a Kiwi accent greets me. Outside the igloo are three snowmobiles with Harley-Davidson motorcycle decals on them. Sitting astride a vehicle marked HUMPY FROM HELL is Paul Fitzgerald, a geologist from New Zealand. Fitzgerald is gathering rock samples for an American National Science Foundation project to determine the mineral composition and age of the Sentinel Mountains. With him are two mountain guides, Rob Hall and Mugs Stump. "We're camped twenty kilometers away," Paul says. "We saw your plane land and thought we should pay a call."

"Would you like some tea?" I ask.

"Naw, not necessary," Paul replies. "We've got a big heater going, melting snow, over at our camp. We're done with our work and are just cruising about, waiting to get picked up. We've waited a week already. It doesn't look like the NSF is coming anytime soon. When you get off your climb, call us on radio frequency 4445 and we'll party. We've got lobster tails, steaks, and Mexican food," he adds with a smile.

Above Camp One our route of ascent goes over the fifteen-hundred-foot ice wall where Klaus and I secure the fixed rope. We carry heavy loads up the steep slope, self-belaying with mechanical ascenders. Ken has not done this kind of climbing before. At ten thousand feet we review basic technique. Klaus climbs with Peter. I stay with Ken, who struggles to keep his balance, alternating between desperate pulls with his arms and hesitant, scratching steps with his crampon points sliding on the ice. We lag far behind Klaus and Peter. Climbing alone, Rob Mitchell, mountain guide, reaches the col at the top of the face by the time Ken and I cross the bergschrund at the bottom. Seven tense hours later I look down on a fairy-tale valley leading to the massive bulk of Mount Vinson. Sweat drips from Ken's forehead. He collapses from exhaustion on top, resting thirty minutes before regaining his feet for the gentle descent to camp.

We descend five hundred feet to a snowfield where Peter, Klaus, and Rob have almost finished building another protective wall. Rob Mitchell, gourmet, flashes his impish grin and yells, "Booty!" while holding up a can of king crab and a jar of black caviar that he excavated from the refuse of a previous expedition. He hands Ken some water.

Despite his dehydration, Ken takes only a small sip before passing the water to me. Then, smiling, he grabs a saw and asks, "What should I do?"

In unison Rob and I answer, "Take off your wet clothes!" I am shocked to see that every layer is soaking wet.

Fortunately the sky is a deep cloudless blue, and Camp Two basks in twenty-four hours of direct sunshine. There is a steady breeze and no humidity. Ken strips and crawls into his down sleeping bag. Rob and I hang the drenched clothes on ski poles. In seconds they freeze solid. Shaking off the ice quickly yields a dry ensemble, but Ken's flagging physical condition and lack of climbing experience are bigger problems.

Mount Vinson towers four thousand vertical feet above us. To gain the peak we must surmount three thousand feet of steep snow ridge to reach the plateau between Vinson and Mount Shinn. Then a long, flat, crevassed section has to be traversed before we reach the summit cone. I anticipate that our summit day will take fifteen hours, which does not bode well for Ken. Seven hours, at lower altitude, nearly pushed him into a coma.

We defrost the cans of caviar and crab in boiling water and enjoy a pleasant soiree despite wine steward Rob Mitchell's inability to produce Dom Perignon. Klaus says, "It is best for Peter to take a long rest, drink, and then climb to the top. With this much cold, at this altitude, waiting will make him weaker. I think we should go to the summit from this camp. Messner told me it is best. There is too much wind on the saddle."

Peter smiles and says, "Ja, this is best." Ken is sound asleep, barely waking long enough to gulp the cups of hot soup we bring him.

Another sleep later Rob, Klaus, and I fire up all three stoves to melt snow and began hydrating. Ken still looks tired, but claims he is ready to go. Peter is determined to leave as soon as possible. I believe Ken would benefit from a rest day, but I also want to keep the team together.

The final factor in the decision to push for the summit is the weather, which seems to be changing. For the first time, high cumulus clouds lace the sky. After discussing the options among the group we decide to leave as a team. But if Ken and I move too slowly on the first snow ridge, the two of us will turn back. We drink as much as possible, fill our thermos bottles (insulated water bottles freeze solid in minutes), and tie into the rope. I am again climbing with Ken. Klaus is taking Peter. Rob Mitchell, mountain guide, starts out breaking trail, climbing solo.

Short-roped with Ken, I reach the col between Vinson and Shinn after five hours. We rest to nibble chocolate, sip warm tea, and put on an additional layer of clothing. A strong wind gusts along the plateau. The mercury in Peter's thermometer retreats beneath the forty-below mark to the bottom of the bulb. Ahead are five distinct summits, and it is difficult to tell which is the highest. Distances are deceiving. We plod ahead for two hours and seem no closer. But as the sun moves behind the peak and we enter shadow, it seems colder. I am wearing two pairs of heavyweight polypropylene underwear, bib overalls, a jacket made of thick pile, a one-piece insulated windproof suit, goggles, a neoprene face mask, three layers on the head and hands, vapor-barrier socks, plastic boots with Alveolite inners, and neoprene overboots. And I am still cold.

"How're ya doing, Ken?" I yell into the wind from two feet away. He just stares straight ahead. I try again. Nothing. Finally I realize that his hearing aids have frozen. He can't hear me shouting next to him. Grabbing him, I get the message across. Ken gives a thumbs-up sign. Climbing on, our team spreads apart. Rob moves faster, vanishing from sight above us; Klaus and Peter slowly drop behind despite the fact that Ken and I are moving at a pace of one step per four raw breaths. Reaching the base of the final impressive summit pyramid, we pause and look around. The sky is still blue with a few high cumulus clouds. Below, two figures are slowly descending into a swirling mist of windblown snow. Another is climbing steadily upward. Five hundred vertical feet beneath the top Klaus joins us. "Peter is so tired, he must go down. Rob exhausted himself climbing the wrong peak and is helping Peter down. I make tracks for you and wait on the summit," he screams into the wind. Klaus moves smoothly and confidently, unroped, up the forty-five degree ice. Ken and I slow down. Ten breaths per step. Ten steps then a sitting rest for Ken. When I motion that we must go down, Ken shakes his head. We have been climbing for sixteen hours. If we were anywhere else I'd insist on turning back. Here the weather is still perfect and we don't have to worry about darkness. If we can't make it now, Ken won't be able to make another bid on this trip. It has cost him a lot of time and money to get this close. He shows no signs of altitude sickness and assures me that he is warm. So we continue, inching for the continental climax.

Above the steep ice we rest and finish our water. There is only a short, easy final ridge to the top. Klaus passes us on the way down. "It is the greatest summit I have made, with the best view. It's better than Himalayas or anywhere," he joyously exclaims. I point to Ken and ask Klaus to please wait and help me bring him down. "I cannot. My feet are so cold. I do not feel my heel. I waited on top for you but it was too cold. I must go down," he insists and begins downclimbing the ice. Ken gathers his incredible inner fortitude and pushes onward and upward. An hour later we embrace on the pinnacle of Mount Vinson. Klaus was right on two counts: The views are incredible, looking down on the jagged summits of the Sentinel Mountains and out over the vast white wilderness. And it is cold.

The descent takes nine careful hours. When we reach the bottom of the ridge, with only a flat walk to the tents, Ken can manage only five steps in a row before sinking to the snow to rest. A quarter mile from camp Klaus meets us with a liter of raspberry drink. Again Ken has only a small sip before handing me the juice. Returning to camp we get warm congratulatory hugs from Rob, who is tending the stove.

Rob Mitchell, solo explorer, confirms that he climbed the wrong summit. He cheerfully tells us, "I was a long way up before I realized it wasn't the highest. But it was a good climb and probably a first ascent. I'll go back up after we sleep. Anyway, Peter needed me to take him down. He was very tired. I'm worried about his right foot. It was frozen solid when we got down."

Klaus adds, "I kept asking him if he was warm enough, every thirty minutes. He always says, *Ja,* fine.'"

Peter snores loudly from his tent. I shake him awake, yelling, "Peter, how is your foot?"

"Good," he mumbles, then he slides his head down in to his bag and resumes snoring.

There is nothing more I can do now. Ken and I drink a few cups of water and quickly join Peter in slumber. Round trip, our summit "day" took twenty-seven hours of continuous climbing.

Eighteen hours of sleep later, I am the first awake. While fumbling to prime the first stove I hear Peter groan. Walking to the tent door I see him staring at his right foot, which is peeking out the side of his unzipped sleeping bag.

"My foot is bad, *ja?*" he asks.

I look. The first three toes are black, the entire foot is swollen to twice normal size, and huge blisters have already formed. "How did this happen, Peter?" I ask, rhetorically, while beginning to think about what to do. It is a serious situation. Peter won't be able to put on his boot or weight the foot. If the blisters break and the foot gets infected, he might die. First we have to get him down.

"It didn't hurt yesterday," Peter mentions flatly, looking in wonder at the deformity at the end of his leg.

"It must have been frozen solid and numb," I explain, to no one in particular, as the full gravity of the situation starts to hit me.

Titus Oates developed severe frostbite on his right foot while returning from the South Pole in 1912. He spoke to his commander, Robert Falcon Scott, saying that he did not want to be a burden to the team. Scott's diary entry from March 16 records that the temperature was minus forty degrees. Oates's famous last words, spoken before leaving the tent to vanish in a raging blizzard, were, "I am just going outside and may be some time."

Klaus, Rob, and I discuss the options. It looks possible to bring a snowmobile around from the next valley to reach us. This will be the least traumatic way to transport Peter. We agree that I should go over the hill behind us and down the steep ice to the Chilean air force camp, where I can radio the geologists for help.

When I top the crest I see a thick layer of clouds rolling in beneath me, stretching as far as I can see. Descending the fixed rope I am enveloped in mist, and it suddenly grows very cold. Visibility is less than three feet. Luckily I can follow our trail in the snow through the whiteout. If I lose the track, I will die. I retrace the route, hoping I've picked the right path to the Chilean camp. Just as my worry starts to escalate into panic, I stumble out of the mist into a warm welcome.

"*Ola!*" Colonel Campos says. "Have some juice. Here, I make you steak. Do you want rice or potato?"

The Chilean radio operator is unable to reach the NSF geological party. However, our message is intercepted by the operator at the American Amundsen-Scott station at the South Pole, who monitors their field team's radio frequency twenty-four hours a day.

"Tell me what you want with them," the operator demands.

"It is for rescue of climber," the Chilean radio operator answers in broken English.

I take the microphone to say, "It's nothing serious. Only a little frostbite that will be a little safer to move by snowmobile." But it is too late. The chain of protocol has started.

"I have to check with the head of operations to see if this is within policy," comes the NSF woman's curt reply. In the next hour, increasingly exaggerated reports of the "dying" climber are the talk of Antarctica. South Pole calls Siple. Siple station calls Rothera base. Rothera contacts Marsh. Marsh radios Punta Arenas. In a giant game of telephone, word of Peter's near-fatal condition spreads. Everyone is contacted except the people we want. The Adventure Network team at Patriot Hills calls the Chilean camp to say they will send a plane carrying a snowmobile for us as soon as the weather improves. Meanwhile there is nothing I can do but drink Chilean coffee with milk and cookies.

Three hours later Mugs, Rob, and Paul roar up to the Chilean camp. "What's goin' on?" Mugs asks. "The American bases are goin' ape crazy over this. You shouldn't of told those jerks a thing. It takes fifty of 'em a week to decide if they can take a shit. They can't get their act together to get us out, yet they try and tell us what we can or can't do. They said not to do anything until some commander reviews the situation. You're climbers. So are we. Fuck them. What do you need?"

I explain the situation to Mugs.

"No problem! Be back with your boys in a few hours," Mugs says optimistically. The rescue squad fires up their engines and sets off into the mist.

I tell my team the plan via walkie-talkie. Peter and Ken will come out by snowmobile with some of the gear. Klaus and Rob will climb down with the rest of our stuff. I'd like to go up with the snowmobiles, but we decide that an additional person will not be needed and might prevent one vehicle from negotiating the steep incline up to camp. There is nothing I can do but settle in for my third major meal in as many hours.

Feeling terrible about Peter's frostbite, I mull over my decisions to this point. Perhaps we should have established a higher camp? Perhaps I should have stayed with Peter and sent Rob to get help? Or maybe we should have just carried Peter down, keeping the team together? As a doctor I want to minimize the chance of infection and don't want to risk popping the blisters by lowering him down the fixed ropes. Then again, I don't want him to stay at high altitude. Perhaps I shouldn't have taken Ken to the summit when I saw two of my teammates descending. All the major decisions were made after extensive discussion with Klaus and Rob, both professional mountain guides. Still, I am the trip leader, and ultimately responsible for the outcome. On a big mountain you have to choose what you think is the best option at the time and go with it. Luckily, I've reached the geologists. They will bring Peter down quickly, without traumatizing his foot.

But no! The snowmobiles can't reach our camp. "The ridge is too steep," Mugs smiles, then quickly adds, "Let's go up and carry him down."

Rob Hall, Mugs, and I climb back up the ice face with Mugs dragging a sled behind him to the top. Meanwhile, Klaus and Rob Mitchell carry Peter to the crest. Ken staggers up on his own. We carefully place Peter in the sled and pad him well. Rob Hall, Klaus, and Mugs lower Peter down the fixed ropes. I belay Ken. Rob Mitchell, sanitation engineer, heads back to Camp Two to clear our camp and carry out all the garbage left by previous expeditions. At the bottom of the face Paul and the snowmobiles wait to take us to camp. Later we'll use the snowmobiles to carry the trash from the mountain.

The rescue is successful, but an Antarctic storm blows in and it is five days before the weather improves. Peter remains optimistic and cheerful, staying in the hospitable warmth of the Chilean camp. Ken and I start him on antibiotics and painkillers and change his dressings twice each day. When my supply of Vaseline gauze gets low, I replenish it from a medical kit left by the first-ascent expedition in 1967. We shuttle between camps by snowmobile and dine like kings. Finally the weather clears enough to try to evacuate. Unfortunately, the fog closes in again while the rescue plane is in the air. The Twin Otter is forced to land nine miles away— which is close enough, as our snowmobile taxi service takes us, our gear, and the garbage to the plane. Mugs is so fed up with the NSF being unable to get him out that he asks to leave with us. Adventure Network says yes, but the "Commandant" tells him no. Since his passport is with the NSF and he hasn't been paid, he stays on the ground.

Back at the White Coffin we again join journalists, Saudis, and sled dogs waiting for a flight. The situation sounds bad.

"One engine is broken. We've sent to Miami for a new one," is the radio message from Punta Arenas. Moreover, they need a mechanic who knows how to install a DC-6 engine. Klaus is going to miss his trip, Ken will have to revise his surgery schedule, and we are all terrified that Peter's foot will become infected. The blisters have popped and we are running out of dressings again. We finish my supply of antibiotics but, fortunately, there are extra antibiotics intended for the sled dogs at Patriot Hills.

The British Imperial Trans-Antarctic Expedition of 1915 appeared doomed. Their ship, Endurance, *was crushed by ice in a grinding tragedy of twisted wood. Twenty-eight men faced food and fuel shortages, the threat of killer whales, and the inevitable crack-up of the ice floes beneath them. Sir Ernest Shackleton and five others repaired a twenty-foot boat and embarked on an eight-hundred-mile voyage across the savage seas of the Drake Passage. After sixteen days at sea the men reached South Georgia Island, where they had to cross glaciers and a previously unpassed mountain range to find help for their mates trapped in Antarctica.*

If it weren't for my concern over Peter's foot getting infected, our wait would be tolerable. Gordon Wiltsie and I climb the Patriot Hills with telemark skis and enjoy some great runs. John Stetson, the trainer for Will Steger's dogs, explains mushing. The cook tent steams with fresh simmering soups and is often the scene of lively international debates. But the camp's mood slowly turns ugly. The journalists aren't going to make it home for Christmas. Everyone else thinks he will lose his job, wife, or girlfriend. Klaus begins insisting that Ken and I declare Peter's condition to be terminal so we can get an emergency military evacuation.

Finally the radio announces that the DC-6 is fixed. But we are then told that the pilot has quit. Only ten hours later the cavalry arrives in the form of a big DC-6 filling the sky above camp. Giles Kershaw is again sitting tall in the saddle. He has "nipped back from Hong Kong" to rescue us from the ice. We reach Punta Arenas at six the following morning. Klaus and Ken fly to Santiago at seven, still wearing their mountain clothes. Giles arranges for a Chilean air force jet to evacuate Peter, who will have three toes amputated back in Europe. Returning to town, I find that all of my clothes have been stolen. Rob Mitchell, haberdasher, insists that I take his extra pants, socks, and shirts.

As the sun sets on us for the first time in weeks we head out, clad in sandals, slacks, and short-sleeved shirts, to celebrate our return to Punta Arenas. A spectacular double rainbow appears in the sky, revealing all of the colors hidden in white light. Rob Mitchell, poet, happily exclaims, "Hey, this isn't Antarctica!"

14

A Climber
of Genius

It's a chilly evening in Yosemite Valley, and when Lou Reichardt and I arrive at the Mountain Room Bar after a day of climbing, the place is jammed. The party doesn't do much for Reichardt, who attempted to skirt this evening by suggesting we stay in camp and eat Hershey bars for dinner. As we make our way through the crowd of mostly young, mostly color-coordinated climbers, I can't help but notice that the forty-six-year-old Reichardt is wearing a patched down coat, torn wool knickers, and thick, black-framed glasses held together by paper clips and tape. He looks like a theoretical scientist. He is.

"Look at Hubel's and Weisel's work on the importance of visual experience to normal cortex development," he tells me at the bar, commencing a forty-minute review of contemporary neurophysiology. That none of the nearby patrons adds his two cents is no surprise. But you'd think somebody would at least recognize Dr. Louis French Reichardt, arguably America's foremost Himalayan mountaineer.

Reichardt was the first American to summit both Everest and K2 and the first to climb three twenty-six-thousand-foot peaks. Moreover, he climbed Everest by way of the East Face—an approach considered suicidal from the time it was first surveyed in 1921—and reached the top of K2 without supplemental oxygen, another first. He's also thought to be the only climber to lug a backpack to the summit of Everest with the airline luggage tags intact, and is certainly the only mountaineer to read *The Universe and Dr. Einstein* at twenty-seven thousand feet on K2.

Until recently, often upon the solution of some monstrous scientific problem, Reichardt would simply hang up his lab coat every three years or so and hike into the mountains to tackle something absurdly difficult. Months after he solved the long-standing mystery of how a cell differentiates itself, he climbed 26,810-foot Dhaulagiri. His widely applauded work on neuronal plasticity preceded an ascent of Nanda Devi, a climb so technically demanding that some characterized it as the best American effort in the Himalayas in nearly a decade.

But alas, Reichardt hasn't climbed a big mountain for more than ten years. In 1992 he scratched from an expedition up Kanchenjunga, the world's third highest mountain, after learning that a research grant might be in jeopardy if he left. He's also passed on expeditions to Cho Oyu, Everest, Broad Peak, and the North Ridge of K2. Since climbing Everest in 1983, Reichardt's principal adventures have been of the purely cerebral kind, in his neurology lab at the University of California, San Francisco. There, at the nether reaches of the in-vitro frontier, Reichardt lays one brain cell next to another and pursues his field's sixty-four-thousand-dollar question: Why do similar nerve cells sometimes grow and sometimes not? Why do they fail to regenerate after a spinal cord injury, yet succeed if the nerve damage is in an arm or leg?

Research in this area is still in its infancy, but Reichardt's previous accomplishments in both cellular biology and brain physiology—his résumé runs to fourteen pages—have made him an academic superstar. "Lou is one of the leading researchers of his generation," says Zach Hall, chair of physiology at the University of California, San Francisco. Reichardt has been awarded two of science's most prestigious fellowships (the Guggenheim and the Howard Hughes), and he recently declined a deanship, an endowed professorship, and virtually unlimited research funds from Baylor Medical School. More than one colleague has mentioned him as a leading candidate for the Nobel Prize.

"If I hadn't lost so many brain cells to high-altitude hypoxia," he jokes, "I'd already have been to Stockholm."

Reichardt's long layoff from climbing, however, may be nearing an end. Several months ago, after learning that a National Institutes of Health grant would fund his lab through 2004, Reichardt pronounced himself ready again. "I am an incredibly fortunate person," he says. "If science and discovery are important to you, there could be no better job. But this is the time to go. I've never been this far from a grant proposal." The challenge of a climbing comeback could be overwhelming, but that's always been the draw for Reichardt. If there has been one clear pattern in his life, it has been his penchant for selecting outrageously difficult problems both in science and climbing. "What is exciting," he says, speaking of mountaineering but perhaps also of science, "is that the challenges almost always come from unexpected places." Would he start back with something moderate, a peak in South America, perhaps, or Alaska? "Maybe Gangar Punsum," he muses, electing a 25,000-foot Himalayan giant, the highest unclimbed peak in the world.

I first met Reichardt as his teammate on the 1981 and 1983 Everest East Face expeditions. When I saw him in San Francisco in 1989 I was impressed at how fit his six-foot-one, 180-pound frame appeared; it looked as though he'd been confined to a gym, not a laboratory, for the last six years. Particularly formidable were his hulking forearms, ridged with thick veins and defined by a Harris tweed jacket a size or two too small. I asked if he'd been working out. "I haven't had any physical exercise in years," he said, smiling. "I've been totally committed to science."

It's moments like these that make climbers wonder about Reichardt. His only regular training is a three-block walk to the bus stop and a one-flight stair climb to his office, yet on expeditions, at severe altitude, he normally carries what seems to be twice the load at twice the speed of anyone else. Some say he must be a physiological freak, a person whose respiratory system is perfectly crafted for work at altitude; others contend that his mind simply drives his body past such niggling distractions as tedium, discomfort, and pain. Finally, there's the rumor that Reichardt *does* train—by spending long hours in his laboratory's cold-room. He denies it, but a coworker claims to have discovered him in the room wearing only underwear.

Reichardt puzzles for other reasons: While other climbers clamor for donations of state-of-the-art equipment and mountaineering clothing, Reichardt prefers a 1969-issue backpack and a collection of hideous sun hats. He seeks no publicity. He's written no climbing books and just a few climbing articles, and he often mumbles about his deeds as if to make sure he'll never be quoted. ("I just wanted to, well, climb some things," he says of his summits of Dhaulagiri, Nanda Devi, K2, and Everest.) He says so little at times, but clearly knows so much, that it can be unsettling. "Lou is the smartest guy I've ever met, but we don't have much to talk about," says John Roskelley, who's been on four expeditions with Reichardt. Once, while waiting out a storm at 24,500 feet on Dhaulagiri, the pair didn't have a single conversation in ten days. "We weren't mad at each other," says Roskelley. "We just didn't have anything to say."

The same might be said by his scientific colleagues, few of whom see the merit in risking one's life on a mountain or the logic of exposing a brain—especially Reichardt's brain—to potential damage from prolonged stays at altitude. On campus, a distracted Reichardt will often scoot right past acquaintances, responding to a bright hello with . . . nothing. Conversely, a joke from Reichardt is liable to leave lab folks pondering for days. "He has a very elliptical, highly condensed sense of humor," explains Zach Hall. "He'll say something, laugh, and then move along. It might be hours before you'll get the link he's made between disparate things. It's as if he's three steps ahead of everyone."

The son of a prizewinning architect and a housewife who later became a peace and civil rights activist, Lou Reichardt was born and raised in Pasadena, California. His parents, both avid backpackers, began taking him along on trips into the Sierras when he was ten. Soon, Reichardt says, "I was wandering off by myself, climbing anything that was nearby. I think it drove my parents nuts."

He attended Midland High School, a tiny, all-male boarding school near Los Angeles. "Lou was tall and awkward, with thick, greasy glasses," says his Midland roommate Joe Esherick, recalling his first impression. "No way, I thought, would he be athletic. But he was." Reichardt, Esherick, and a third classmate took a Sierra Club climbing course and made forays to nearby Taquitz Rock. "We were pretty unsophisticated," says Reichardt, an average beginner. "I remember this one long, crazy climb. It was before we started using nuts and things, and at one point I was sixty feet above my anchor. I had no business doing anything like that, but I finally made that damn thing. It made me appreciate the certain thrill in living beyond where someone should rationally live."

Perfect scores on his math SATs and his French boards earned Reichardt a National Merit Scholarship and a spot at Harvard in the fall of 1960. "It was kind of embarrassing," he says. "At Harvard they put me into third-year French. When I came to class they started reading poetry, and I didn't understand a word of it. It was clear I'd scored twice what I should have on the test." Reichardt intended to major in philosophy. ("I was never in high school science fairs or anything like that," he says. "I had endless ideas, but I could never get close to the finished product.") But he changed his mind soon after taking a class taught by James Watson, one of the discoverers of DNA. "The things he was saying were tremendously exciting. It was obvious that society was becoming driven by science."

He joined the renowned Harvard Mountaineering Club but never went on an expedition. "I had school to worry about, and I had to work in the summer," says Reichardt, who did fit in some rock climbing and tried ice climbing during summer vacations back in California.

In 1964 Reichardt went to Cambridge on a Fulbright scholarship, then to Stanford, where he first attacked the problem of how the myriad cells of a human body, all of which are genetically identical, differentiate to become muscle, nerve, bone, and blood. His academic elders considered the problem of gene expression far too complex for a Ph.D. candidate in physiology; Reichardt persisted anyway, taking the topic on in his doctoral thesis.

It was at Stanford that Reichardt got a reputation as a promising mountaineer and rock climber. He would unwind from an eighty-hour week in the lab by marching fifty miles in a weekend, typically climbing three ten-thousand-foot summits en route. His fortitude was spectacular, but there was perhaps no uglier stride in all of North America, the result of a college knee injury and his habit of taking one stride to anyone else's two. He also climbed in Yosemite with a Palo Alto crowd that included Paul Gerhard, one of the Bay Area's best climbers. Gerhard invited him on an expedition to Mount McKinley in 1967, the first of three trips they would take to Alaska.

The weather was unusually bad that year—six people died in a storm that kept most climbers from reaching the top—but Reichardt and Gerhard made it. "Mentally, going to McKinley was a much bigger step than going to the Himalayas," says Reichardt. "It was the first time I was really away from everything." Afterward Gerhard pushed to get Reichardt on a 1969 American team to Dhaulagiri. Three weeks before the team departed, a spot opened up for him. "I think I got to go because I was the only one without a real job," says Reichardt. "The Himalayas weren't really in my life plan."

The expedition went well at first. But on April 28, Reichardt was on the glacier beneath Dhaulagiri at 17,500 feet, taking photographs while his teammates worked to bridge a crevasse. Later he would write in his diary:

> It began with the noise of an avalanche, then a mutual realization that it might hit us. Then there was silence. No screams, just silence. First came the realization that I was not hurt. It couldn't have been that bad. Then came the discovery that nothing was there—no tents, no cache, no ice ax, and no friends. A moment of hope. It was just a snow avalanche. Hey, Boyd! Hey, Dave! Hey, Vin! I'm alive and okay; here to dig you out. Just let me know where you are. No answers.

Reichardt performed two exhaustive searches—first by himself and later with the expedition members who had been at base camp at the time of the avalanche—but no bodies were recovered. Seven of the finest climbers in the world were dead. By a quirk of fate, Reichardt, who had been in the midst of them moments before, was left to tell the story. He returned to America and traveled from San Francisco to Connecticut to visit the friends and families of the victims. "I wasn't ready to go back to the research," he says. "I was pretty blown away."

Reichardt resumed his graduate work several months later and published *Regulation of Repressor Synthesis and Early Gene Expression by Bacteriophage and*

Lambda Virus in 1972. The dissertation provided a model to explain how one cell develops differently from the next. The understanding of gene expression was radically altered by Reichardt's work, and today it is one of the basics in any medical school curriculum. "I think all of my promotions and appointments still come from my dissertation," he says. "It's the only really important thing I've done." Hall, along with others, thought it worthy of Nobel consideration.

In 1973 Reichardt went back to Dhaulagiri with another strong team. Many climbers were stunned to hear that he was returning to the mountain where he had witnessed one of American climbing's worst tragedies. "Lou carried the heaviest loads, pushing hard day after day," says Roskelley, who was amazed by Reichardt's strength and intensity. Teammate Jim Morrissey remembers a day when he and Reichardt hiked into base camp. Subtly, they both accelerated the tempo, turning the trek into something of a race. It ended in a dead heat. The next day, while hiking at sixty-five hundred feet, they learned that a teammate at fourteen thousand feet had cerebral edema. They took off, and at eleven thousand feet Morrissey doubled over sick. As his partner raced on, Morrissey asked, "God, Lou, how can you keep going?" Reichardt put it this way: "Mind over matter."

They pushed on to 24,500 feet and waited out a storm for ten days; then, well into the "death zone," Reichardt and Roskelley bulled their way to the summit without supplemental oxygen. On the way down, Reichardt's suspenders snapped and his thick glasses fogged; in a kind of Himalayan Charlie Chaplin skit, his pants fell to his knees whenever he reached up to wipe his glasses. He also suffered a mild case of ataxia, a loss of coordination and sense of balance. Though Morrissey offered help, mostly he observed in bemused wonder as Reichardt stubbornly marched into base camp under his own power, tail bared to the wind. There, Reichardt diagnosed his ataxia as resulting from a minor stroke in the cerebellum. At that moment, it occurred to him, his vocation and avocation were for the first time in perfect harmony.

"In mountaineering there's real discovery, pushing of limits," says Reichardt, who counts Dhaulagiri, his first Himalayan peak, as his favorite. "You live on the edge, figuring out what you need to do to stay on the right side of the line. Science is sort of similar."

In fact, when he returned from Dhaulagiri, life on another edge—the scientific edge—was foremost in Reichardt's mind. "After my dissertation, I could have coasted," he says. "I could have stayed in cellular biology for the rest of my life or go into something new and wild. I decided to go into neurological biology even though I didn't know much about it. It was considered really far-out, the wildest type of biology there was. It was a risk—I might not have ended up under an avalanche, but I could have been left without a grant, which is scientific death."

As it turned out, Reichardt made the right decision, producing brilliant work as a postdoctoral fellow at Harvard from 1974 to 1976 and attracting job offers from the major research centers and universities across the country. He put them all off—at least for the summer—and went to India instead.

The infamous Nanda Devi expedition was a tortured one from start to finish, culminating in the tragic death of co-leader Willi Unsoeld's twenty-one-year-old daughter. Reichardt generally stayed out of the number of squabbles that afflicted the expedition and partly for that reason was elected climbing leader. He toiled at shepherding the large, feuding team up the 25,645-foot mountain, and eventually he, Roskelley, and Jim States—each carrying seventy-five pounds of gear over the route's most difficult section, a thousand-foot sheer vertical buttress beneath the summit area—pushed to Camp Four. When it was time to summit a few days later, Reichardt balked. According to his altimeter, the trio had fifteen hundred feet to go; it was already midday, and if the altimeter was accurate, they'd probably have to bivouac without any gear. Reichardt trusted the reading and wanted to retreat. The others refused. Against his better judgment, Reichardt made the ascent. The three summitted at two o'clock on the afternoon of September 1, returned to camp before dark, and proved Reichardt wrong about the altimeter and right about his theory: The beauty of an expedition begins when things start to screw up.

Harvard, MIT, and Cal Tech had offered posts to Reichardt back in the spring, but only the University of California, San Francisco, agreed to let him take prolonged leaves of absence to climb. "He was the first person I hired," says Zach Hall, who started the university's neuroscience program, now regarded as one of the best in the country. Hall signed Reichardt on the strength of his Harvard work—he had pioneered a technique to distinguish among the many types of brain cells, allowing the neuroanatomists to study rare populations of neurons—but the two had been friends since meeting at Stanford in 1967.

"His stamina is amazing," says Hall. "His style has never been slick or graceful, but he has this tremendous ability to focus his energies and get things done, to cut right through to what's important." The parallels to his climbing style are unmistakable. Reichardt has often said that when he's on the mountain he thinks of nothing but climbing, and when he's in the lab, nothing but science. Nothing. When climbing with him, it's not unusual to have to holler simply to capture his attention. "He'll appear oblivious sometimes," says Hall, "but it's more that he's recognized that what's going on is not important."

In 1978 an American expedition was gathering for an assault on K2. Americans had been trying to climb the world's second highest mountain since the 1930s, and though Reichardt was at the crux of his new research, he couldn't say no.

The Karakoram Range suffered from a series of terrible storms in 1978. As the American group trekked in, they met a beleaguered British expedition that had already given up on K2. The Americans went on, changing strategy daily to account for the weather. Reichardt was again the pacesetter. "Without him, we probably would have turned back," expedition member Rick Ridgeway wrote later. When it came time to make a summit bid, Reichardt's oxygen system failed and he fell behind Jim Wickwire, his summit partner. He discarded the seventeen-pound unit, dumped his pack and parka, and caught Wickwire just below the summit. "Tell me if I exhibit any bizarre behavior," said Reichardt, worried that the lack of oxygen would impair his judgment. A short time later the pair walked onto the 28,250-foot peak. "He lacked what, to the rest of us, was the main limiter of our efforts; feedback from the body to the mind," Ridgeway wrote. "Lou's body just carried out the mind's orders."

Lou Reichardt is at the helm of the family minivan, calmly piloting his four children home from a church dinner. In the backseat Anna, Ben, Christian, and Isa, ages four to twelve, are attempting to lever a heavy pack up to the front seat. Cries of "Louie! Louie!" drown out conversation. Seven-year-old Ben begins to scale the front seat when Reichardt spies him in the rearview mirror. "Now Ben, it is imperative that you remain stationary and fasten your seat belt," he says. By the time the Reichardt clan arrives at its modest stucco home in the hills overlooking the Cal–San Francisco Medical Center, the noise has approached the supersonic.

Reichardt's wife, Kathy, is away this afternoon, and he valiantly attempts to attend to a visitor as the four precocious youngsters spread out. Outside in the driveway, one has inexplicably dropped a rotten Halloween pumpkin on the hood of Reichardt's Toyota truck. Inside, Isa confronts her dad. "Louie," lectures the twelve-year-old, "you have already inflicted severe psychological damage by missing my birthday. Don't you think it would be a mistake to miss my school play?" Reichardt agrees that it would.

These days Reichardt is much more reluctant to take large chunks of time away from his wife and children. "My first priority is my family," says Reichardt, who rarely goes anywhere socially without the gang. "Ever since I became a father, I'm not as willing to stick my neck out."

There are occasional exceptions to this rule, such as Reichardt's trip to Everest in 1981. Hidden in Tibet, the mountain's East Face is its largest and steepest side. It was first seen by Western climbers during the 1921 British Everest reconnaissance, when George Leigh Mallory declared it to be unclimbable, concluding that "other men, less wise, might attempt this way, but emphatically it was not for us." The British moved around to the north, where all subsequent Tibetan assaults on the mountain took place.

But in 1981 the Chinese sold Americans a permit to make the first climbing attempt on the East Face, and Reichardt was named the climbing leader. The standard expedition bickering soon erupted into open warfare. Unaccustomed to the role of massaging overamped egos and disinclined to referee the disputes, Reichardt instead showed his leadership by hefting double loads up the mountain. His understated diplomacy failed, and six climbers, including Roskelley, abandoned the effort. Some on the expedition suggested an easier route, but on that subject Reichardt was uncompromising. "There is no greater challenge for a climber than an untested face," Reichardt once said, and clearly he had no intention of substituting anything less demanding. The handicapped squad did find a route up the initial forty-five-hundred-foot sheer buttress but stalled from lack of support at twenty-two thousand feet.

Reichardt returned to the East Face in 1983, so determined to climb it that he had actually run "up to five miles in a single day," worked out on pull-up bars, and squeezed a grip exerciser. Led by Jim Morrissey, veteran American alpinist George Lowe, and Reichardt, the team members quickly worked their way up the mountain. When it came time to choose a summit team, Reichardt was picked along with Carlos Buhler and Kim Momb. Equipment problems delayed Reichardt on the morning of the summit push, and he was forced to climb hurriedly to catch his partners. He finally tracked them down, six hours later, where the East Face merges with the southeast summit ridge at 27,500 feet. From there, Reichardt broke trail through deep snow all the way to the South Summit. For the sake of speed, the trio climbed without a rope, knowing what a slip on the exposed ridge would mean. At two o'clock in the afternoon, thirteen hours after leaving camp, Reichardt, Momb, and Buhler completed the first ascent of the East Face. "Nobody ever believes this, but I never go on any of my trips expecting to reach the summit," says Reichardt, who has been the first to the summit each time one of his expeditions landed someone on top. "In the case of Everest, I'd never in my life dreamed I'd actually get up the thing."

Reichardt's strength on Everest gave rise to still more theorizing about how he could be so good at altitude. Reichardt disputes the notion that he is some kind of genetic freak uniquely adapted for high-altitude work. "One of the first times I went high, I had a terrible case of altitude sickness," he says. "I was dehydrated when I started the climb, and forgot to bring a water bottle. I had a splitting headache and dry heaves."

Reichardt knows that less oxygen in the air can be compensated for by deeper, more rapid breathing. But faster breathing means you exhale more, losing moisture and acid. Your blood becomes alkaline, a problem that the kidneys deal with by selectively excreting alkaline urine and saving acid. Together, the heavy breathing and the kidneys' compensatory mechanism lead to dehydration. Old climbers' lore holds that at altitude you should "drink until your piss is gin-clear."

Reichardt lives by this rule. "On Everest, I never saw him without a water bottle in his hand," says Buhler. Proper hydration is one part of Reichardt's systematic, ever-logical approach to altitude. He starts his daily carries of supplies before dawn and pushes himself to go twice as fast as most climbers in order to finish his chores early. He then spends the rest of the day melting snow to drink, making sure to shield his head from the high-altitude sun. Never one for small talk, he eschews most expedition socializing to rest in his tent. He often forces down huge gulps of high-calorie food with his liquid, even if he's not hungry. On Everest, Carl Tobin says, it wasn't uncommon to see Reichardt stuff four or five Almond Roca candy bars into already bulging cheeks. Reichardt says this regimen of maximum exertion followed by concentrated drinking, eating, and rest allows him to work hard each day. And that when it's time for a summit bid, he's both acclimatized and fit.

Reichardt's climbing partners remain unconvinced that it's as simple as he makes it sound. "Lou is a thoroughbred at altitude," says Roskelley. "Put him on a mountain and it's like he was born to run." Physiological research supports that notion. People who acclimatize best to altitude breathe harder and faster when the oxygen content in their blood drops even a little bit. That explains why marathon runners, who endure maximum exertion with a minimum of huffing and puffing, often fare poorly at altitude. Reichardt, who sprinted in high school, breathes heavily with the slightest exertion, even at sea level, giving the impression that he's horribly out of shape. To the contrary, his overactive respiratory response combines with what must be a genetically humongous lung capacity to make him superior at altitude.

Jim Morrissey, a partner on five expeditions, has another theory: "Lou is unstoppable, not because of physiology, but because of attitude. He's one of the most powerful, capable, and determined mountaineers in the world because he's more focused and driven than anyone else. He also has an incredibly high pain threshold." Says Reichardt: "Science and climbing are intellectual exercises. There are specific things in each that you just suffer through."

Reichardt's laboratory is awash in centrifuges, microscopes, and science journals. He supervises a dozen graduate students and postdoctoral fellows, who daily, from eight in the morning to eight at night, try to discover what makes nerve cells live or die. It is new scientific territory. "This is like cancer research ten years ago," Reichardt says of the ongoing struggle to understand the human brain. "It's intense, but the pressures aren't the same as on expeditions, where people will literally hate each other. People aren't scared in the same way.

"Basically, my job is to figure out how things work, to try and think of good ideas, raise new questions. The stuff I do in the lab is in some ways not so different from, say, the problem of how to get two food bags from Camp Two to Camp Four."

In the years since Everest, Reichardt's mind has been exclusively devoted to science. Early in his tenure at Cal–San Francisco Medical Center he did pioneering work with nerve growth factors, the proteins that decide whether neurons live or die. Their existence was cause for much optimism in the scientific community. If scientists could stimulate nerve cells to grow, they could regenerate damaged brain tissue. "Most solutions are only half solutions," Reichardt cautions about the immense problem before him. The research could occupy a lifetime, maybe much longer, which may be why Reichardt is ready to go climbing again. "One reason he likes to climb," says Kathy Reichardt, "is that when you climb a mountain, the problem is either done or not done."

Since 1983 Reichardt's work and family schedule has allowed for exactly one weekend of rock climbing each year. Still, nobody doubts his ability to knock off another Himalayan giant, be it Kanchenjunga or Gangar Punsum. Even with the long respite, he has spent more time above twenty-four thousand feet than any other American. And he isn't unusually old for a Himalayan climber, many of whom reach their prime in their thirties, even early forties. "If you can climb one," he says, "you should be able to climb them all." Reichardt may again prove his mastery over both science and climbing, but that isn't ultimately what he cares to be known for. "My goal is to have children who remember me fondly," he says, the dizzying complexities of two brilliant careers unerringly simplified to the most obvious and important of responsibilities. "There is nothing that gives me more pleasure than being with my children."

Recently Reichardt returned to Yosemite for a full week. The object was to relax, but there was something else to do, too. Twelve-year-old Isa Reichardt had told her father she wanted to climb Mount Rainier. He agreed to lead her up the mountain if she met his criteria: First, she would have to hike an advanced trail in Yosemite. Next would come a climb of Mount Shasta, which would reveal her capability on snow and ice. Finally, she'd have to summit Mount Whitney, California's highest peak, to determine how she fared at altitude. While the park burst with early-spring dogwood and a thousand waterfalls, Reichardt timed his daughter as she hiked up to the Yosemite Falls Trail. He reports that she knocked off the three miles and twenty-seven hundred vertical feet in well under the allotted time. Mount Shasta is next. Though the preparation may seem excessive to Isa, she should be thankful. They could be going to the cold-room.

15

THE ULTIMATE
HARDMAN

George Lowe is the real-life version of the image that Clint Eastwood attempts to project in his westerns. George has the cold steel eyes. George has the calm demeanor and the can-do attitude. He is the freethinking western gunslinger who knows what's right and wrong and quietly does it. Since his teenage years, George Lowe has been breaking through psychological barriers. In the 1970s most climbers agreed that rock climbs could only be done up to a certain difficulty, after which it was essential to use pitons as aid. At the time, the limit of unaided climbing was thought to be grade 5.10. George Lowe quietly went out and, unaided, climbed whatever he felt like climbing. Many of his climbs are now listed as 5.12s. George ignored the general consensus about what was possible and consistently broke through current standards and limits. Once George pioneered the way, others could follow—most of the time, anyway.

George, along with Chris Jones, climbed the North Face of the North Twin in the early 1970s. More than thirty years later this route is unrepeated and is still considered among the most difficult and serious in the Canadian Rockies. Similarly, his climbs of the Infinite Spur on Mount Forker, the North Face of Mount Hunter, and the North Ridge of Latok, as well our route on the East Face of Mount Everest, are all standards for difficulty that have stood the test of time.

More importantly than his physical achievements, George Lowe exudes a quiet confidence and strength of mind in the harshest of situations. He is the ultimate hardman who has hovered near the cutting edge of climbing for three decades. Even as he gracefully ages, George retains a keen sense of what he can and cannot do. He continues to embark on climbs that, if no longer absolutely setting the limit of human possibility, certainly continue to expand his own abilities. While in his fifties, George solo climbed the twenty-six-thousand-foot giant Dhauligiri. With Alex Lowe, he climbed the nose route on El Capitan in one day.

I first met George on Everest. In both 1981 and 1983 he was the driving force on our East Face expeditions—so much so that in 1981 the team affectionately named the six-thousand-foot vertical ice and rock buttress that is still the most difficult technical climbing ever attempted on Mount Everest the Lowe Buttress. No matter how severe the weather, no matter how bad the rock, George never lost his enthusiasm or his optimism. He quietly went out and led the most difficult pitches under any conditions. With the scream of falling rock hailing around him like bombs around the small wooden houses of Dresden during the worst air strikes, George led with composure and control. On rock so crumbly it could well have been molded of eggshells and Scotch tape, George delicately picked his way higher and higher. In a position where a fall would have dire consequences and the climbing was nearly impossible, George calmly figured out how to engineer a small piece of aid and gently balance out. Cool as a cucumber, he could crack whatever code needed to be broken to conjure up a route through the overhanging bands of our upper headwall.

When the weather gets bad on any climb George has the tenacity to dig in and wait as long as needed; yet in dangerous situations he has the good sense to know when it's time to head back. He pushed our route up the East Face of Mount Everest in 1981, but when weather conditions and lack of a coordinated team made it apparent that it was too dangerous to push on to the summit, he cheerfully agreed to go down. A similar situation occurred when George did what may still be the most amazing route ever in the Himalayas on the North Ridge of Latok with his cousin Jeff. The pair were through all obstacles and ready to go to the top when Jeff became ill. George quickly abandoned the summit and calmly figured out how to get Jeff down the seven thousand feet of technical climbing that they had just pioneered. George focuses on the moment rather than the ultimate goal—although when the summit is in sight he's unstoppable.

Once our 1981 attempt on the East Face had been abandoned, the team retreated to base camp to wait a few days for yaks to come and evacuate our loads. On the first day back at camp, George quietly asked me, "Geoff, do you want to come climb Kartse tomorrow?" Kartse is one of Everest's sister peaks and, at twenty-two thousand feet, a beautiful and dramatic summit in itself. It had never before been approached from the east and we had no maps, charts, or information. We knew little

Chomolungma—Mount Everest—Mother Goddess of the Universe.

Rock climbing in the Shawangunks.
(John Sherman photo)

Dani tribesman Wanimbo, using organic needle and thread in Irian Jaya, New Guinea.

Seppanus always wanted to be a writer, too.

Mount Kilamanjaro, Africa's highest peak.

Sam Moses on the North Face of Cartensz Pyramid.

Me, left, and fellow adventurer George Lowe, atop Utah's Moses. (Neal Beidleman photo)

Heading to the top of Mount Vinson, Antarctica.

At the apex of North America, Denali, with Scott Woolems.

Ascent to the top of Europe, Mount El'brus, 18,481 feet.

The Kangshung Team, 1983. First row, left to right: Dan Reid, Lou Reichardt, me, Jim Morrissey, George Lowe, Dave Cheesmond. Second row: Carlos Buhler, Andy Harvard, Kim Momb, Jay Cassell, Carl Tobin, Dave Coombs, Chris Kopczynski.

The East Face of Mount Everest.

The rock headwall on the East Face of Mount Everest. (Jay Cassell photo)

The Bowling Alley—East Face of Mount Everest.

In the Khumbu ice-fall, Everest, 1988.

Everest avalanche, 1988.

Flying Frenchman J.M. Boivin descending from the summit of Mount Everest, 8,000 feet in nine minutes.

The first plastic flamingo to the summit. Stacy Allison, the first American woman, and Pasang, Gyalzen Sherpa. (Stacy Allison Photo Collection)

Me on top of the world. Mount Everest, October 2, 1988.

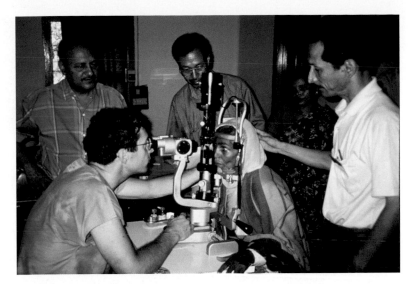

Back to more earthly matters.

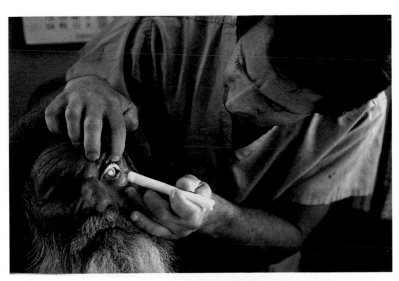

An elderly patient in need of help. (Neal Beidleman photo)

Another satisfied customer. (Neal Beidleman photo)

Not your usual operating room security. (Neal Beidleman photo)

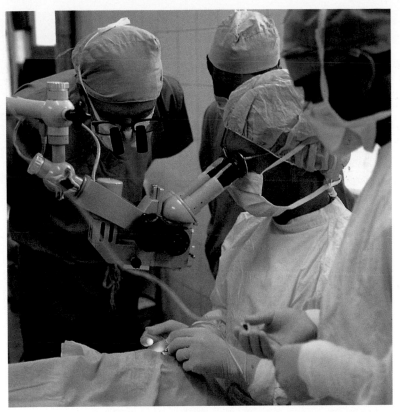

Teaching surgical technique—a lesson that will keep on giving. (Neal Beidleman photo)

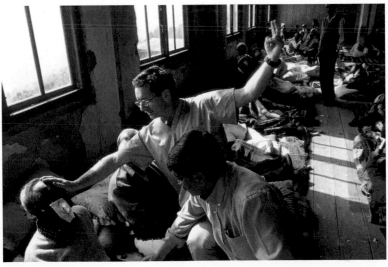

An assembly-line examination while others wait patiently. (Neal Beidleman photo)

The doctor is in. Back in the mountains on one of my annual trips. (Neal Beidleman photo)

about the mountain, other than having seen its beautiful pyramidal summit from our high buttress camp. George and I set out at one in the morning, hiking in the general direction of Kartse. An enormous icefall and a jumble of crevasses thwarted our approach at one point. Undaunted, George said in his quiet voice—a cross between John Wayne's and Donald Duck's—"Okay, let's rope up." In the shimmering half-light of early dawn, George, with the aid of a headlamp, picked an unerring line through the wild labyrinth of broken ice. We reached the upper slopes of Kartse by first light. We chose a line up a steep ice slope and continued upward. We had not brought enough equipment to set belays for the entire route or to protect the leader: If one of us fell while we were roped together, we would both die. George suggested we unrope and began climbing the ice slope in a methodical style. I followed behind. By eleven o'clock in the morning, we had reached the summit. George is a believer in absolute honesty but has a sly, quiet sense of humor that allows him to play by the rules while ignoring some when necessary. We did not have a permit to climb the Kartse, and George was concerned that he would offend the Chinese. Thus he stood with one foot on each side, straddling the summit, without ever standing on top of Kartse. George could honestly answer any Chinese interrogation by saying he had not climbed to the top of the virgin mountain. After not reaching the summit, we soloed down the mountain's steep face. George was cool and calm as always. We returned to base camp by late afternoon and agreed that we had just completed one of the most enjoyable days of mountaineering either of us had ever experienced.

When the yaks came to help us evacuate camp, George asked our Chinese liaison officer, Mr. Wang Fu Chow, the man who'd made the first ascent of Mount Shishipangma, whether we might attempt a late-season, early-winter assault on the highest mountain completely within Tibet. Wang Fu Chow was incredibly accommodating. After a quick discussion among our team members, Jim Morrissey, Eric Perlman, and Lou Reichardt signed on to join our attempt on Shishipangma. The five of us veered off from the main road in Kharta after a final farewell dinner with the rest of the team. Everyone else was headed for Lhasa. We moved west toward the highest peak. The climbing was much easier than on Everest, and we were all well acclimatized. We made rapid progress up the slopes. The winter winds, however, had moved in, and their constant shriek blew over the col at our high camp. Our tents buckled and flattened like junked cars being trampled by a monster truck at a county fair. We spent several nights awake, pressing our backs against the tent walls simply to keep them from collapsing. It became apparent to everyone that it was impossible to continue with the winter jet stream winds being what they were. This was apparent to everyone, that is, except George. George was absolutely content to wait as long as possible for a chance at the summit. Like a western gunslinger playing a hand of poker, George's face never revealed any worry or gave away any sense of fear or futility. When the rest of the team left, however, George calmly departed with us.

It was with his signature cool, calm demeanor that George returned to the East Face of Everest in 1983. Again he was the driving force pushing our team upward. He was never rattled by anything throughout the trip, and when the time came for him to go to the summit, George found himself spending an exhausting night at High Camp taking care of our first summit team. Despite a complete lack of sleep, at three in the morning he quietly said, "Well, it's time to go." Off he went, easily summitting Everest, completing his ascent of the Lowe Buttress to the top of the Kanchung Face.

When I returned to Colorado for my internship, George and I became regular rock climbing partners. Again he embodied the essence of the cool. George did, however, gain certain aspects of wisdom from his age. Although I never heard him complain on a climb, he would launch a wonderful dialogue prior to any ascent. Beginning by telling me about how, as he was getting older—now in his mid-forties—his body was no longer quite holding up, he would always continue, "Ya know, Geoff, my shoulder's just not quite coming around and well, I really want to do this route and well, maybe at my age it might not be possible for me to lead it, so when it comes to the crux pitch, you might have to take the lead today . . ." Then invariably, when we reached the crux pitch, George would continue the same dialogue with a new twist: "Well, ya know, it's feeling a little looser now and, well, at my age I may never be able to lead a pitch quite this hard ever again, so you wouldn't mind too terribly, would you, Geoff, if I just went ahead and led this next pitch?" It happened every time; when it came to the hardest, scariest pitch, George figured out an excuse to put himself in the lead. Once in the lead, he never again moaned or complained.

—

The two of us went on several speed trips from Denver with the aid of his plane. George had long ago learned to fly and purchased his own Cessna, which he kept at an airport near his home. Once we decided to fly to Canyonlands National Park to make a one-day round-trip ascent of a route called the Primrose Dihedrals on Moses Tower. We knew from friends and the guidebook description that a 5.11 off width was the most daunting obstacle to the route. As a precaution, we brought Neal Beidleman, who was at the top of his rock climbing form. He would serve as a rope gun for the scary off-width pitch. When it came time to lead the scary wide crack, however, it was George who, as always, finagled a way to place himself in the front.

George holds himself to the absolute highest standards. He pushes himself hard but does not necessarily expect his partners to adhere to the same level. Although he does not drink excessively or engage in any sort of wild behavior, he never has a harsh word for those who do, as long as they hold up their end on a climb. The only place that George is less than a joy to be with is in his plane.

George's Cessna 185 helps him maximize his climbing time. The weekend after we climbed a route on the Diamond Wall of the East Face of Longs Peak, we flew to Moab, Utah, to climb. Our flight took us over Rocky Mountain National Park, and George was eager to photograph the route we had just completed. As we approached the Diamond Wall, we experienced an excessive amount of turbulence. The Cessna 185 bounced in the unsettled air like a pinball. I felt a little bit nervous that the plane constantly dipped between two and three hundred feet. Fortunately, George's face looked extremely calm, and I was able to reassure myself that, as long as George stayed cool, there must not be a serious problem. Suddenly, to my dismay, George tilted the plane completely on its side. We hovered perpendicular to the wall, approximately two hundred yards from the granite face. To my horror, I saw that George was leaning out the window with his camera, taking photographs of our route. The tiny plane, meanwhile, bobbed and weaved like a cork on the rough seas. George glanced over and, seeing my discomfort, allowed the plane to dip down several hundred feet before rapidly pulling it back up again. With a wry grin, he passed a vomit bag to me. To his great disappointment, I did not regurgitate the contents of my lunch.

When we finally deplaned in Moab, George pointed out the notches on the side of his plane. Like World War I fighter pilots who used to put notches or symbols on the side of their plane for every enemy plane they shot down, George had made notches for every person who needed to use a vomit bag while flying with him. He proudly regaled me with a litany of the famous adventurers and climbers who had blown their cookies in his plane.

Over the next several years George and I flew the Cessna to the sites of many climbing adventures. We were able to complete weekend climbs on routes in areas as far from Denver as the Bugaboos and the Tetons. George remained calm no matter how serious the flying situation became. Whether we were trapped above clouds unable to find a landing site while the fuel gauge dropped dangerously—or if perhaps turbulence was high and approaching thunderstorms made it difficult for us to return to work the next day—George's complacent demeanor always made me feel secure no matter how much we bobbed and bounced.

The only time I ever saw him lose his cool in any situation was thanks to my job as the "adventure editor" for *Penthouse* magazine. After climbing Mount Everest in 1988, I wanted to write a long article about the changes occurring on Everest. I was hoping to include both of the East Face expeditions and my own summit in 1988 as well as a history of the mountain and a discussion of the effects of guided expeditions. I had published feature articles in *Outside, Playboy,* and many climbing specialty magazines. The only magazine publishing articles of the length I hoped to write, however, was *The New Yorker.* I asked Julian Bach, a literary agent and friend of mine, to help sell my idea to *The New Yorker.* Julian called me a few weeks later and said that *The New Yorker* had turned it down. He had, however, been able to sell it instead to *Penthouse.* I would be making much much more money than I ever had on any previous article.

As it turned out, the editorial team at *Penthouse* is a joy to work with. Moreover, they pay on completion of my articles, rather than months later like all of the other magazines I had worked for. My Everest article was bumped at the last minute when the mistress of a baseball player gave an exclusive story about how boring their sex life was, but the editors at *Penthouse* asked me to be their "adventure editor at large" and write a regular column. I would be able to think up crazy adventures, invite friends along for a free ride, and then write a few pages about each trip. It was pretty much the best journalism job ever.

One of my many *Penthouse* adventure ideas was to go on a dogsled trip from Crested Butte, Colorado, to Telluride. We would ski and ice climb along the way, and then camp each night in the finest style, with gourmet cooking and fine wines. Having a dogsled team along would be a novel experience and would free us from having to carry any supplies.

I thought it was going to be a great adventure. Rick Meinig, a buddy of mine from my surgical internship who trained and raised sled dogs, would be the leader. Neal Beidleman quickly signed on, and as a fourth I thought of George. Unfortunately, when I told George's wife, Liz, about our proposed trip, she hit the ceiling at the word *Penthouse.* I don't know what she expected from a *Penthouse* adventure, but I suspect she pictured scantily clad pets riding beside us on dogsleds. I tried to explain that none of my articles for *Penthouse* had any sexual content whatsoever, but she was skeptical. In a final effort to convince her, I photocopied every single article I had ever written in my life, highlighting all of the ones from *Penthouse* and *Playboy.* These I sent to Liz. Nevertheless she stood firm in her wish that George not participate. She explained that her decision was based on the principle that *Penthouse* is evil and exploits women. It took a considerable amount of begging on George's part to tip the scales so that Liz reluctantly agreed to let her husband join our expedition. After all our work at persuading her, it was unfortunate that just prior to our departure, the Gulf War broke out and George resigned from the trip. He claimed he had to "work."

The type of work George Lowe does has always been a mystery. When he was a younger man, George earned a doctorate in physics. Between his cool, quiet demeanor, his steely blue eyes, his Ph.D., and his amazing climbing skills, he embodies the Hollywood image of a superspy—the real-deal James Bond. Yet he's never really let on what he does. All he will say is that he "works for the government." When pressed further, he explains that he works with computers and will say no more. Occasionally he jokes that, if anyone found out what he really does, he would have to kill them. No wonder many of his closest friends privately hint that he's a spy. What *is* known is that he has a high-security government clearance and has a considerable amount of free time, which he utilizes for climbing. Plus that bit about the Gulf War.

The dogsledding trip turned out to be somewhat disastrous. When I wrote it up for *Penthouse*, I decided that George really should have been included in it. So sitting at my computer late one night, I inserted a few sentences about him into each paragraph. In the first paragraph, where I described my teammates, I typed in, "The final member of our team was to be George Lowe, a CIA agent well known for the massive size of his genitalia." In the next paragraph, I added, "I knew our trip would have problems from the start when the Gulf War broke out and George had to drop from our team to go on a supersecret spy mission to the Middle East with his larger-than-average love snake still coiled expectantly in his ever-bulging trousers." Later on I brought George's wife, Liz, into the picture. "It was a very cold morning and the only thing that gave us pleasure was thinking of how the frigid temperatures would make George Lowe's wife, Liz, who has 44DD breasts, nipples firm and erect, the way we like them." I then sent a copy to George with a short note: "Here's the final article. I hope you like it. It should be published in *Penthouse* soon." The only sexual references in the entire piece were about George and Liz. I thought what I had written was so over the top that George couldn't possibly believe it.

A few days later, George called me. He was absolutely livid. I could almost feel him trembling with anger on the other end of the line. "I will lose my government clearance! How can you do this? My wife will divorce me! God damn you, Tabin!" For the first time in more than twenty years, I heard George Lowe lose his cool. He was so upset, I was afraid he'd have a stroke over the telephone, so I immediately told him it was all a joke. Nothing about him or his wife was in the real *Penthouse* article. After a lot of reassurances and apologies on my part, I finally got him calmed down. I had one notch on the side of my plane.

A few months later, climbing at the Shawangunks, I ran into a guy named Rich who was a close friend of George's. Rich was only a casual acquaintance of mine, but we shared a beer at the Mountain Brauhouse in New Paltz and spoke of our day's climbs. When he asked, "Have you heard from George lately?" I told him the story of my joke article. Rich fell off his chair laughing. In the forty years he had known George, he'd never heard of the man having a conniption. Within five minutes we were together at the restaurant pay phone.

Rich began, "Hey, George, this is Rich. What's going on?"

"Not much," George answered.

Rich continued, "George, I was flying cross-country, and I picked up a *Penthouse* to read on the plane, and the next thing I knew I was reading about you, George. It says you have the world's biggest penis and that you work for the CIA. What's going on?"

A forceful scream shot out of the phone, blowing Rich's ear at least two feet from the receiver. "That son of a bitch Tabin!"

I had a second notch on my plane.

16

KAY
GUARNAY

Five days after Dawa Tsering, Nima Tashi, Phu Dorje, Peggy Luce, and I stood together on the summit of Mount Everest in 1988, Nima Tashi said to me in halting English, "Dr. Geoff come Pangboche, okay?"

"Why?"

"My wife has baby," he replied, his head bobbing from side to side.

"When?"

"I think today."

We raced down from base camp to Pangboche, covering in six hours what had taken us three days to trek up. Arriving at his two-story stone and wood home, we rushed inside before I had a chance to catch my breath. The lower floor housed his animals. We pushed past a goat and two small yaks and climbed upstairs to the smoky living area. Nima Tashi motioned for me to sit down on the long wooden bench that lined the wall next to the wood-burning cooking area. The opposite wall had shelves filled with large copper pots, expedition sleeping bags, stuff sacks, and a small shrine with a *thanka* painting and a small statue of Buddha. The center of the single-room house was empty except for three wooden columns supporting the carbon-stained ceiling.

We were immediately attended to by a slender Sherpani. She filled both our glasses to the rim with home-brewed *chang* then pushed mine to my lips, admonishing me to drink. "*Shay-shay-shay.*" After every sip my glass would be refilled, and I would be urged to drink again. Relief from the forced consumption of alcohol came only when she went to cook potatoes and a hot chili sauce for us. After several min-utes I asked, "Nima Tashi, is this your wife?"

"Yes."

"I thought she was having a baby?"

"Yes."

"When?"

"Three hours ago."

We stepped over to the pile of yak wool blankets on the sleeping portion of the bench on the other side of the stove. Sleeping peacefully in the covers was a new-born girl.

That evening most of the village crowded into Nima Tashi's home. Everyone brought offerings of Kata, blessed silk scarves, and *chang*. Dawa Tsering and Phu Dorje came down for the party. We celebrated the birth of a baby and the four of us reaching the top of Chomolungma and returning. Four generations of warmth glowed in the dim candlelight. People began singing and then dancing. The Sherpas locked arms, singing the melody and creating the beat with an intricate series of steps that resonated on the wooden floor. I joined in the dance line, swaying from the drink, unable to pick up the steps and only avoiding crashing onto my face from the support of Sherpa friends holding me by the shoulders. Turning to Dawa Tsering, I slurred, "Someday you must come celebrate in America."

Two weeks later, at Namche Bazaar, I said good-bye to my Sherpa friends. Dawa Tsering headed for his home in Gumella, a poor village with a population of thirty, three days' walk away. As a child Dawa had spent a year in Khumjung going to school but had to quit at age seven to work as a porter and yak herder. Now, as a top climbing Sherpa, he owned six yaks and a small plot of land where he hoped to build his own house. Our expedition over, Dawa planned to see his parents and then join a French trekking group.

The American members of our team flew from Lukla to Kathmandu, where we spent a week celebrating and tying up expedition business. On our last day in Nepal I found Dawa Tsering waiting at our hotel holding a vinyl carry-on bag less than half full.

"Dawa!" I greeted him. "I thought you were trekking with the French?"

"I go America with you," he said with an even smile. "You say, come see my fam-ily, okay," he added, bobbing his head from side to side.

"Dawa, do you have a passport?"

"Passport?" His face was blank.

"Do you have a visa?"

"Visa?"

We found an interpreter who explained to Dawa that he needed special papers to visit America. I called the U.S. embassy and was assured that with a letter from me, my summit partner could have a visa to visit America. However, they cautioned, it is very difficult for Buddhist Sherpas to obtain passports from the Hindu-dominated government. When the translation was finished, Dawa smiled and quietly said, "*Kay guarnay.*" I promised Dawa that if he got a passport and visa I would buy him a plane ticket. We parted with hugs and smiles at the Kathmandu airport.

Dawa had shown no outward signs of disappointment. He had given up a lucrative trekking job and walked for eight days from his home to the nearest road, where he took a crowded, bumpy bus to Kathmandu, only to find out he could not come to America after all. "*Kay guarnay.*" Unless you've spent a great deal of time with Sherpas it is difficult to comprehend their complacency at times like this. Once again the four essential truths came to mind. Man suffers, suffering is caused by unfulfilled desire, overcoming desire eliminates suffering, and to eliminate desire you must follow the eightfold path to wisdom. They do not preach this way of life. The Sherpas just live it.

The Sherpas migrated from Tibet to the highlands of Nepal some five hundred years ago. They number about six thousand, all of whom share the same last name— Sherpa. In addition to cultivating the high fields and raising yaks, the Sherpa people traditionally worked as traders, carrying goods between Nepal and Tibet over the high passes.

Three months after returning to the United States I received a telex: "Mr. Dawa Tsering Sherpa has visa and passport and awaits ticket to your home." Two days later Dawa took his first airplane ride—Kathmandu to Delhi, Delhi to Singapore, Singapore to Los Angeles.

At the Los Angeles airport Dawa was to be met by my climbing friend David Dossetter and his wife, Susan. Two hours after all other passengers had cleared customs, Dawa was still nowhere to be seen. Worried, Dave spoke to an official. A short search revealed a Sherpa sitting quietly on a bench in the luggage area. He had with him just his small vinyl carry-on bag, a passport, no money, and less than a hundred words of English. Dave and Susan took Dawa directly from the airport to Disneyland, where Goofy's fiftieth birthday party was in full swing. Dawa ascended "Space Mountain" for a roller-coaster ride and swing danced with Minnie Mouse on Main Street beneath the fireworks. That evening he attended a black-tie party in Bel Air, complete with a sushi chef on the lawn. He had barely five hours of sleep before scoping the outdoor brunch scene amid roller-skating grannies and steroid muscle men on Venice Beach. Susan later told me, "We wanted to show Dawa as much of California as we could. I was amazed. Nothing seemed to surprise him. He laughed a lot at Disneyland. Otherwise, it was as if he did these things every day. He's so calm."

That night Dawa flew to Chicago's O'Hare airport, where I picked him up. He had no plans or expectations other than that he was going to live with me for two months. Having already spoken to Dave, I excitedly asked, "Did you like Los Angeles?"

"Yes."

"What did you like best?"

"Susie is very nice."

Initially Dawa accompanied me wherever I went. He always tried to pick up on what was going on and help out whenever he could, insisting on carrying any packages that I had. No one ever questioned his following me into the emergency room, wearing a green scrub suit and carrying my medical bag. When I had to leave him alone he was seemingly content to watch videos or the television, even though his English was not sufficient to follow most conversations. His favorite movie was *E.T.*, which he watched a dozen times with joy. Whatever was offered, he always smiled and said, "It's okay," with a little bob of his head.

I finally asked Dawa what he wanted to see or do while he was in America. "Maybe, work for money?" he replied.

It was not easy finding employment in Chicago for a man without a green card whose only proven skills were herding yaks, building stone fences, and carrying heavy loads up steep mountains. We tried a fancy restaurant called the Everest Room to see if they wanted a Sherpa greeter who had been up Everest, but received a firm no from the stuffy manager.

Eventually we found a man who installed aluminum siding. He hired Dawa for minimum wage but gave him a raise after one week. His employer said that he did the work of three people. Dawa soon found a second job as a busboy in a restaurant. In two months he made more money in America than he made in a year as a top climbing Sherpa in Nepal.

As Dawa and I became better friends and his English improved, he slowly revealed more of himself to me. He was surprised that I regularly asked him how he liked his jobs or what he thought of things.

"Things are what they are." And he would shrug.

To Dawa, America was not better or worse, only different. This contrasted sharply with my own Western judgmental mind. He saw change in Nepal the same way. My American friends and I *judged* the changes that we thought we saw in

Nepal. Dawa said we did not understand. More tourists in the Khumbu were not bad or good, they just were. *"Kay guarnay."* More money, better medical care, and schools are balanced against the erosion and garbage. *"Kay guarnay."*

There was no hint of jealousy, envy, or pity as I observed America through Dawa's eyes. One of his favorite finds in America was running water. He enjoyed taking a hot shower or turning on the tap for a cool drink. With the money he made in America, Dawa planned to start building his house in Gumella. He happily told me that his land was only a ten-minute walk, up a hill, from a river.

There were, of course, certain things that impressed even an accepting Buddhist mind. The glitzy, high-tech, and luxurious aspects of Western life did not fascinate him as much as strange creatures, like big fish. At the Shedd Aquarium, Dawa pressed his face against the first tank with a wide-eyed look. He began laughing and shaking his head. After fifteen minutes I grabbed his arm to drag him to the next exhibit. He held his ground laughing and then turned to me, saying, "Fish like goat, as big as goat." I finally succeeded in getting him to the next tank, where giant turtles had an equal effect. The next weekend we went to the Lincoln Park Zoo. Dawa had heard legends of big animals when he was growing up, but this was beyond his imagination. He particularly liked the African elephants, giraffes, and hippos. He also was happy to see the yaks in the zoo, a bit of home. And the size of the buildings impressed the man of the Himalayas. I tried to get permission for Dawa and me to walk the stairs to the top of the Sears Tower so that we could climb both the world's highest mountain and tallest building together. After wasting several hours with various building officials we settled for the elevator. Dawa said the view from the top of the tower was "the best."

Nothing fazed Dawa. He seemed happy in every setting, until we went to the Chicago Lyric Opera to see *Salome*. First, he did not like having to wear a tie. He asked me why everyone in America wears them. I could think of no good answer but still insisted he wear one. The music he found fine. But when they brought out John the Baptist's head on a silver platter, Dawa turned to me and said, "I think we must go now, okay."

The opera was one of the only two times that Dawa appeared uncomfortable. The other occurred a few nights later when, in an attempt to expose Dawa to the breadth of American experience, my friend Bruce Goldstick and I took him to a Jell-O wrestling night at a biker bar on Chicago's Northwest Side. A ring with three feet of foam rubber was covered by a slick plastic tarp coated with oil and then two feet of Jell-O cubes. Four girls came out and did striptease dances, down to G-strings. Each had her own distinctive wrestling motif, like "Machine Gun Molly" or "Amazon Annie." Then the matches began. The combatants attempted to duplicate the moves of professional wrestlers on television, but basically just slipped around in the Jell-O. The emcee, a comedian, announced the bouts and insulted the men in the audience. Dawa sat in the front row, mesmerized by the action. The emcee announced that an auction would be held for a man to wrestle the girls.

Before the final match I spoke to the emcee, gave him a bribe and begged for a short intercontinental match with Dawa Sherpa. He agreed. After Machine Gun Molly won, the loudspeaker announced, "We have a special event. A three-minute match between our champion and Mr. Sherpa, who trains by climbing Mount Everest!" The spotlight turned to Dawa. I sensed the same fear in him that I felt when I first confronted the Khumbu Icefall.

Dawa dived under the table, hugging my leg saying, *"No! No! No!"* It took several minutes of coaxing by Bruce, Molly, and me before Dawa agreed to go. He was led to the changing room by a typical bouncer at a rough motorcycle bar: six feet, six inches tall with a big gut and a face that looked like it had taken its share of crowbars. I still didn't know exactly what Dawa thought was going to happen when this giant brought him into a back room and told him to strip. The thin, five-foot-three-inch Sherpa bolted, wide-eyed, from the room. He picked the bouncer up and threw him out of the way before dashing back to our table. The bouncer crashed through a table like a stunt man in a western movie. A wave of terror spread over me. But before the hulk could get up, the emcee had the whole crowd chanting, "Sherpa! Sherpa! Sherpa!"

It took another ten minutes of cajoling to finally get Dawa to enter the ring, fully clothed, and square off against a bikini-clad Machine Gun Molly. Dawa stood, looking confused. Molly rushed him, bouncing off and slipping away as Dawa firmly kept his footing. On her fourth try she knocked him off balance. Dawa picked her up and threw her onto the mat. The crowd erupted into new chants of, "Sherpa! Sherpa! Sherpa!" A lifetime of Buddhist pacifism melted away as Dawa Tsering Sherpa began to attack. He picked Molly up above his head and hurled her down into the muck. Two other girls came into the ring and were body slammed, airplane spun, and pinned as the crowd went into a frenzy. Dawa was declared the Intercontinental Intergender Wrestling Champion of the World.

Before he returned to Nepal we had a farewell party for Dawa. He cooked a big Nepali dinner and tried brewing *chang*. The dinner was great—spicy curry, hot chili sauce, and mo-mos. The *chang* didn't work, however, so I bought vodka and sake, mixed them together, and told everyone it was *chang*. I pressed it to Dawa's lips, saying, *"Shay-shay-shay."* Everyone got a little drunk and Dawa was his most talkative ever in English.

Dawa said he was going home to start building his house in Gumella before the spring climbing season. He was also scheduled to marry during the monsoon. It was arranged by his father. He had only seen the girl once.

We discussed love and lust for a while before I asked, "Dawa, will you marry her?"

"Kay guarnay!" he replied. Of course. He must marry her. People at the party asked Dawa if he liked his stay in America. He quietly bobbed his head and said yes. When pressed on what his favorite things were in America, Dawa said, "Many people are nice." He was then asked if he would like to stay longer. "I must go."

My mother gave Dawa Tsering a gift as we prepared to drive to the airport. She then asked him, "Dawa, what will you miss the most about America when you are back in Nepal?"

Dawa paused for a moment, smiled broadly, and said, "I think Jell-O wrestle."

17

DAN
REID—
A LIFE

The bodies of Dan and Barbara Reid were found in late September 1991 at the base of the Ice-Window Route on Mount Kenya. No one knows exactly what happened. There was a storm and they separated from the other rope team. Barb was on her first technical climb on a big mountain as part of her fortieth birthday celebration. Dan had not climbed in eight years. Yet it still seems inconceivable that Dan Reid died in the mountains, or died at all. I expected him to call me to join him in adventures when he was a hundred years old. He died a few weeks before his fiftieth birthday, looking half his age, but having lived more than any three people twice as old. Reid lived life on his own terms, with unbridled enthusiasm and full-throttle pedal-to-the-metal overdrive at all times. He did not simply march to the beat of a different drummer, he sprinted to the sounds of his own bagpipe orchestra.

I met Dan on the East Face of Everest, where he was a doctor on the first American climbing expedition into Tibet in 1981. The slight, bespectacled cardiac surgeon was supposed to be our base camp physician, but he moved onto the steep initial buttress to belay George Lowe when others demurred because of the weather. Later Reid attempted to solo an icicle at twenty-one thousand feet on a day too nasty for even Lowe to leave his tent. No matter that Reid had never attempted to climb vertical ice before. He self-belayed on three forty-foot whippers on "Reid's Nemesis" before giving up. A few days afterward a falling rock hit Reid as he was descending an ice gully known as the Bowling Alley. He received an implosion injury exposing his tibia. It required thirty-eight stitches to close the wound. Two weeks later, after the rest of the team retreated, Dr. "PercoDan" popped some of his own medications and headed up the ropes, vanishing into a cloud. He descended after thirty-six hours of continuous climbing. With a big grin he said, "I had to check the snow conditions above our high point for a summit attempt another year."

Reid returned to his wife and busy heart surgery practice in Diablo, California, and did not climb for two years. His next outing was a return to the East Face of Everest. This time he came fully prepared. He wore a formal kilt for the approach trek and had THE LITTLE ENGINE THAT COULD embroidered on all of his climbing clothes. Reid, team doctor, was supposed to stay at base camp. No one on our team was surprised when he reached the summit of Mount Everest on October 9, 1983, completing the first ascent of the Kangshung Face.

Everest was the culmination of thirty years of fanatical climbing that also included first ascents in Patagonia with Don Whillans, a solo ascent of the University Wall on Squamish Chief in 1969, the sixth ascent of the North American Wall on El Capitan in 1971, and the first ascent of the South Taku Tower in Alaska's Coast Range in 1973. But he was always fanatical about life.

Reid challenged the medical establishment with his frequent absences into the mountains. Yet he was such a good physician and surgeon that he ascended the medical hierarchy to become a highly respected cardiothoracic surgeon. Intelligence and skill aside, it was his honesty, caring, and ability to give of himself that made Dan beloved by his patients, climbing partners, and friends from all walks of life. He was always upbeat. Even after forty-eight sleepless hours in the operating room he always had his silly grin and sense of humor. His laughter was infectious. He was genuinely excited about what his friends were doing. Then again, by most of our society's standards, Dan Reid was crazy.

He decided to run the Western States 100. No matter that he had never run more than ten miles at a single stretch and that to qualify you must have completed both a twenty-six-mile marathon and a fifty-mile race in good times within the previous year. Dan flew to New Orleans and ran his marathon. The next week he jetted to Baffin Island for a fifty-mile run that he finished just under the twelve-hour limit. Two weeks later Dan completed the Western States 100. He missed winning a silver belt buckle for a time under twenty-four hours by only eighteen minutes. With a grin he related, "If I hadn't doubled up vomiting for an hour at mile seventy-six I could have made it."

Reid decided to learn how to play the bagpipes. He spent two months in Scotland practicing twelve hours a day under the tutelage of a master. He soon called me to play his bagpipe rendition of "Hava Nigila" over the phone, offering to entertain if I had ever a traditional Jewish wedding. He dived into fly fishing. On the river he became the embodiment of a green drake, or whatever the fish were feeding on that day. He tried polo. Soon Dan had a practice cage built onto his house, owned eleven ponies, and was housing a top player he brought up from Argentina.

At home he supported his wife, Barbara, a remarkable person in her own right, helping her realize her goals. Barb was a registered nurse who specialized in cardiac rehabilitation. With Dan's help she started her own fitness consulting business and became a leader in preventive and sports medicine in her community. She was also an accomplished marathoner, running much faster than her husband, and a skilled horsewoman.

Dan was loyal to his friends. He was generous with his time, his skills, and his assets. He was also fiercely patriotic. Reid put his climbing career on hold in the early 1970s while the war in Vietnam was still raging. Dan did not simply sign up to be a military surgeon. He became a full-combat Green Beret. At age forty-nine he left his lucrative cardiac surgery practice to join Operation Desert Storm. Despite the intensity of his actions, Reid was one of the most easygoing, humorous, and fun people with whom I have shared a climbing rope. Don Whillans, who called Dan the "Mad American," loved to tell of the time Dan was leading a horrendous pitch of loose overhanging verglas in a raging storm in Patagonia. Whillans and the other British wanted to retreat. Dan smiled and said, "Come on! This isn't as bad as Vietnam!"

Dan Reid lived by the doctrine of "Cram as much into life as possible and maximize your fun doing it." He was chronically late from always trying to squeeze in one more thing. He had the courage to accept life's challenges and a zest for life itself. His real contribution, however, was his smile and the way he cared about people. His friends knew that he would be there if they needed him.

18

An Evanescent Presence

I've shared many of my favorite climbing moments with the irascible Rob Slater. With his bug eyes and a constant Cheshire cat grin, Robby had both a cocksure confidence and a totally irreverent and novel way of approaching virtually any problem, in climbing or in life.

Rob was best known in the climbing world for his ultraserious, ultracommitted, and ultradangerous aid climbs. On these routes he would use equipment to tenuously secure his body weight to the rock, then carefully balance upward and attach another temporary anchor into the rock surface. Often Rob would go hundreds of feet on crumbly, overhanging rock without a single point of attachment to hold more than his body weight. Any slip or fall would lead to all of his attachments zippering out, causing a long, or even fatal, plunge.

Rob pioneered the first ascents of two of the hardest routes on El Capitan in Yosemite and was the first person to climb all of the crumbling sandstone and mud Fisher Towers in Utah. Even in the most desperate situation his sense of humor came through. He also enjoyed throwing people off if they took themselves or their climbing a bit too seriously. For one of his climbs on El Capitan, the Wyoming Sheep Ranch, Rob overcame a completely blank section of overhanging granite with a homemade device he termed the "love-tron." The love-tron was a series of telescoping PVC tubing through which he could place a small spring-loaded camming device. This was attached to a ladder of webbing. Utilizing his devious technology, Rob was able to place a tenuous attachment into a crack overhanging thirty feet above his last stance. He then monkeyed up his ladder and moved on with the climb. Needless to say, in the route description, Rob never mentioned his use of the love-tron. Many top teams failed in desperate attempts at making a second assent of Rob's routes.

Rob's father was a surgeon in Wyoming, and Rob was fascinated with medicine. He often asked to spend an evening with me on call to observe what I did. Initially I told him no, since it's against the law and I would lose my medical license if I brought a climbing buddy, impersonating a medical student, into the hospital. As in everything he did, Rob was so persistent that, eventually, I relented. One night when I had no medical student working with me, I dressed Rob in surgical greens and brought him along on night trauma call as a "medical student." I told Rob that he could watch whatever he liked, but he would not be allowed to touch any patients. It was a typical busy night in an inner-city hospital, more exciting than any *E.R.* episode. Rob watched as I cared for patients from car accidents, falls, beatings, gunshot wounds, and a wide array of orthopedic trauma. At three o'clock in the morning, I was seeing a woman who had been involved in a knife fight and had lacerations on her arm that cut all of the deep tendons in her forearm. I repaired her tendons in the minor operating room adjacent to the E.R. and was just beginning to close her skin when I was stat paged to the major trauma room. A man had been involved in a terrible motorcycle accident; I had to assess the situation and decide which X-rays would be required. I told the lady that I would be back to finish sewing her arm as soon as I handled the emergency. She yelled, "What the hell do you mean, *emergency?*" She then pointed to her own arm and screamed, "Ain't this an emergency? What about my arm; ya gonna finish my arm?" I told her that her tendon repair was finished, I only needed to sew her skin, and I would do it as soon as I returned from the major trauma. The lady kept protesting as I walked out the door. I assumed Rob was right behind me. The situation with the motorcycle accident was grave, and it took me several minutes to decide what needed to be done and in what order. I conferred with colleagues from both the general surgery and neurosurgery teams and helped place a collar on our patient to secure his neck. Once the life-threatening problems were stabilized, I returned to finish sewing the lady's arm.

From thirty feet down the hall I could hear my female patient screaming, "You ain't no fuckin' doctor are you? If you're a doctor, how come you can't tie a stitch? Are you a doctor or not?" I rushed into the room to find Rob, with a characteristic grin plastered on his face, staring at the howling lady. He had placed a perfect suture across the wound, but his mountaineering knots were not applicable to the tiny 6–0 sutures we use to close skin wounds. Rob did not know how to instrument tie.

I had visions of a nurse rushing in at any movement and discovering that Rob had been sewing on a hospital patient. I would lose my medical license and be kicked out of my residency program for certain. I quickly explained to the lady that Rob was my medical student and that he had placed a perfect stitch. Now I would continue the job, and the arm would be as good as new. Rob smiled at me with the innocence of a four-year-old boy caught with his hand in a cookie jar.

When he wasn't practicing on my patients, Rob spent his days attempting to win his fortune on the Chicago Board of Trade. He had previously worked as a mountain guide and rock climbing instructor. A few guided clients who were successful commodity traders had suggested to Rob that, with his cool head, he could easily make a fortune on the trading floor. Rob had thus moved to Chicago from his home in the mountains of Colorado and Wyoming. He had big plans that his commodity winnings would allow him to pursue his Himalayan and Antarctic dreams. On weeks when Rob traded successfully and he was flush with money, he would fly to Yosemite or Utah to climb. On weeks when he lost money, he would keep his quiet Cheshire cat grin and work other odd jobs. Rob and I bouldered together and often linked up for weekend trips to Red Rocks in Las Vegas, the desert towers of Canyonlands in Utah, or Yosemite. We also frequently drove to train on the short rock walls of Devil's Lake, Wisconsin. Rob's climbing always impressed me; it was not just the cool head with which he led the absolute hardest and most dangerous routes, but his amazing natural talent, that allowed Rob to climb hard right off the couch.

I needed to train constantly to maintain a moderate level of rock climbing skill. I installed pull-up bars on every ward we rounded on in the hospital and one just outside both the operating room and emergency room. I forced myself to do ten pull-ups every time I came to any floor on the hospital and ten more before I left any floor. I did twenty-five pull-ups before and after seeing any patient in the emergency room, and another twenty-five after every surgery. With this regimen, I was doing more than three hundred pull-ups per day. I also ran to and from the hospital every day and sprinted the stadium steps at Soldier Field. Sometimes I went to Northwestern University's Dyke Stadium and trained with Brad Werntz, another Wyoming climber. Rob did little more than eat and ride the subway. Nonetheless, every three weeks, when Rob and I would get together to climb, I would find that I struggled to maintain my level while Rob effortlessly seemed to climb harder every time. When Rob and I went for twenty-mile training runs along Lake Michigan, he would lope along effortlessly while I panted behind him.

Rob had two main fantasy trips. He wanted to make the first unsupported crossing of Antarctica, and he wanted to climb K2. He never made enough money on the Board of Trade to fund his Antarctic journey. He eventually went bust, sold his seat, and moved back to Colorado at roughly the same time that I quit my residency and returned to Everest.

Over the next several years Rob and I remained close. In Boulder he hung out with and climbed extensively with my old Yale climbing partner, Henry Lester. Whenever I passed through Colorado, the three of us would get together and climb. Rob worked as a climbing guide and then as a bond trader for a Denver bank. As he began to achieve a semblance of financial solvency, his dream of K2 returned. Just as I was about to depart for a corneal fellowship in Australia, Rob called and said I had to come with him to K2 the following summer. I tentatively signed on.

I .spoke with Rob frequently from Australia. He continued to organize his K2 expedition. As he had planned it, Rob's trip would require that I leave my fellowship two months prior to completion. I had also begun to organize eye surgery work in Nepal that would have conflicted with the climb. Thus, with some regret, I dropped out of the K2 expedition four months prior to the team's departure.

I was working in Biratnagar, Nepal, and had been completely isolated from news for almost two months when I went for a weekend trip across the border to Darjeeling, India. In Darjeeling, for the first time in weeks, I saw a newspaper. I was horrified to see the *Times of India's* front-page headline: K2 DISASTER. I looked at the paper with mounting terror. Allison Hargreaves, a British mother of two, had reached the summit of K2 and disappeared on the descent along with expedition leader Rob Slater. Apparently a storm was fast approaching while they were en route to the summit. A third member of their summit team, Peter Hillary, the son of Sir Edmund Hillary, had seen the approaching clouds and turned back a few hours below the top. Rob and Allison pushed on to reach the summit. According to Hillary, the winds hit the top of K2 at a force well over a hundred miles per hour. Hillary estimated that the storm struck almost at the same time as Rob and Allison were on the radio stating they had reached the top and were about to descend. Whether they were blown off the mountain, fell, or tried to bivouac and did not survive the storm that lashed the mountain for five days, will never be known. Rob's manic life and spirit, however, live on in all of us lucky enough to have shared some of his evanescent time on earth.

19

A NEW
DIRECTION

Sir Edmund Hillary is one of my heroes. But it is not only his climbing that makes me admire the man. It is also the way that his life as a climber has smoothly segued into a lifetime of helping the people of the Himalayas. Everyone knows of Hillary's first ascent of Mount Everest with Tenzing Norgay Sherpa. Many also know of the amazing adventures he undertook in his post-Everest years, including a dramatic first crossing of the Antarctic continent and becoming the first person to reach both Poles. In addition, Hillary continued exploring hard climbing throughout New Zealand and the Himalayas, completing a string of additional first ascents on Himalayan peaks after Everest.

Less well known is Hillary's incredible service to the people of the regions he visited. Hillary has built schools and hospitals for the Sherpa people. He not only raised the money for the construction of these buildings where none existed, but himself came to help dig the foundations and work constructing the walls. Once the schools were established and the hospitals equipped, Hillary worked tirelessly, giving slide lectures throughout the world to raise money to pay for the upkeep and support of these projects.

On a walk toward Mount Everest in Nepal you move up from Namda Bazaar toward the Tengboche Monastery. A short detour to the village of Khumjung will take you past Hillary's first great contribution to the Sherpa people, the Hillary School. Sherpa children sing and play games as they walk anywhere from forty-five minutes from Namda Bazaar to two and a half hours from Thame or Pangboche to get to school. Initially the teachers were from New Zealand, and Hillary's foundation supported their travel and stay. Now, thirty years later, all the teachers at the Hillary School are Sherpas who have been educated there. Similar progress has occurred at hospitals Hillary and his foundation established in Kunde and Phaplu. The hospital in Phaplu is now run by Dr. Mingma Sherpa, one of the first graduates from the Hillary School in Khumjung, who earned a scholarship to university and medical school in India. Hillary has given an amazing amount back to the people of the region. His life, his writings, and my personal interactions with him inspired me to look for some way to follow in his enormous footsteps.

After our successful Everest climb in 1988, I continued working primarily as a full-time climber, guiding expeditions and exploring. When I was in Nepal on a climbing trip, however, I had the opportunity to fill in as a physician at Phaplu. The doctor there had to return to New Zealand for medical leave. I had recently graduated from medical school, having caught up after my repeated climbing leaves, though I had even more recently quit a residency in orthopedics to climb Everest in 1988. With these credentials, I jumped into work as a primary-care doctor. I was the only physician within a five-day walking distance. It was exciting and rewarding to provide such a needed service. Then again, it was also often frustrating, scary, and sad. Poor nutrition, poor hygiene, and dirty water were the big enemies, and high-tech modern medicine was not the answer.

—

In the midst of all this, I watched as a visiting team of Dutch doctors performed cataract surgery. One Sherpa woman named Dolma, who had been totally blinded by cataracts for three years, was brought to be seen by the Dutch team. Dolma's vision was limited to only discerning light and dark. She was unable to detect the motion of a hand waving just in front of her face and had never seen her grandchildren. The day after her cataract surgery was performed, she was able to see, and her joy was endless. As tears of joy ran down her cheeks, I began to develop a focus for my life in medicine.

A few months later I returned to America, still thinking about how much I would like to work on restoring eyesight. I finally felt I was back on a clear medical path, but realized that a large obstacle to pursuing ophthalmology would be the extreme competition involved in getting an ophthalmologic residency. Given my checkered medical history, I doubted whether I would stand any chance of obtaining another residency.

It was just after my then girlfriend Beth and I had had a long conversation regarding my future plans that Beth found herself riding up a chairlift at Snowbird with a doctor from Rhode Island. During the course of their conversation, he mentioned that he was an ophthalmologist in academic practice at Brown University. Beth, a plastic surgeon, replied that she was a doctor as well, visiting Snowbird with her boyfriend. "Is your boyfriend also a doctor?" Beth was asked. In her soft North Carolina drawl Beth answered, "Well, he graduated from Harvard Medical School, but he's just a bum! All he does is climb mountains." At this, the doctor mentioned that he was very interested in the effects of high altitude on the retina, and that he had read several interesting articles about the eye at altitude. Beth told him her boyfriend had worked on the articles. "No, they were by Dr. Mike Wiedman from Harvard Medical School," he assured her. Beth explained that I had worked with Dr. Wiedman doing a research project that allowed me to go back to the East Face of Mount Everest in 1983.

That evening Beth and I met with the ophthalmologist for dinner. It was toward the end of the meal that the doctor told us a position had just opened for an ophthalmology residency at Brown to begin in July. Normally, people apply for an ophthalmology residency during the start of their fourth year of medical school. There is a two-year lag between the time you apply and the beginning of your residency. The doctor at Snowbird suggested that since I would be available immediately in July, it would be worth my while to send in a résumé and call the chairman of the ophthalmology department at Brown. The next day I telephoned the secretary of Dr. Bill Tsairas, the department chairman, and had my CV faxed to his office. I was scheduled to leave to guide a climb on Mount McKinley the following Friday. On Tuesday I flew from Utah to Rhode Island to meet with the program chairman. The interview went fairly well, and Dr. Tsairas told me they would get back to me, as the program was also considering several other candidates.

Two hours before I left for Alaska, Dr. Wiedman called to say he might be able to help get me the residency. His encouraging words came with a warning. If I ever quit, he would "hunt me down like a dog, and kill me dead!"

One month later I returned from Denali, where I had brought two clients to the summit in absolutely perfect weather. As soon as we got to Talkeetna, before I even had my first celebratory beer, I went to a pay phone to check my answering machine. I found a message saying my job at Brown would start in two weeks. I called the secretary to confirm my acceptance of the university's offer. To prepare for the work ahead of me, I quickly read a book titled *Clinical Ophthalmology Made Ridiculously Simple* and headed to Providence, Rhode Island, to start my residency.

20

THE ROAD TO JIRI

My next trip to Nepal brought me back to Jiri, the town at the end of the road on the way to Mount Everest in the Khumbu region. It was from Jiri that in 1988 I had begun my trek to the base of Everest. I remembered the village fondly, because we had stayed there for several days while organizing our 493 porter loads to be carried to Everest base camp. Jiri was a bustling, thriving Nepali town, where people and goods congregated before beginning the walk into the remote mountainous regions.

Now, instead of being surrounded by porters and climbing gear, seven hundred people from Jiri and its surrounding villages pressed around me. They all were either pulling down on their lower eyelids and poking at their eyes or pulling down the lower eyelids of blind relatives and pointing at *their* eyes. The mayhem slowly gave way to examinations. In twelve hours I managed to examine 735 people. The next day, in a pristine operating theater that our ophthalmic assistants had created from a previously squalid schoolroom, we began to perform surgery. Over the next three days, 224 totally blind people had their sight restored. It was like a religious revival meeting—a gospel church where the choir never stops. I was a convert.

My road back to Nepal began in 1993 after I completed a residency in ophthalmology. It was then that I decided to pursue advanced surgical training in corneal transplant surgery to further my surgical skills before seeking my place in international ophthalmology. The cornea is the clear window at the front of the eye, and corneal blindness caused by an infection called trachoma is the second leading cause of blindness worldwide. By becoming a corneal specialist, I hoped to improve my chances of infiltrating the tight-knit community of international ophthalmology and international medical aid.

At the time I was also interested in getting a master's degree in public health, which would be important for making large-scale impacts on health care in the developing world. Johns Hopkins, which offered one of the best corneal fellowships around, also had a premier public health program that included a branch in international ophthalmology. It seemed like the best place for me. I applied for a fellowship position at Hopkins, hoping to combine my work in corneal surgery with a course in public health.

A few weeks after my interview at the university, I attended an American Academy of Ophthalmology meeting in Chicago. I was walking through the enormous convention hall when I ran into Dr. Walter Stark, head of the corneal program at Hopkins. We had a nice conversation in which Dr. Stark mentioned that I was high on the applicant list for the university's corneal program and said he hoped I would be coming to Baltimore. As we spoke, a tall Australian gentleman approached and gave a warm greeting to Dr. Stark. I quickly recognized Professor Hugh Taylor, Australia's most prominent academic ophthalmologist and a protégé of Fred Hollows, one of the initial leaders in international eye care. Professor Taylor had spent many years at Johns Hopkins, first as a corneal fellow and then as Dr. Stark's colleague, during which time he helped start the Dana Center for International Ophthalmology. He had also been involved in many of Fred Hollows's early projects in Australian Aboriginal health care. Taylor was a world authority on both trachoma and onchocerciasis, the parasite responsible for river blindness, the fourth most common cause of blindness in the world. He had done extensive work on both throughout Africa and Asia. The relaxed warmth of your typical Aussie was apparent in Professor Taylor. He had thinning hair, slightly tilted glasses, and a gangly smile. When we were introduced, he extended a warm, "G'day!" and exuded none of the pomp or ceremony of a typical, high-powered American academic. Walter Stark mentioned my interest in international ophthalmology and my hope of combining a program in the school of public health and his corneal fellowship. Professor Taylor nodded, exchanged a few more pleasantries with Dr. Stark, and disappeared into the crowd. I was pleased to have met him.

The next day Professor Taylor gave a lecture on the fight against trachoma, and as I listened, I was impressed both by the substance of what he had to say and again by his animated personality. After the talk, I ran into Professor Taylor in the hallway outside the lecture theater. Without hesitation, he struck up a conversation, "So you're interested in a corneal fellowship and getting into international ophthalmology?"

"Yes!" I said.

"Well, why don't you come to Melbourne?"

I looked at him for a second without responding. He continued, saying that Melbourne University had, in his opinion, the best corneal fellowship in the world. In addition to himself, they had five outstanding corneal surgeons, and as the only referral hospital in Victoria they saw a wide range of pathology and interesting cases. Moreover, if I wanted to become involved in international ophthalmology, he would arrange for me to work with the Fred Hollows Foundation during my fellowship and spend time working in Nepal. He looked at me and said, "What do you think?"

Now, of all the international charity programs around, the Fred Hollows Foundation, based in Australia, impressed me most. Fred Hollows, who passed away in 1993, was an amazing man with an amazing career in ophthalmology and international health care. He was a Robin Hood of modern medicine, especially in his efforts to set up medical services for Australian Aborigines. In his autobiography Hollows described his less-than-conventional methods for beginning such services:

> We plundered the Prince of Wales Hospital for equipment—stethoscopes, ther-
> mometers, scales, all the accoutrements of a medical practice, we shamelessly stole.
> And we learnt as we went along. . . . We backed a truck up to the pharmacy at the
> hospital and loaded it half full—tens of thousands of dollars worth of pharmaceuti-
> cals. It wasn't always a matter of clandestine raids, there were some sympathetic
> people around. Pretty soon we had more doctors volunteering than we could handle.
> The medical service was a great success and there are more than sixty of them now
> Australia-wide . . . all owing something to that original model and the principles on
> which it was based. One of the most important of those principles was that the
> Aborigines staffed and managed it to the fullest extent possible.

In addition to his work in Australia, Hollows went on to help begin modern eye-care programs in Eritrea, Vietnam, and Nepal. In all his efforts, Hollows was a strong proponent of providing medical training to local doctors, technicians, and nurses, and empowering them to become self-sufficient. He strongly advocated this as opposed to outside doctors flying into poor countries, performing surgeries, and departing, leaving no resources for sustained long-term medical assistance.

I was excited by the prospects of becoming involved with the Fred Hollows Foundation, which I much preferred to programs like Project ORBIS or SEE International, the primary American charities working on international eye care. While both of these bigger charities had good intentions, the programs were, in my mind, very cost *in*effective, producing much more flash than actual results in targeted countries. Project ORBIS, for example, had a fully tricked-out DC-8 aircraft flying around the world with a team of American surgeons and their state-of-the-art techniques. This was wonderful for the lucky few who were chosen and cured out of the sea of blindness in their poor countries, but it did little to provide a sustainable solution for curing the majority of the population.

"Shall I send you a résumé as soon as I get home?" I asked Professor Taylor, eager at the invitation to join him in Australia.

"No worries. If you're good enough for Walter Stark, you'll do for us. What do you say?"

I looked him in the eye. In an act of serendipity, I shook the hand he offered me and said, "Okay!"

"Right. We'll look forward to having you." With that, Professor Taylor walked off.

I was now left with the dilemma of whether to remain in the American fellowship match, or withdraw and count on the job in Australia. When I didn't hear from Professor Taylor for a few weeks, I began to get nervous. I sent a CV and my support letters to Melbourne, and called Professor Taylor's office. The first time I called, he was lecturing in Manila and would return in a week. I called back ten days later. He was now lecturing in Brazil and would be back in one more week. With some trepidation, I withdrew my name from the American fellowship match. When I finally tracked Professor Taylor down, he was reassuring and calm. "No worries," he said.

I continued to wait for paperwork. I indeed began to worry as the months dragged on and I watched friends in ophthalmology training programs finalize plans for the coming year. Still no formal letter arrived about my job. Then, only a few months before I finished my training, a letter came. When I completed my residency in July, I was on my way to the Antipodes. From there, Professor Taylor, true to his promise, made plans for me to work in Jiri, Nepal. The trip would be part of my fellowship, and I would get to work with the legendary Dr. Sanduk Ruit.

21

DR. RUIT'S DREAM

I eagerly went to the Nepali consulate in Melbourne to procure a visa for my trip to Jiri. I filled out the requisite paperwork and handed my passport to the official behind the desk. The counsel who processed the application smiled cordially.

"You can pick up your passport in a month, sir," he told me.

Smiling, I explained, "I really need my visa immediately. I'm leaving for Nepal in one week."

"I am very sorry, sir, but processing is always taking at least two weeks."

I told him that I was going to do eye surgery in conjunction with the Fred Hollows Foundation. He said he was familiar with the Fred Hollows Foundation, but, unfortunately, that didn't change the fact that visa processing always took a full two weeks.

Sensing my disappointment and frustration, the counsel hesitated, and then gave me a second option. "For an additional fifty dollars, sir, we can expedite the process."

I groaned inwardly and wearily took fifty Australian dollars from my wallet. Looking pleased, the counsel took a rubber stamp, pounded it into an ink sponge, and slammed it down twice on my passport. Then he smiled and handed me my passport with a newly stamped visa.

"I hope you are having a wonderful trip, sir."

—

In Kathmandu I found an amazing increase in street traffic and roadside garbage since my last visit. It was still reasonable for me to commute around the city by bicycle, but now it was necessary to exercise caution. I stayed at a friend's guest house called the Tushita at the edge of Thamel. I then bicycled around visiting old friends before riding over to the new Tilganga Eye Center.

The Tilganga Eye Center is a diamond in the rough of Nepal's dirty medical facilities. Walking in, you feel you've entered the Emerald City. The center itself is the result of Dr. Sanduk Ruit's dream to bring superb, first-world quality eye care to the region. Dr. Ruit was Fred Hollows's protégé in Nepal, but he is an absolutely self-made man. Ruit was born in a small, hillside Nepali village. His town, a three-day walk from the nearest road, sits in the shadows of Kanchenjunga in the far eastern corner of the country. His parents, devout Buddhists of Tibetan decent, worked tirelessly to give their children an education. Early on, Ruit showed himself to be exceptionally gifted. He earned a position at a prestigious school in Kalimpong, India, on the other side of Kanchenjunga. Ruit excelled in every aspect of school life, from academics to cricket. He won an ace award on his school exams, earning himself a scholarship to medical school. Ruit topped his class again in medical school and earned a position to train in ophthalmology at the prestigious All India Institute of Medical Sciences in Delhi, the Harvard Medical School of India.

Ruit returned to Nepal after completing his government and military medical duties. There he began to practice at the Nepal Eye Hospital. His brilliance and exceptional surgical hands were noticed by Dr. Pokhral, the leading ophthalmologist in Nepal and the hospital's director. Dr. Ruit worked with Dr. Pokhral on a blindness survey of Nepal. He also kept up with ophthalmologic advances around the world. He traveled to Madurai, India, to observe the Aravind Eye Hospital, where an innovative charity program was being developed where paying patients subsidized free care for the destitute. At Aravind he met Dr. Dick Litwin, a hippie ophthalmologist from Berkeley, California, who was at the forefront of American ophthalmology and used lens implants for cataract surgery. In America it is now standard to use a small man-made lens as an implant to replace the cloudy cataract inside the eye. Without this lens, the cataract patient must wear thick, Coke-bottle-like glasses to focus light on the retina. In the best of circumstances, patients may get clear central vision, but the distortions from these thick glasses create horrible problems in peripheral and side vision, making activities such as walking on steep mountain trails treacherous. Ruit sensed the importance of lens implants. He asked Litwin to help and join forces with him in Nepal.

Over the next few years, Dick Litwin and Sanduk Ruit began organizing remote eye camps in Nepal. For the first time ever, intraocular lens implants were used in Nepali patients. The operating conditions and the quality of the microscopes and other equipment were often horrible. Ruit assembled a strong team of assistants and nurses. Led by Nabin Rai, they learned, through trial and error, to perform complete epidemiological surveys of the regions where they worked. Everyone with an eye disease was brought forward for screening by the doctors. Schoolrooms and other semiclean buildings were sterilized and converted into surgical suites. When no buildings existed, Ruit and his team learned to perform sterile surgery in tents.

The innovation of intraocular lenses was not initially well received by the other ophthalmologists in Nepal. Ruit was initially seen as a heretic. His concept of surgery and his vision of ophthalmology for Nepal were not shared by his colleagues at the Nepal Eye Hospital. There were those within the community who hoped for infections and complications allowing them to prove that Ruit was performing dangerous, harmful surgery. During this initial period, Ruit met a doctor from the Netherlands named Jan Kok, a corneal and cataract specialist in Amsterdam. Kok encouraged and supported Ruit, and suggested that Ruit come to the Netherlands for further training. When Fred Hollows later visited Nepal on a fact-finding mission for the World Health Organization, he was amazed by Dr. Ruit. The man's brilliance was obvious to Fred, and he was equally impressed by Ruit's gentle surgical hands, his impeccable surgical technique, and his vision for eliminating blindness from the Himalayan region. Fred realized that in Ruit he had found a true kindred spirit. He suggested that Ruit come for further microsurgical training in Australia. The situation at Ruit's maverick eye camps with their newfangled intraocular lenses was becoming increasingly tense, so he took his young wife and set out, first for the Netherlands and then for Sydney, Australia. After honing his microsurgical techniques and learning where state-of-the-art of eye surgery was in Amsterdam, Ruit spent three months visiting the top eye hospitals in the United States. He then migrated to Australia where, for a year, he lived with Fred Hollows and performed surgery, perfecting his technique. He also had the pleasure of spending many late hours with Fred and many a bottle of whiskey discussing politics, humanity, and how to change eye care for his people.

Ruit returned to Nepal in 1992 with a clear vision of what needed to be done. One of his first tasks would be to establish a base for his operation. His vision was the Tilganga Eye Center. This would encompass both a state-of-the-art clinical facility and a teaching wing in which other doctors could be trained. The final element necessary for the success of his vision was a low-cost source for intraocular lens implants. This was Fred Hollows's final contribution to improving the world's eye care. Fred had been diagnosed with cancer and the outlook was bleak. Despite the constant wrenching pain of terminal cancer that had spread to his bones, Fred used the last of his energy to raise money for building intraocular lens factories to provide high-quality inexpensive lenses for cataract surgery in Asia and Africa. The two locations he chose were the Tilganga Eye Center in Nepal and a hospital in Eritrea. Funding from many sources around the world, including the Fred Hollows Foundation and the Third Jangmon Kongtrul Rimpoche Trust, led to the establishment of both the best medical family in Nepal and the intraocular lens manufacturing facility at Tilganga.

The Tilganga Eye Center sits along the Bagmati River just downstream and adjacent to the Holy Pashupatinath Temple. The Hindu faithful are cremated at the edge of the river at Pashupatinath, and their ashes float past the eye hospital. To get to the hospital from the airport, you head down the main road to Kathmandu. Just beyond the bridge over the Holy Bagmati River, a small turnoff leads down to a common waiting area where hundreds of patients and their families squat in the sunshine waiting for their turn to be seen. On my first visit I pushed through the crowds and made my way to the registration desk. I introduced myself as Dr. Tabin, the ophthalmologist who had just been sent over by the Fred Hollows Foundation. The jovial Mr. Baniya, the hospital's administrator, immediately greeted me. Baniya spoke fluid but not quite fluent English. He effusively gave me a tour of the facilities, including the impressive intraocular lens factory. The hospital had only had its opening ceremony a few months before, and it was choked with patients. Nevertheless, the facilities were spotlessly clean—no garbage, no dirt, no dust. It reminded me of an American or Australian hospital, not a third-world facility.

I was also introduced to Nabin Rai, a wiry and energetic man who was trained as an ophthalmic assistant. Nabin had been Ruit's right-hand man at his maverick eye camps. Now he was the all-around troubleshooter for Tilganga. With a wide smile displaying his single gold tooth, Nabin told me I would be leaving for Jiri in four days. Toward the end of my tour, I was brought to the main examination room, in which a huge number of people waited to be seen. Patients scooted along a long wooden bench until they reached the head of the line. They were then walked to a stool, where they were positioned at a slit lamp microscope. The man at the opposite end of the microscope dominated the room. With hunched shoulders and an enormous, square head, Dr. Ruit sat examining the patients one by one. Before the patients had a chance even to get comfortable on their stool, Ruit had made a clinical diagnosis and planned a course of treatment. His two assistants moved each diagnosed patient away and placed the next patient in position for Dr. Ruit. The line of patients extended around the room, out into the hallway, and down the hall. An even longer line of patients sat outside, still waiting to register. After registering, patients walked through an area where ophthalmic assistants checked their vision, refracted them for glasses, and performed ancillary tests before sending them to join the queue waiting to see the doctor.

Ruit looked up at me with only a cursory glance and nod. It was clear that he was too busy to spend much time with another young ophthalmologist from the Western world. A steady stream of both trainees and ophthalmologists from the West had already begun to visit Ruit to observe his legendary surgery. He clearly had too much on his mind to make a production of welcoming each visitor.

The next day I was able to observe Ruit in surgery. Like many before me, I was amazed by his skill. He performed absolutely perfect cataract surgery in only seven minutes. The turnover time between patients was virtually nil. In a few hours, he had restored sight to more than thirty people. Every surgery was performed with the smooth, effortless grace Michael Jordan displays when completing a breakaway basket. The outcome was never in question. Again, I only had a short audience with Ruit, but I spent a considerable amount of time meeting with his ophthalmic assistants.

The hospital put me to work on my second day. I was seated at the single slit lamp microscope; with a nurse acting as interpreter, I began to examine the unending line of patients that continued to shuttle past. In a few short hours I saw more pathology than I normally encountered during several months of work in America or Australia. Every manner of unusual disease presented itself. Moreover, many of the diseases had reached their end stages, something rarely seen in the Western world, where everything is treated early. Here I found people blind from complications of tuberculosis and leprosy, people with tumors that had completely engulfed their eyes, people who had sustained horrendous trauma weeks or months before and had received no treatment. Beside the sad group of patients for whom nothing could be done, however, were large numbers of people totally blind from cataracts. These patients could be spotted from across the room because their pupils, the black circles in the centers of their eyes, were now an eerie white. When we dilated the pupils with drops, the cataract patients stared back at us with glowing eyes like characters in a cheap horror movie. These people could see only light and dark, but after Dr. Ruit's seven-minute surgical procedure, full functional vision was restored to them. A few weeks later, if no other eye diseases were present, Ruit's cataract patients could see twenty-twenty!

On my fourth day of work at Tilganga I was brought to the operating room to perform a cataract surgery. I sat in the same magical chair where Ruit had effortlessly restored perfect vision to countless patients in seven minutes each. I found that these fully developed cataracts were much more challenging surgically than any I had previously encountered in my residency or fellowship. Moreover, the microscope I was using was a five-thousand-dollar model rather than the seventy-five-thousand-dollar instrument I was accustomed to. Every aspect of the surgery, in fact, was more difficult than I expected. After nearly an hour of concentrated struggle, I completed a reasonable sight-restoring surgery.

The next day I embarked for Jiri with an ophthalmic assistant. We would be setting up an eye camp in this remote village. Since 1988 the road to Jiri had been fully paved, but our progress was constantly hampered by a large amount of traffic. The sudden stops and starts on the windy road made for an unpleasant ten hours. It was good to finally arrive in town and stretch my legs on the muddy roads. Assistants had prescreened nearly a thousand patients for the eye camp. During the next day, my task would be to see each patient and determine who was and who was not a candidate for cataract surgery. With M. K., my affable ophthalmic assistant at my side, I used the only tools I had—a penlight and an ophthalmoscope—to examine the throng of patients. Each patient pressed forward in the crowd, often accompanied by several family members. M. K. had previously been in the military and used all of his experience to impose a semblance of order upon the confused group. We methodically began to examine the never-ending line of patients.

As in Tilganga, we encountered an overwhelming quantity of deformities and diseases. For the first time I saw many rare congenital disorders that before I had only read about. For example, I encountered families in which all the children were blind from retinitis pigmentosa or congenital glaucoma and other untreatable problems. Mixed in among the throng were 248 people totally blinded by treatable cataracts. These we screened and took aside. Their faces had to be washed and antibiotic drops had to be instilled before surgery.

The next day Dr. Ruit arrived with Nabin in the Tilganga jeep. Two other ophthalmic assistants and two scrub nurses accompanied them. Also in Ruit's entourage were Dr. Dick Litwin and two Tibetan doctors whom Ruit had convinced the Chinese government to allow him to train. Litwin had returned to join Ruit for his first eye camp in several years. He had a round face with snow-white hair and a snow-white beard. He could have been a fit, Himalayan Santa Claus.

Ruit was clearly the captain in charge of camp. In addition to a massive head, almost disproportionate to his body, Ruit had enormous ears, a barrel chest, and a bearing that made him seem much larger than his five feet six inches. I watched him supervising his troops. They showed absolute respect, love, and reverence, mixed with a sense of awe and fear. The ophthalmic assistants and nurses immediately set out to convert an old dusty schoolroom into a sterile operating theater. The two Tibetan doctors, Dr. Olo and Dr. Kesang, simply smiled and observed the general hubbub.

Six months earlier, Ruit had been the first person ever to perform cataract surgery with lens implants in Tibet. He was the first outsider allowed to perform surgery in Tibet, the product of a long struggle with Chinese officials. The results of his surgeries were absolutely overwhelming. For the first time ever, blind people in Tibet were cured. With the enormous success of his first surgical camp at the Lhasa City Hospital, Ruit was able to convince the Chinese health authorities to let him train Dr. Olo and Dr. Kesang, the two ophthalmologists at Lhasa City Hospital. Their prior training was very modest. Both had only two years of health sciences education after high school, followed by one year of specialty training in eye diseases. Both had arrived in Nepal eager to learn and eager to follow Ruit's example.

During the eye camp, Dr. Ruit and Dr. Litwin stayed with the head school administrator in a house with electricity above the main school building. I stayed with the Tibetan doctors and the ophthalmic assistants and nurses in the student barracks at the bottom of the hill. For the next four days both of the two microscopes we had were constantly in use. Dr. Ruit commanded one, performing another perfect surgical miracle every seven minutes. Dr. Litwin and I took turns struggling at the other microscope. We both took considerably longer to complete cases than Ruit. On several occasions, I needed to ask Dr. Ruit to intervene and take over my case to ensure a good result.

Every morning in Jiri, bandages came off the previous day's patients, and people who had been blind for years were suddenly able to see. Tears of joy flowed freely. The harshness of life for the blind in the mountainous Himalayan areas is incredible, and their life expectancy is short. Many of the blind we operated on were young enough that they would be able to return to work. Others could now resume household tasks such as cooking and helping to care for young infants, thus freeing another family member to work.

Each day at the camp was a joy. At first light we began with dressing changes and application of antibiotic drops. This was followed by a quick breakfast and a rescreening of the day's surgical patients. Next, the ophthalmic assistants would prepare each patient for surgery. Local anesthetic had to be administered, and each eye sterilized prior to surgery. Then the patients lined up and waited quietly for their turn on the operating table. As one surgery was completed and the patient was rolled off the surgical table, the next was rolled on from the other side. The surgeon represped the new eye with Betadine while the scrub nurses sterilized all of the instruments. Then surgery began again. Each break between surgeries lasted less then two minutes. We worked well past dark each evening and then made the rounds, checking all of our post-operative patients again. By the time we were able to sit down, Dr. Ruit's cook staff had prepared the first of what was usually a six- or seven-course meal. Like a general who knows that his troops fight best on full stomachs, Ruit ensured an amazing array of Nepali delicacies every evening. An abundant supply of alcohol always flowed with the food. Beer, local rum, local whiskey, and usually a supply of Western whiskey accompanied dinner. At the conclusion of each meal, people were called forth to sing a local song or perform a local dance. Dr. Kesang had trained in classical Tibetan opera and each night ended the festivities with amazing songs.

By the end of the camp, I was absolutely a convert. I had slowly developed a rapport with Dr. Ruit. He had some admiration for mountaineering and mountaineers. One of the board members of the Tilganga Eye Center was Gombu Sherpa, who had been to the top of Mount Everest twice. Fred Hollows had been an avid mountaineer and had spoken at length with Ruit about the virtues and pure challenges of mountaineering. Ruit was excited to hear of my climbing Mount Everest. He was impressed that, after the eye camp, I planned to run up to Everest base camp at a Sherpa pace. I told Ruit that when I finished my fellowship I wanted to return to Nepal full time to work with him. Ruit told me that there was lots to be done, and he had lots of work for me.

When I returned from Jiri and my trip to Everest base camp, I asked Ruit what his plans were for me. He told me to come back in July, and we would figure something out. Upon completing my fellowship in Australia, I shipped some of my belongings back to the United States and brought the rest to Nepal. Ruit first had me work for several weeks at Tilganga seeing patients and operating where he could give me pointers. I continued to stay in the Thamel region and commuted daily to Tilganga by bicycle. By now there was a copious amount of raw garbage lining the streets of downtown Kathmandu. The tiny avenues were always choked with traffic. It became a dangerous sport commuting by bicycle through the crowded roads. Motorcyclists weaved in and out of traffic jams. Cars frequently crossed lanes at any opening or any chance to move ahead. Despite the drenching monsoon rains, which came virtually every day in July, the air of Kathmandu Valley was now thick with pollution from the increase in motor traffic. The ring road, which had been gloriously empty in 1988, was now choked with truck traffic moving in both directions around the city.

The one large improvement technology had brought the city was in communication. It was now easy to arrange a phone line from Nepal to America, and I was able to speak with loved ones easily. After a month, Dr. Ruit said he had found a position for me. A charity hospital had been built in Biratnagar, the second most populated area in Nepal. Ruit wanted me to spend several months in Biratnagar improving the quality of care at the Golchha Eye Hospital. Two senior ophthalmologists were already working there. Neither had ever performed surgery with intraocular lens implants or under a microscope. Ruit told me that if I could only convert these two doctors to microsurgery, I would be making an enormous contribution to eye care in Nepal. I flew on an old prop plane from a domestic terminal in Kathmandu to the grass runway of the Biratnagar airport.

22

GOLCHHA
HOSPITAL

A thick, humid fog engulfed the plane as we descended into Biratnagar. The city's mid-July atmosphere was a heavy quagmire that foreshadowed the tropical monsoon season. Beads of sweat collected on my forehead when I stepped onto the grass runway. The temperature was a hundred degrees Fahrenheit with 100 percent humidity—I felt I could almost drink the air. A representative of the Golchha family, Mr. Dugar, was waiting for me at the airport. He wore a crisp long-sleeved cotton shirt and didn't seem at all uncomfortable with the weather. He briskly led me to a Golchha family van, which whisked me to my new home in the Golchha compound.

Biratnagar, a sleepy town that seems to have been frozen in time four decades ago, has one paved road running at its outskirts along the main trucking route from Delhi to Kathmandu. The streets turn from pavement to rutted mud as you enter the town proper. Traffic switches from trucks and automobiles to flatbed oxcarts pulled by two water buffalo yoked side by side to a large log. Occasionally a bicycle, and more seldom a motorcycle, swerves around the lumbering buffalo. Three-wheeled bicycle rickshaws are the main mode of transportation for the people of Biratnagar. On every street corner you can see the lean, blackened bodies of the bicycle rickshaw drivers who drape themselves across their front seats in languid positions while waiting for customers. In the intense heat and humidity people remain as motionless as desert lizards. As we passed through town, the locals occasionally twisted their necks and stared at my white face—mainly they just followed me with their eyes.

The Golchha family vehicle honked sporadically as it made its way along the rutty roads leading to the gated entrance of what appeared to be a palace. Together, six boys who work for the Golchha family pulled back the thick iron gate, and we rolled onto a smoothly paved driveway. My bags were collected, and I was led to an immaculate three-room marble suite, complete with modern furniture, a modern television and VCR, and one of the only air-conditioning units in all of Biratnagar. The suite's ornate bathroom included a marble tub-and-shower area, and the spacious bedroom housed a king-plus-sized bed draped in satin sheets from India. Fresh-cut flowers added color and sweetly scented the air.

The Golchha family is one of the wealthiest and most powerful industrial families in Nepal. They control five major industries in Biratnagar, including everything from a sugarcane factory to a factory that makes the shock absorbers for most vehicles in Nepal. They are devout believers in the Jain sect of Hinduism, committed to total *anhimsa* or nonviolence. I was repeatedly amazed as I watched family members gently shoo away mosquitoes that were actively biting them instead of squashing the pests. The Golchhas keep a strict vegetarian diet but with more variety and flavor than anyplace else I have ever had the pleasure of dining. Meals consist of multiple courses served in small silver bowls and chalices. Four of the new generation Golchha sons lived with their wives and children and myriad servants in the enormous communal house, which towered above the three-suite main guest headquarters. Behind the house acres of flower, vegetable, and fruit gardens spread in all directions. Nestled among the gardens were barns full of cows, goats, and chickens, and small one-story dwellings that housed the hundreds of servants.

The Golchha family strongly believes in charity, and their affluence has allowed them to make important contributions in many areas. In 1990, in the name of their senior founding grandfather, the family built the Ramlal Golchha Charity Eye Hospital. The Golchha Eye Hospital is a large four-story structure two blocks down the main road from the family's home. It consists of several examination rooms, several layers of dormitory-style wards, and an operating theater. In 1993 the senior Golchha management asked Dr. Ruit to upgrade the quality of care at their hospital. Dr. Ruit had sent me to help.

After my first lunch at Golchha house I was driven the one block to the hospital. It took several weeks for me to convince the family that I did not need a chauffeur. I was never able to convince them that I did not need a servant by my side twenty-four hours a day. When I arrived at the hospital, the two chief technicians, Bupendra and Makesh, eagerly greeted me, each embracing my hand in both his own. The reception from the two doctors, on the other hand, was polite but a bit cooler. Dr. I. C. Biswas was an affable, round-faced man. He was graying at the temples, thinning on top, and had exceptionally smooth skin for a man who appeared to be in his early sixties. A pillar of the community, generally beloved for his warmth and compassion, Dr. Biswas had previously been president of the Nepal Ophthalmology Society. Despite his accomplishments, I would soon discover that the surgery Dr. Biswas performed made his name, *I. C.,* a wonderful misnomer, as few of his patients could see. His partner, Dr. D. B. Joshi, was approximately ten years younger. He had lighter skin and wore a taut expression. He greeted me warmly but maintained a somewhat reserved, distant air. Both Dr. Joshi and Dr. Biswas seemed wary of a young physician who had come to tell them what to do. Dr. Biswas quickly pointed out that he had been in Biratnagar as an ophthalmologist for more than twenty-five years. He had seen virtually all there was to see and bragged that he had not needed to look at a medical book in nearly twenty years! He knew every diagnosis in the region. His past accomplishments described, Dr. Biswas went on to say that I would have trouble helping with the flow of patients, as I knew little Nepali. He suggested that I do all the surgery instead. Dr. Biswas explained that he still did excellent cataract surgery—not only could he remove cataracts without using a microscope, but his eyes were so excellent that he could do so without any magnifying glasses—but had done so much over the years that he could now turn the task over to me.

I visited the filthy inpatient wards where postcataract patients typically spent five to seven days. All of the cataract surgery being done by Dr. Biswas and Dr. Joshi was intracapsular surgery, which involved slicing an eye in half and forcibly wrestling out the entire lens using large forceps. The eyes were stitched shut with sutures the size of those used for general surgery in America. Patients remained in the hospital for a week and were issued thick, Coke-bottle glasses before being discharged. Only a small amount of vision was recovered in the first few weeks. Even those patients who could see well after surgery suffered from horribly distorted peripheral vision due to the thick lenses. Only the totally blind came for surgery at the Golchha Eye Hospital. Yet there was a constant stream of patients being led here by relatives. It was generally considered a good result if, after surgery, patients could see shadows and avoid walking directly into objects in their path.

Just a few hundred cataract cases were done per year even though the hospital was the only eye-care facility available to 1.2 million people. Over the next several weeks I began doing cataract surgery using Dr. Ruit's technique. I operated with a microscope and replaced the cloudy lens with a modern intraocular lens implant. I moved slowly and carefully and averaged approximately ten surgeries per day.

Patients were able to see reasonably well the day after surgery, even without glasses. They were able to go home, even to remote locations, after a few days. Soon people began requesting that the Western doctor examine them. By the end of two months, both Dr. Biswas and Dr. Joshi started to take an interest in my surgical procedure. They began watching me in the operating room and then began scrubbing in on my cases. Finally they admitted their interest in learning the new techniques and opened up to my instruction. Both doctors had done a phenomenal amount of surgery in their careers and had excellent surgical hands. It took only a short time before they were performing microsurgical cataract operations with lens implants and achieving markedly improved results. Concomitant with this, more patients began coming to the Golchha Hospital for treatment, and the surgery volume increased.

With the increased flow of patients, we had to face the task of directing them through the hospital as efficiently as possible. The majority of those who came required only refraction for mild glasses or artificial teardrops for eyes irritated by chronic smoke. I taught the ophthalmic assistants to perform better refractions, to prescribe glasses, and to recognize and care for most minor eye problems. This would free the doctors to see a much lower volume of patients, allowing them to perform complete exams including the use of an ophthalmoscope and slit lamp microscope. Both Makesh and Bupendra proved to be incredibly bright and were able to perform excellent screening examinations and refractions. They learned to give good anesthesia for cataract surgery and also to coordinate the flow of patients through the hospital. The assistants thrived on the additional responsibility, and the doctors' skills improved markedly when they were able to take their time—finally, Dr. I. C.'s patient's could see. In general, everyone's morale improved.

As a last measure, we began to introduce the concept of cost recovery at the Golchha Eye Hospital. The plan was modeled after Ruit's Tilganga Eye Center in Kathmandu, where one-third of the patients paid approximately $120 for full surgical care, one-third of the patients paid between nothing and $120, and one-third received completely free care. In Biratnagar we had difficulty recovering as much as we would have liked because of the high percentage of absolutely destitute patients. Still, with cost recovery instituted, we were able to improve several aspects of care for the patients and improve overall conditions in the hospital.

I was, in general, ecstatic with my workdays. A servant brought me tea and fresh-squeezed tropical fruit juices in bed each morning. After a refreshing shower, I walked upstairs to the Golchha dining room where my cooks had three types of homemade breads, two types of cooked cereals, and fresh milk from the house cows waiting for me. In addition I was served potato and vegetable curry, and omelets with Marsala chilies, onions, and fresh cheese from the premises. An enormous plate of fresh mangoes, papaya, and pineapple always decorated my table. After breakfast I would assure the chauffeur that I need not be driven and walk the single block along a rutted dirt road to the hospital. I was unable to carry even a small ophthalmoscope—my personal servant insisted upon doing everything for me. After a brief look at my post-operative patients, I would go upstairs to the operating room to commence a day of surgery. Every few hours my loyal servants brought me food and tea. In the afternoon, when I went back to the palace to take a shower, any article of clothing I changed out of was taken away and returned forty-five minutes later fully cleaned and pressed. The summer weather brought torrential monsoon downpours interspersed with days of smothering heat and 100 percent humidity; thus there was little to do besides work, eat, and hold evening ophthalmology teaching sessions for the doctors and assistants.

—

Despite our successes, there were continued frustrations, some of which I still find difficult to reconcile. In this poor region of Nepal, with its high mortality rate, I found only a weak focus on the importance of each individual patient. A typical upsetting incident occurred one day when a father brought his frail, eight-year-old daughter to the hospital. The pair had walked three days from their village to do some essential shopping in the big city of Biratnagar. While in town, the girl had been playing with a stick and had received a sharp cut across her cornea. The corneal laceration was plugged by a knuckle of iris prolapsed outside the eye. The girl was in tears when she was brought to me. I explained to Dr. Joshi that this needed to be repaired urgently. I asked him to tell the father that most likely, the girl would lose vision in this eye. However, I instructed him to translate, we needed to operate immediately simply to save the eye. It had to be enclosed and an infection prevented. If nothing was done, the girl would absolutely lose all vision, most likely lose her eye, and infection could continue along her optic nerve to the brain and kill her. Surgery was the only option. Dr. Joshi translated this to the father, who seemed to understand. I told Dr. Joshi to prepare the operating room and to bring the girl to the operating table. We had to do surgery with injectable Ketamine anesthesia, and I needed to get a book back in my room to check the exact dosage. I also had a few vials of artificial vitreous in my room and a set of finer instruments, which I thought would improve the surgery. I ran to my apartment, grabbed the book and instruments, and ran back to the hospital. I arrived back no more than twenty minutes after leaving. I was surprised to find Dr. Joshi sitting and quietly drinking a cup of tea. "Where is the girl?" I queried. I had been rehearsing exactly what I would say to calm her, remembering her large brown eye that had looked back at me with fear.

"They are gone," Dr Joshi said simply.

"What do you mean, *gone?*"

"They have returned to their village." Dr. Joshi was very calm.

"Dr. Joshi, didn't you explain that the girl needed urgent surgery, otherwise she would lose her eye and possibly die?"

"Yes," he replied, "but they decided it was best not to have surgery. They need to go back to their village and, besides, it's only a girl." He resumed sipping his tea.

—

Life at the Golchha residence continued to be interesting. My quarters were adjacent to the family's communal home. Being the wealthiest family in the region, they were the first to have several modern luxuries. In 1994 this included satellite television. The installation of a satellite television receiver in the family yard was accompanied by great ceremony, and the programs from India and the rest of the world became available. One night, a few weeks later, Mrs. Golchha came running to my room in a panic. She looked at me very gravely and said, "Space invaders have attacked the earth and have destroyed America and Washington, D.C. What should be done?" She was in an absolute frenzy. I went to the main house to find all of the Golchha family in a similar state of alarm. These were the educated elite of the region. I pressed for details. Mr. Golchha, a man who runs several multinational companies, told me, "It's true, Washington, D.C., has been destroyed and all of America's transportation is shut down." When I said this was impossible, they insisted that they were watching CNN and that indeed, it must be true. Fortunately, the Golchhas also had one of the few phones that allowed international calling from Biratnagar. I suggested that I call my parents. It was four o'clock in the morning in the United States when I woke my father and said, "Dad, this may sound a bit crazy, but have you heard anything about space invaders attacking earth?" He groggily replied that, no, he hadn't heard any such news. I related what the Golchha family had seen on CNN and asked him please to check. He awoke, turned on the radio and the television, and found that all was well. When I got off the phone, I insisted that I come to see the television to hear updated reports. As it turned out, the same satellite that received CNN also broadcast movies. The family had been watching *Independence Day* with Will Smith.

—

As Dr. Biswas and Dr. Joshi became increasingly adept at surgery, I took the opportunity to travel to some of the other eye hospitals that cater to the impoverished population on the border of Nepal and India. I went to one hospital where there had recently been an epidemic of post-operative infection. Again, I wanted to help the local surgeons change from operating without magnification to operating with a sophisticated microscope. In addition, I needed to teach them extracapsular cataract surgery and ocular lens placement. At one particular hospital I noticed that the water was blocked in the squat toilet used by the surgeons, nurses, and ophthalmic assistants. This was a typical Asian facility, and as in most Asian toilets of its kind, there was no toilet paper. Generally, the people use their hands and then wash afterward. In this case, however, there was no running water, and there clearly hadn't been any for some time. I tried to discuss the situation with the doctor in charge. I was going to suggest that possibly, just possibly, this toilet and the lack of running water to wash hands were the sources of their high infection rate; but when I confronted the doctor and told him the lack of running water in the toilet was the problem, he smiled broadly and said in a complacent tone, "Oh, this is not a problem. You see, every day I wash my ass in the river." With that, he walked away.

—

Every two years since leaving Biratnagar, I have returned for a visit. Whether I happen to be traveling to Sikkim, Darjeeling, or eye camps in northeastern Nepal, I always arrange to see my friends at the Golchha Eye Hospital. The hospital has continued to improve with every passing year, and the cost recovery system has been fully implemented. Although more of the patients are destitute in Biratnagar than in Kathmandu, many are able to pay a small fee for the hospital's services. The number of surgical procedures performed in the hospital has steadily increased as more and more people see the benefits of intraocular lenses and microsurgery. As more surgical procedures are performed, the doctors become better surgeons. Both Dr. Biswas and Dr. Joshi are now performing impeccable surgery in approximately ten minutes. Nearly three thousand people have their sight restored at the Golchha Hospital each year. Meanwhile the ophthalmic assistants have improved their diagnostic skills, and they prescreen a large number of patients so that the doctors are able to concentrate on those for whom they can do the most. The hospital has also begun its own outreach programs with community screening efforts to bring in patients.

In 1990, when Dr. Ruit was the only Nepali surgeon performing microscopic surgery with lens implants, fewer than fifteen thousand cataract operations were done annually in the country. Less than 10 percent were performed using microsurgical techniques or intraocular lens implants. A decade later, virtually every ophthalmologist performing surgery in Nepal is using a microscope and intraocular lenses. Nearly a hundred thousand cataract surgeries were performed in the year 2000 and, of those, 95 percent were done with lens implants. This contrasts impressively with the case in India, a much wealthier country, where less than forty percent of cataract surgery is performed with a microscope or intraocular lenses.

23

CHANGES:
TIBET

Over the past twenty years I have seen dramatic changes in the lives and lifestyles of the Himalayan people. On my first expeditions, going to the Himalayas meant becoming totally isolated from the rest of the world. When I arrived in Tibet in 1981, a rough, rutted dirt and gravel highway connected the Lhasa airport to the center of the city. The airport itself was strategically located to facilitate Chinese plane landings during the military takeover of Tibet. More recently, however, this same airport has been used for a different kind of invasion, the invasion of Tibet by Han Chinese as well as Western tourists, trekkers, and adventure seekers like myself.

In 1981 Lhasa was a split city. Low wood and mud structures crouched together in the center of town, housing the native Tibetans. These were traditional nonheated homes without running water. Their design had not been altered for the past two hundred years. On the outskirts of town, hastily built army barracks extended in all directions. Because there were no tourist facilities in Lhasa at the time, our expedition was housed in one of the barracks. The Chinese in Lhasa could be picked out of any crowd because they all wore official uniforms. The vast majority were clad in full military fatigues and carried firearms. Any Chinese person not in a military uniform, such as our drivers and cooks, wore a blue Mao suit. The tension between the Chinese, who dominated the streets militarily, and the Tibetans, who appeared to have maintained a spiritual superiority, was palpable. The major Buddhist temples and monasteries, such as the Jokang and the Sera, had become veritable museums in 1981. Chinese military troops guarded the entrances, and life inside was carefully regulated.

In Lhasa my teammates and I interacted mostly with the Chinese. Mr. Wang Fu Chow, who in 1975 became the first Chinese man to summit Everest, was our liaison officer. Mr. Tsao, a thin chain-smoking Han Chinese man from Beijing, was our affable translator. These two were our constant companions. We had minimal contact with the Tibetan people.

Once our expedition flew from Chengdu to Lhasa, all communication with the outside world ceased. It was nearly two months before we were able to contact anyone. There was a certain thrill in thinking that we were adventurer explorers off on a quest, completely isolated from outside interactions.

—

When I returned to Tibet in 1983, the amount of Chinese construction had increased dramatically. Several wide, paved roads now stretched into Lhasa, and the main streets of the city had been widened. As in 1981, the central Barkhor region remained an enclave of traditional Tibetan homes where smoke from wood fires escaped through the roof slats. In place of the crude army barracks on the outskirts of town, however, cinder-block-style Chinese housing had begun to sprout up.

As in 1981, our expedition drove from Lhasa onto Xigase and then to Xegar on bumpy gravel and dirt roads. The Chinese influence progressively lessened as we continued moving away from Lhasa. The flow of Chinese military trucks and vehicles, however, remained impressive. The cultural split between the uniformed Han Chinese and the Tibetans also remained stark.

In 1983 there was still virtually no chance for communication with the outside world in Tibet, and none whatsoever after we left the capital.

After the Everest expedition in 1983, I didn't return to Tibet again until 1994. When I went back, it was for an eye camp that Dr. Ruit arranged. This would be the first time Tibetan surgeons actually performed microsurgery and cataract surgery themselves. Dr. Olo and Dr. Kesang from our Jiri camp had returned to Tibet, where they had prescreened a large number of people who were totally blind. The plan was that initially, Dr. Ruit and I would operate, restoring sight to the first eyes of most of the patients. Starting on the fourth day, Dr. Olo and Dr. Kesang would begin operating under our supervision on the second eyes of the patients who had sight restored to their first eye. I flew in to Lhasa with the team from Tilganga. The Lhasa airport, once a primitive hangar, had become a modern air terminal. A large statue of Mao dominated the entrance. Wide, well-paved roads made for a quick trip into the city.

Although the Potala Palace still dominated the skyline, the road in front of the Potala was now six lanes wide. A large Chinese-style paved park and garden covered the opposite side of the road. Wide blacktop roads crisscrossed throughout downtown Lhasa with many multistory steel Chinese buildings on all sides. It was clear that by 1994, all barriers between the Tibetans and the Chinese in Lhasa were being eliminated. No longer were Mao suits visible. Instead everyone, Chinese and Tibetans alike, wore modern Chinese clothing. The monasteries and temples were once again alive with activity, and pilgrims circumambulated and prostrated themselves before the Potala and the Jokang. Walking through the temples, we found a large percentage of Han Chinese tourists armed with expensive cameras. The temples, shrines, and monasteries had become museums. The Chinese military was no longer an obvious presence. Still, every midlevel position seemed to be filled by Chinese. A large number of clean guest houses had sprung up along the main road as well as several large, modern hotels. We stayed at a small Tibetan-run guest house and worked at the Lhasa City Hospital during our first week in Tibet.

The Lhasa City Hospital, despite the grandeur of Lhasa relative to Kathmandu, was far behind Tilganga in terms of cleanliness and order. I watched, horrified, as poorly trained Chinese surgeons attempted to perform an appendectomy on a young man. They were unable to find the appendix and were extremely rough with the bowels. There was no general anesthetic. The patient was under a spinal anesthetic, and the excision had been extended above the level of the anesthetic. The patient was howling in pain. Several small blood vessels were ruptured in the doctors' efforts to find the appendix. The abdominal cavity filled with blood, thus making it impossible for them to find the infected organ. Pus oozed from the abdomen as the infected appendix ruptured. I, meanwhile, was kicking myself because I still probably could have performed a reasonable appendectomy had I taken over at the point where I walked in to observe the case. By the time I realized the dire state of the situation, however, it was well beyond my general surgery skills to be certain that I could save the situation. After another hour of fumbled attempts, the bleeding in the abdomen was beyond what the surgeons could control. They finally sewed up the infected, bloody abdomen, leaving a drain. I later found out that the doctors had informed the family that the boy had cancer and was likely to die.

—

Dr. Ruit and I had no such dire problems during our own cases. The success of the surgery at the Lhasa City Hospital was overwhelming. Both the health department and doctors were amazed by the speed and quality of our results, and Dr. Olo and Dr. Kesang began doing surgery on their own.

We then moved by bus to the more remote Medrokongga County Hospital, where our surgery continued. Medrokongga County, three hours north of Lhasa, is one of the poorest areas in Tibet. The main highway, a rutted dirt and gravel road, snakes along the mighty Tsong Po River. On both sides the arid and desolate Tibetan plateau rises steeply into the jagged foothills of the high Himalaya. A few scattered settlements of bare wood and mud hovels cling to the flat bed of land along the river. While Buddhist prayer flags flap in the wind on top of each boxlike dwelling, yaks and goats graze on the sparse grass in the brown remnants of barley fields. Medrokongga County has one of the highest rates of cataract blindness in the world. Cataracts are responsible for the blindness of an estimated two hundred people in this county of only four hundred households.

Our bus bounced to a halt at a small one-story building with peeling white paint that served as the Medrokongga County Hospital. Rumors of our cataract camp had begun to circulate in Medrokongga County almost a year before our arrival. When we arrived, hundreds of elderly Tibetans and their families had already gathered at the county hospital. Many had traveled sixty miles or more by tractor or on the backs of family members. Some had been waiting for months. Their gazes were a mixture of hope and doubt. No one here had ever been cured of blindness.

The hospital itself was plagued by the sickly smell of many such third-world facilities. The acrid odor of stale urine combined with the pungent smells of excrement and antiseptic. The halls and tables were dusty. A welcoming committee of flies buzzed in every room. There was no heat and no power. As the microscope, portable generator, and other supplies were unloaded, Dr. Ruit looked across the barren dirt courtyard and gave me a broad smile. Pointing at the blind crowd, he excitedly explained that everything was perfect: "This is where the people need us."

Our ophthalmic team from Tilganga sterilized the room where we operated. In addition to training Dr. Olo and Dr. Kesang, we had trained two nurses and two ophthalmic assistants from Tibet for the eye camp. For the next three days, twelve hours a day, Dr. Ruit and I performed surgery side by side in a makeshift operating room without any high-tech equipment beyond a microscope. When the generator failed, we continued working through the microscope on eyes illuminated by flashlights. Technicians injected local anesthetic to numb the eyes and prepare the patients for surgery. When an operation finished, the patient was rolled off one side of the table and the next patient rolled on from the other. The new patient's face was painted with antiseptic and surgery continued. The turnover time between patients was less than one minute.

Dr. Ruit had no trouble sustaining a rate of seven perfect surgeries per hour for a twelve-hour operating day. For a cost of about twenty dollars, these Tibetan patients got approximately the same surgery that was state of the art in America ten years before. While patients needed a month to recover fully and had to wear mild glasses to obtain perfect twenty-twenty vision, in the first post-operative day they went from seeing only shadows to having ambulatory vision, roughly twenty-eighty.

"There is a new sky for my eye! I am free from the hell of darkness!" exclaimed Sonam Detchen moments after the white gauze patch had been removed from her left eye. Tears of joy streamed down her bronze cheeks. The day before, the sixty-three-year-old widow had been unable to see the shadow of a hand moving in front of her face. Today she could see her family for the first time in five years. With no living sons, she had no one to take care of her, often falling into ditches and going days without eating. Sonam was certain she would soon die. "Now," she said proudly, "I will be able to take care of myself."

In three days Dr. Ruit and I performed nearly two hundred such "miracles" in Medrokongga County. The gratitude of the local populous was overwhelming. Every night banquets were prepared that made me feel like royalty. Anything that crawled, flew, swam, or slithered was slaughtered and prepared with a variety of sauces for our pleasure. Local alcoholic beverages as well as Mao Tai liquor were constantly offered. At 14,500 feet, the alcohol quickly went to our heads.

At our final banquet, we renewed our ritual of cultural music and dance exchanges. Two of our ophthalmic assistants were expert Nepali dancers, and several of our staff had wonderful voices. Late in the evening, when everyone had had a bit too much to drink, a modern tape player was brought out and Michael Jackson pop music turned on. One svelte, effeminate Tibetan body came forward and began to dance. Clearly, he had watched Michael Jackson videos in the past and had memorized every move. He appeared to be triple jointed and displayed moves that surpassed even Michael Jackson's. Ruit watched in amazement and then began to command his troops. He first turned to Nabin and ordered him to go out and beat the dancer at his own game. Nabin tried, but alcohol combined with high altitude and the furious pace of the Tibetan Baryshnikoff quickly left him out of breath and crumpled on the floor. Next it was Latou's turn. Ruit directed him to battle, ordering him to "kick ass!" Again, the Michael Jackson of Tibet wore him down and blew him away in a few minutes. With this, Ruit heaved himself onto the dance floor. In the past few years, Ruit had gained a large gut that hung well over his waistline. He still had the soft hands and athletic shoulders and legs of his youth, and for the next four or five minutes Ruit and the Tibetan Michael Jackson engaged in a furious dance-off. Then the Tibetan Michael Jackson grabbed Dr. Ruit and, rather than competing, they began dancing together, twirling each other in jitterbug fashion. When the song ended, they hugged. Peace was restored. At the end of song, Ruit returned and sat next to me with a satisfied smile.

When the dancing had calmed, Chinese officials poured more Mao Tai liquor into our cups. Ruit added to the festivities by pulling a bottle of Glenfiddich malt whisky from his bag. He poured two long glasses. A few drinks later Ruit and I were swimming with satisfaction and alcohol. Ruit looked at me, "Did you see the way Olo was doing surgery?" he asked enthusiastically, "He's really getting it! Ya know, I think we can overcome all the cataract blindness in Tibet if we're allowed to train these doctors."

Several glasses of Scotch later, Ruit and I made a pact. Together, we would overcome all of the preventable and treatable blindness in the Himalayan region. We would be certain that every doctor in Nepal was able to perform cataract surgery under a microscope with intraocular lenses. We would train and equip doctors in Tibet. We would then turn our attention to the Himalayan regions of northern India and northern Pakistan. Moreover, we would provide free intraocular lenses and medicines to patients who could not afford them.

—

My head throbbed as we bounced along the rutted road back to Lhasa the next morning. Despite the hangover, Ruit and I remembered our pledge of the night before. As we flew back to Nepal, we formalized our plans for the Himalayan Cataract Project.

Our standard technique for the Himalayan Cataract Project proved to be incredibly successful. We trained teams of one doctor, one nurse, and one technician at the Tilganga Eye Center in Kathmandu. Here each team would learn the basics of cataract surgery, diagnosis, and pre- and post-op care. The surgeons would go through a microsurgery training course and the nurses would learn how to care for and prepare the instruments. Each team would then return to their local regions and prescreen a huge number of people bilaterally blind from cataracts. Dr. Ruit or I would operate on the first eyes of each patients with the local doctors assisting. A few days later, the local doctors would operate on the second eyes, under our supervision. Before leaving, Dr. Ruit and I would donate all of the equipment, supplies, and intraocular lenses needed for the doctors to continue sight-restoring surgery.

In its initial phases, this program was an unbelievable joy. The problem I soon discovered was that, once a surgeon has been trained, he needs continued teaching and follow-up. As we continued teaching more doctors, more doctors asked to be trained. Our program expanded from Nepal to Tibet. Over the next five years, we trained an additional twenty-four surgeons in Tibet. We expanded to Sikkim, the Darjeeling region of northern India, Bhutan, and northern Pakistan. Either Dr. Ruit or I needed to return frequently to each area to continue working with the doctors we had taken under our wings.

24

CHANGES: NEPAL

When I climbed in the Khumbu region near Mount Everest with Steve Ruoss and Jim Traverso in 1985, we found ourselves cut off from the outside world the day we left Kathmandu. Kathmandu, at that time, was a quiet, lush green city. Its pungent air hung heavy with the smell of cows, which roamed freely throughout town. The streets were narrow, the buildings were low, the traffic was minimal, and the cows were plentiful. In the few streets downtown where traffic congregated, all movement would periodically be blocked for hours if a sacred cow chose to lie in the street. The roads in the center of the city were paved, as was the main road around town, but the remainder of Kathmandu's streets were dusty dirt tracks where the bustle was all pedestrian. A majority of the traffic consisted of bicycle rickshaws. Motorcycles, three-wheeled diesel-burning putt-putts, and the infrequent car or truck also shared the streets. Steve, Jim, and I rented bicycles and rode freely throughout the city without a single moment's worry about traffic. Pedaling around to visit the myriad temples, we only occasionally encountered a rumbling truck carrying goods to or from India. Whenever we left the main tourist enclaves of Thamel and Freak Street, we became a curiosity. Everywhere, men wearing brightly patterned Hindu Toby hats turned their colorful heads to stare and women and children giggled and smiled. I breathed in the pungent, spicy odors of the city and returned the locals' smiles. Small children often ran alongside us, chasing wooden hoops down the road. A few times, I stopped and lifted a child onto the handlebars of my bike to give him a short ride, a treat that gave rise to squeals of delight.

The city would not remain so innocent. By 1994 Kathmandu's roads were packed wall to wall with people. The population of the Kathmandu Valley had soared to the point that crowds were everywhere. Three cars abreast jostled for position on narrow one-and-a-half lane roads with two-way traffic. It required absolute vigilance and attention simply to avoid being hit. The road accident rate and trauma fatality rate in Kathmandu reflected this increase in traffic. Sacred cows were still free to wander the city. With no improvement or widening of the roads, a single cow lying in an intersection could back up traffic for miles in every direction. By 1996 I had had a couple of close calls, jumping off my bicycle to avoid swerving cars. It was at this point that I decided it was no longer safe to ride a bike in Kathmandu. In addition to the danger of oncoming cars, the traffic-generated pollution hanging low in the Kathmandu Valley made even mild outdoor activity unpleasant. Ironically, I had no choice but to begin commuting to Tilganga by car.

The pollution problem in the Kathmandu Valley has continued to escalate with an exponential growth in population and motorized vehicles. The frequent changes in the government of Nepal make it nearly impossible for any single policy to remain in effect long enough to have a significant impact on the problem.

—

Even the more remote regions of Nepal have changed significantly in the less than two decades I have known them. In 1985, after leaving Kathmandu, Steve, Jim, and I were able to enjoy the hiking trails that wound their way through the quiet Sherpa villages of the Khumbu. These paths were kept pristine; a majority of the people who used them were local traders. No village beyond the end of any road had electricity or running water. Lack of such basic conveniences did not, however, hamper the generosity of the people. We were welcomed openly into many Sherpa homes. These houses tended to be two-story wooden structures. Yaks and other animals lived on the first level, while the family lived in a dark, upstairs room. Situated at one end of the room upstairs was a cooking area with an open woodstove. The stove was surrounded by flat benches covered in Tibetan rugs, which served as seats by day and beds by night. A Buddhist shrine for worship was neatly tucked at the far end of the room. Three and often four or more generations of a Sherpa family lived together in a single long room. Sexual encounters were carried out discreetly on the flat wooden beds. All aspects of life were shared together in this one room. During the winter, wood fires and warmth from the animals down below were all that heated these houses.

Once you ventured from the edge of the main road, all communication occurred via mail runners, fit Sherpa men who carried messages for miles over the rough dirt track into Kathmandu, where letters could be mailed. A single radio relay station had just been erected in the main Sherpa village of Namche Bazaar. It was controlled by the government and military, however; no civilian access was allowed.

By the time I returned to the Khumbu in 1988, significant changes had begun to occur in the Sherpa world. The hiking and trekking traffic had grown exponentially each year through the 1980s. The more this traffic increased, the harder it became to control the effects it had on the natural surroundings. A dramatic increase in garbage along the trekking trails had already begun. By 1988 it was not uncommon to see toilet paper tangled in the branches of a rhododendron tree, strangling its beautiful flowers. No one was working on any sort of policy to remove the trash buildup. Erosion caused by an increased cutting of trees also had become a problem. Sherpas were cutting down their forests for firewood to keep a fresh supply of hot tea ready for sale to trekkers.

Despite the negative changes with respect to the environment, positive advances were also being made through improvements in basic housing in the Khumbu region. Sir Edmund Hillary had built several schools and two hospitals, one in Phaplu and one in Kunde. The hospitals had gas-powered generators and were small bastions of electrical lighting. When we trekked out from Everest, another development project was working on utilizing hydroelectric power to provide light and warmth for the monks in the Tengboche Monastery. An American charity was sponsoring the project, and we met with the program's head engineer. Sadly, the Tengboche Monastery, holiest shrine of the Sherpa people and home to a priceless collection of books and art, burned to the ground in an electrical fire several months later. The charity that had funded the hydroelectric project spent the next several years raising funds to rebuild the monastery.

As in 1985, the communication in the Khumbu region in 1988 was still carried out only via mail runner. As a large expedition, we had hired our own private mail runner. In the tourism industry hierarchy, the most able Sherpa workers gravitate toward high-level positions such as Sirdar, or expedition leader. Those a tiny notch below become climbing Sherpas. Next in line is the important job of cook. Below cook you find the cook boy, and below the lowly cook boy, the mail runner.

In 1988 we hired an extremely cheerful, strong young man named Pemba as our chief mail runner. Pemba was always smiling and eagerly observing all aspects of the expedition. One of his favorite things about the expedition was all the shiny climbing equipment and clothes that we had brought from America. In particular,

Pemba fell in love with the rose-colored reflective sunglasses given to us by the Revo Company, one of the expedition's sponsors. He coveted our Revo sunglasses and asked if we would give him a pair.

On his first mail run from base camp, Pemba was to deposit postcards for all of our sponsors as well as letters for our loved ones at our trekking agency in Kathmandu where they would be mailed. He was also supposed to pick up any mail that our friends and relatives had sent to us via the trekking company. Our hike from Jiri to base camp had taken twenty-four days. We had been resting at base camp for another four days before Pemba set out. We had heard no news from the world we had left behind for a full four weeks, and we encouraged Pemba to go quickly.

As of 1988, the Sherpa land speed record from Everest base camp to Kathmandu and back was nine days. This required running a full marathon with an altitude change of nearly fifteen thousand feet up and down to Namche Bazaar on the first day, and then running over three separate mountain ranges back down to Jiri, reversing the twenty-four-day walk into base camp. The runner would take the night bus from Jiri to Kathmandu, a jostling ten-hour journey. He would then return by bus from Kathmandu to Jiri and repeat the run, only now going uphill from four thousand feet over three separate high passes to reach Namche Bazaar at twelve thousand feet. From here he continued on the up-and-down marathon back to base camp at seventeen thousand feet.

We told Pemba that if he could beat the existing speed record on his mail run, we would give him a pair of Revo sunglasses. Pemba set out from base camp at a fast jog. We watched him disappear quickly into the moraine of the Khumbu Glacier. When he left, we turned our attention to fixing the route through the Khumbu Icefall, which we would be sharing with a Korean team. We had just completed our route through the icefall when exactly eight days later, a thin, exhausted Pemba sprinted back into camp with an enormous smile. We patted him on the back and congratulated him heartily on his speedy run. Then we asked him for our mail. Pemba looked at Jim Frush, our expedition leader, complacently. He smiled, and complacently said, "No mail, sir."

"What do you mean, *no mail?*" Frush asked.

"Office closed, sir."

Pemba had made his journey taking the night bus to Kathmandu. The night bus arrives at six in the morning, and Pemba had gone directly to our trekking agency's office, arriving at six-thirty. Of course, it was closed. In order to break the speed record, Pemba knew that he had to take the day bus back to Jiri. It was due to depart at eight o'clock. Determined to set the land speed record, Pemba went back and took the day bus.

Using an interpreter, we took a long time explaining to Pemba that he had been hired as a "mail" runner, not simply a "runner." The purpose of his run had been to deliver mail that we wanted to send and pick up mail that had been sent to us. Speed was only of secondary importance. We hammered the mail aspect into Pemba's head and gave him a pair of Revo sunglasses for his second trip. After five days' rest he set out again. Four days after Pemba disappeared, a support trek came into our base camp. One of the ways our expedition had received funding was through organizing support treks for trekkers to hike into base camp. These treks were led by friends and family of the team members, and part of the profits from the trek were given as a tax-deductible donation to our expedition. When the trek arrived, we had been without any word of the outside world for nearly six weeks. We were eager to receive some. We asked the trekking leader if he had our mail. "You should have the mail by now!" he told us. "Four days ago we encountered your mail runner. He introduced himself as the official mail runner for the American Everest expedition and told us that his job was to bring all of your mail to you. He insisted that he must have all of your mail. The trekking agency had given us two large bags of mail and we turned them over to your mail runner. We expected that the Sherpa boy could easily make it back from Tengboche in one, or at the most two days."

Pemba, of course, had not returned. A week later he staggered back into camp with an enormous load of mail. He had taken the bags from the trekking group and carried them with him all the way to Kathmandu. In the city he picked up a new, smaller, bundle of mail and brought back the entire load to base camp.

—

After my 1988 trip I didn't return to the Khumbu region again until 1993, following our eye camp in Jiri. I had ten days to spare before I needed to return to Australia, and I knew that several of my old friends, including Peter Athans, Dr. Ken Kammler, and Nima Tashi Sherpa were at Everest's base camp. I decided to run from Jiri up to base camp to say hello.

The changes in five years were astounding! Dusk had just set in when I jogged into Namche Bazaar. The entire city was alight with electricity. Dozens of new trekking hotels and lodges had been erected; several were four stories high. Many of the lodges advertised hot showers inside. In addition, the village now had telephone lines reaching back to Kathmandu. The advent of hydroelectric power had even spread through remote villages and into the lower reaches of the Sherpa world.

In general, the trekking and climbing industry has brought a new prosperity to the Sherpa people. Certainly even the most nostalgic person who cries out against the unfortunate loss of culture and spirituality in the modern Sherpa must recognize that if one is living in a wooden hut at thirteen thousand feet in the Himalayas, it is nice to have electricity and higher-quality food products shipped in by airplanes. Also, it is preferable that children receive a formal education rather than remaining illiterate.

Such prosperity, of course, came with its own price. Because trekking and climbing traffic had continued to increase unchecked, problems with sanitation, garbage, and deforestation had intensified throughout the entire Khumbu region between 1988 and 1993. As I continued my quick trip to base camp in 1993, I was disgusted to see metallic candy bar wrappers reflecting the light of the sun and crushed plastic water bottles poking out of mountain streams. Luckily, news of the increasing amount of garbage at base camp and of the sad effects of the tourist industry on the general environment has stretched back to the Western world. Several expeditions were organized in the 1990s as Everest cleanup expeditions. Beyond bringing needed publicity to the problem, these expeditions actually made significant progress in cleaning up the area. The amount of garbage on trekking routes and at base camps has improved in recent years.

When I finally arrived at base camp in 1993, I entered a veritable city of tents. The amenities were amazing. Satellite telephones and computers now rang and beeped and buzzed, linking climbers with the outside world in a way that had never before been possible—instant communication to anywhere on the globe. When I visited Ken, Nima, and Peter in their spacious base camp tent, I enjoyed not just the warmth of their friendship, but also the warmth of solar heat panels. I wondered what had happened to poor Pemba, whose profession was now obsolete.

25

DOLPO
DREAMS

For twenty years my world had focused on climbing. Then I became more serious about medicine. No big adventure—no big mountain. My angst was building. I needed to bite back—a final dream expedition.

I began to conceive the plan for such a trip at the end of my stay in Nepal. I had just accepted a permanent position on the faculty of the University of Vermont College of Medicine in Burlington, Vermont, and did not know when my next extended mountaineering trip might take place. I formulated my dream trip. It would include a few close friends, an unexplored area of the Himalayas, and a previously unattempted peak. Virgin big-mountain enclaves still exist if you look for them. Pakistan, Afghanistan, Bhutan, Sikkim, China, Tibet, and Nepal are all home to the type of raw, pristine mountain that both reduces and inspires humanity. I made my choice carefully, settling upon the Dolpo region of northwestern Nepal. The Dolpo and its people first entered my imagination while reading Peter Matthiessen's book *The Snow Leopard*. I knew the area contained the Kanjiroba Himal, one of the least explored big mountain ranges in Nepal. Japanese teams climbed its two highest peaks in 1969 and 1972, and a French expedition came in 1973. The region was then totally closed by the government for nearly twenty years. It had recently been reopened as the Shey-Phoksundo National Park, a wildlife refuge for blue sheep and snow leopards. My friend Phil Lieberman trekked into the Dolpo in 1993 and returned with photographs of fantasy mountains. No mountaineers had applied for a permit to climb in the Dolpo since 1973.

I scoured the maps and the photographs and decided on a peak named Kang-Chunne. At 6,443 meters, or 21,138 feet, it was a perfect height for me to climb a hard technical route yet still feel good. The access appeared to be straightforward. It is just north of a pass on the main trekking route.

Having chosen my mountain, I began the arduous process of getting the Nepalese government to open a new peak. To make the first ascent of a mountain, you must have a joint expedition with at least three Nepali climbers. I recruited my close friends Nima Tashi Sherpa and Dawa Tsersing Sherpa, who had summitted Mount Everest with me in 1988.

While working as a doctor in Nepal, first in Kathmandu and then in Biratnagar, I had made the acquaintance of several people in official government ministries. I also, through the Golchha family, had met many people important in Nepali business. I spoke to several people highly connected in the Ministry of Tourism, who felt that opening a virgin peak in the Dolpo was a distinct possibility. Several times the phrase "It would be my honor to help you, Doctor," was repeated to me. Dawa suggested that I use the trekking agency he worked for additional help in navigating the permit process.

I filled out masses of forms. The opening of a mountain first requires the approval of the Nepal Mountaineering Association. My application passed this hurdle, and I was told that the rest was just a formality. The Ministries of Tourism, Mountaineering, and Home each had to endorse the application. Then the Ministry of Defense had to give its okay. Finally the entire cabinet needed to unanimously vote to allow the mountain to be climbed. Encouraged by a first interview at the Ministry of Mountaineering, I invited some longtime climbing friends: Ed Webster, a rock climbing buddy and mountain guide living in Colorado; Steve Ruoss, my partner on Kusum Kangruru and Everest; Bruce Norman, a Scottish climber; and Mike Sinclair, a fellow Everest summiter.

Time passed, and in the quagmire of Nepalese bureaucracy our application dragged on. My trekking agency kept saying not to worry. Having operated successfully on the mother-in-law of one of the top government ministers in Nepal, and having developed a close relationship with the Golchha family, I didn't feel I had to be concerned. Meanwhile Ed asked if his close friend, rock star Billy Squier, could join the party and help him with expenses. As the costs of the expedition mounted, we also invited George Waring III and his son, George IV, two accomplished kayakers who were able to assist with the budget. With the influx of cash came an increased responsibility to make certain the trip happened on schedule. More than a year had passed, and I still didn't have my permit.

Four months prior to the proposed start of the trip, I was still working in Nepal. I personally walked my application from ministry to ministry. When all that was left was the defense approval and cabinet vote, I faxed my team that everything was set and told them to buy their nonrefundable plane tickets. Two weeks later, I heard that the Defense Ministry had said no.

"*Kay guarnay*" is the all-purpose Nepalese expression for "What to do when there is nothing to do?" I panicked. If it weren't for the high rollers on my trip, I could have just come up with an alternate plan. If I had kept it small, I could have gone "trekking" with a friend and wandered off to climb. But our group was too large not to be seen. What to do?

I desperately scrambled and used a very high source I knew in the government of Nepal to intervene on my behalf. Success seemed assured when I was able to override a midlevel military administrator's decision and win military approval for my expedition. But before the matter could be brought to the entire cabinet of Nepal, a vote of no confidence successfully shut down the entire government. I was back to square one. I would need to restart the entire process as soon as a new government convened.

Now I was stuck big time. The permit could not be approved without complete approval from the government, and now there was no government. Moreover, if a new government were elected, they would have to appoint a new cabinet. Then I would have to win approval from the new minister of tourism, the new minister of mountaineering, and from the new security council from the military. Elections were not scheduled for at least another four months. It would be impossible for me to obtain the permit in time for our plans. I thought back to a conversation I had had with Chris Bonington, the noted British mountaineer and explorer. Chris had lamented his two-year struggle to get the government of Nepal to open a new peak. After two years the rug had been pulled out from under his feet. Since then he had concentrated on first ascents in India and Tibet, where he found the governments more manageable. I had been chuckling to myself, thinking that with my newfound connections as a doctor, I could do what Bonington couldn't. Clearly, I was wrong.

I walked, feeling a gloomy despair, through the thick monsoon air that hung in Kathmandu. Sweat dripped through my third T-shirt of the day as I made my way to the office of Ang Tsering Sherpa, who runs one of the most successful Sherpa-run trekking agencies as well as a helicopter air service. He was also the head of the Nepal Mountaineering Association. Ang was mystified as to why the military had vetoed Kang-Chunne. His best guess was that the midlevel officer had been too lazy to look at a map and see that the mountain was near the main trekking route and in the middle of the currently open Dolpo mountains. He told me that with proper documents and his help I could get a new permit for a virgin peak.

I switched trekking agencies, losing Dawa from my team in the process. Still, with less than two weeks to spare, I did obtain a permit. The permit was for a mountain called "Shey Shikar." This posed a problem, as there was no "Shey Shikar" on any map. I thus sought the counsel of Elizabeth Hawley, the Grande Dame of Nepalese mountaineering history. Ms. Hawley has lived for nearly forty years in Kathmandu and keeps meticulous records of all mountaineering ascents. She interviews all climbing expeditions who obtain permits to climb in Nepal and keeps detailed records of what and where they have climbed. She is also a close friend of Sir Edmund Hillary and administers his Himalayan trust in Nepal. I had met with her previously during my trips to Everest and also through my work as a doctor. Ms. Hawley spread out an amazing record of all the climbing ever done in the Dolpo region. She showed us that, on one map, a peak otherwise listed as Junction Peak was called Shey Shikar. We determined that this was almost certainly the mountain. She also pointed out three adjacent twenty-thousand-foot mountains had never before been attempted. From the maps, it appeared that the best approach for Shey Shikar would be from the north. We thus ended up with a permit to attempt the first ascent of Shey Shikar from the north.

Ang Tsering arranged transportation and a cook staff. We found two new Nepali climbers, B. D. Shresta and Naga Dorje Sherpa, and set out for our climb.

Our team was supposed to unite in Kathmandu on September 10 and fly to the Dolpo on the twelfth. However, I had also been working for several months to arrange a cataract camp in Tibet. Dr. Ruit and I had done a phenomenal amount of preparatory work for the camp, and then the Chinese had notified us that we would have to come two weeks later than we had planned. The camp was now scheduled to last until September 17. Not to worry. Being acclimatized from working in Tibet, I expected to finish the camp and trek quickly to catch my expedition. Instead, I arrived from Lhasa to a frenzy of activity at the Kathmandu airport. "One of your teammates is dying and the government will not allow us to fly a helicopter into the Dolpo," I was told.

I joined the fray, telling officials that they would be reincarnated badly if my teammate died. I yelled and threatened to ruin careers. The counsel at the U.S. embassy finally got involved, and I soon hopped into a charter helicopter piloted by K. C. Madan, who would later gain worldwide acclaim for his daring rescue of Beck Weathers in 1996 from twenty-one thousand feet on Mount Everest.

The scenery was fantastic on the four-hour flight across Nepal, but I was too worried to enjoy it. I wondered who was ill, and with what. It was too early for altitude problems. I assumed something had happened to Billy Squier or one of the George Warings. Everyone else was too fit and experienced to be having trouble. Yet when we landed, it was Ed Webster who had to be helped into the chopper. He had lost muscular control and had been having irregular heartbeats. I flew back to Kathmandu with Ed and arranged for his evacuation to America. A month later Ed had surgery to remove a tumor from the base of his brain.

I returned to the Dolpo, now a full week behind my group. Nima Tashi met me at the airstrip in Dunhai. The trek in was gorgeous and pristine. We encountered no other Western sojourner. We followed the raging Suligad River through deep canyons to the village of Ringmo. It was as if we had stepped back three centuries, even in relation to the rest of Nepal. The smoky houses had no chimneys or stoves; cooking fires crackled in the center of dirt floors. Leaving Ringmo, we wove around the aquamarine water of Phoksundo Lake. The ice fortress of Kanjilaroba, the second highest peak in the Kanjiroba Himal, loomed above us as we started our ascent toward Shey Shikar.

I caught up to my teammates the day after they arrived at base camp, on a beautiful grassy knoll at the head of a valley. Further walking was blocked by a huge rock wall and three hanging glaciers. These features protected the highest mountain in the vicinity, which was labeled "Tso Karpo Kang" on all three of our maps. Our maps suggested that "Junction Peak" was back down the valley.

With our first crisis with Ed behind us, we now faced a second problem. The Ministry of Tourism had sent a liaison officer with us. He was a stern and righteous little fellow named Mr. Shresta. Mr. Shresta had never previously spent time camping. He had never trekked in the mountains. He was not happy about his assignment, but felt an earnest duty to perform what was needed for his country. He felt he needed to ensure that we only climbed "Shey Shikar" by the North Face, North Ridge. At base camp it became apparent that access to our slated mountain, the one we thought was Junction Peak by the topographic map, would be difficult, or even impossible. Fortunately, three other giant peaks loomed ahead and seemed more approachable. To actually reach Shey Shikar or Junction Peak, we would have to backtrack eight days around a large massif and attempt to negotiate a valley on the other side of a large ridge.

Fortunately, Mr. Shresta was feeling the effects of the altitude. It was also clear that he was not enjoying our mountain walk. He complained of a headache and lethargy, classic symptoms of acute mountain illness. I told him, as a doctor, that the only treatment for his mountain sickness was to drink large quantities of alcohol. This is, of course, the absolute worst treatment for altitude sickness. High altitude causes you to hyperventilate, which leads to a respiratory alkalosis—a shift of the blood chemistry that makes you feel an overall malaise and loss of appetite. The cure is to rest at the same altitude and drink large amounts of water so that the kidney can correct its acid–base shift. Drinking alcohol decreases the oxygen-carrying capacity of the bloodstream, greatly worsening altitude sickness. Moreover, drinking alcohol causes dehydration, which exacerbates the condition. As expedition leader, however, I felt that the appropriate therapy for our team was to give Mr. Shresta alcohol. We had with us Kukhri rum and plied Mr. Shresta with large amounts of it. We also had one excellent bottle of malt whiskey, which, as expedition leader, I felt needed to be sacrificed for this important cause.

The next morning Mr. Shresta felt worse. His head pounded from the combination of acute altitude sickness and a hangover. I told him the only choice at this point was to drink more whiskey. We gave him the hair of the dog, and after several more shots, he fell into a listless sleep. When he awoke a few hours later, not surprisingly, he felt much worse. A few shots of whiskey later, I made a difficult decision. For medical reasons, I concluded that Mr. Shresta must return to Kathmandu. In many ways, Mr. Shresta was greatly relieved. He could now keep his honor without remaining at a cold mountain base camp. The Hindu festival of Desai was coming up in one week, and he had several times expressed his dismay at missing the holiday.

I assured Mr. Shresta that we would not climb any mountain not named Shey Shikar, nor would we climb any mountain by any route other than the North Face or North Ridge.

The day after Mr. Shresta departed, we met a yak herder who only spoke one word of English. I was able to ask him if the large peak at the head of the valley was called Shey Shikar. "Yes!" he emphatically answered. Satisfied with his response, I then pointed to a second twenty-six-thousand-foot peak that loomed behind a small ridge and asked "And this mountain over here, would you also call this Shey Shikar?"

"Yes!"

I pointed to a third peak and posed the same question. "Is this Shey Shikar as well?"

"Yes!" he answered with absolute certitude.

Excellent. We now had our objectives safely in sight. I just had to make certain that our routes would all be on the North Face. I posed a few more questions to our affable yak herder. I pointed toward the setting sun and asked if this was the North Face, North Ridge direction. The yak herder smiled and nodded, "Yes!"

I quickly confirmed that the direction where the sun rose each morning was also considered the North Face, North Ridge of the valley. Finally, the southern flanks of our second Shey Shikar were confirmed to be the North Face, North Ridge.

We could now comfortably settle back into our beautiful base camp at the head of the valley and begin our exploration and reconnaissance. The binoculars came out, and we scattered on hikes to all the accessible ridges and glaciers. The views were glorious. The peaks south and east of us glistened with snow and ice; their valleys were lush and green. North and west stretched the arid landscape of Tibet. Rich, dark brown and red earth tones blended in a jagged mosaic to the horizon. We hiked to the top of several seventeen- to nineteen-thousand-foot hills and attempted to figure out what and how to climb. The three topographic maps were all different and all inaccurate. We had several heated debates about our objectives.

A consensus was finally reached. Junction Peak appeared to be suicidal from this side. To reach the mountain, we would first have to cross a rock ridge two thousand feet high. The rock, a friable, crumbly shale, was guarded by huge hanging glaciers with unstable ice cliffs. An enormous cornice loomed above the cliffs. There was no way around the ridge, because it eventually merged with a summit ridge of Kanjilaroba on one side and the Tso Karpo Kang Massif on the other. Fortunately, the local yak herders kept saying that "Shey Shikar" was definitely the big peak at the head of the valley, not the one over the ridge.

Bruce and Steve were not convinced, but agreed that we had no other good options. We set out to find a feasible route up our new "Shey Shikar." Three large icefalls descended from the mountain. All had extreme objective danger, with avalanches and rockfalls sweeping the approaches. A two-thousand-foot-high rock wall between two of the hanging glaciers could possibly provide a safe route.

A hike to base camp revealed a couple of possible lines. It seemed that once we surmounted the rock, we would be on a relatively flat glacier leading to the base of the mountain. The Nepalis, Mike, Bruce, and I scrambled around and found a hidden line of broken gullies that provided an easy, if somewhat dangerous, path to the mountain's base.

We returned and fixed a few ropes to make the route safer with loads. The next day everyone but the Georges headed up to the higher glacier. We brought three light bivy tents, set camp, and assessed our options. Shey Shikar (Tso Karpo Kang) dominated the scene. Directly above our tents was a fantastic ice buttress that rose at an average angle of fifty degrees. Farther around was a steeper ice wall that looked as if it topped out directly on the summit. Bruce was keen to go for the direct line, which—with vertical ice at more than twenty-one thousand feet—would provide a state-of-the-art challenge.

Our permit, of course, gave us permission to attempt Shey Shikar from the north only. The map, sun, and compass all suggested that we had a big problem deciding on either route. Still, Naga Dorje Sherpa was certain that the beautiful ice slope above us was the North Face of Shey Shikar. Much relieved, we melted snow, brewed up, and planned to start the climb at three o'clock in the morning.

—

Climbing by moonlight and headlamp, we broke trail through knee-deep fresh powder to the start of the technical climbing. We roped up and began climbing the best ice I had ever seen in the Himalayas, blue and as firm as soft plastic. Every placement set with a reassuring *thunk*. The slope meandered from forty-five to sixty-five degrees with plenty of bulges to rest the calves. Unfortunately, both Steve and Mike felt a bit ill. They, along with Bruce who still hungered for the steeper line, returned to camp.

The three Nepalis and I made quick progress. By midmorning we had sur-mounted the steep ice and moved onto a very long, low-angled summit ridge.

The snow was again knee deep. Our progress slowed. We took turns breaking trail. I led for two minutes and then doubled over, gasping for breath. Nima Tashi took over and led for twenty minutes. Then Naga Dorje did the same. I soon found that I was doubled over, gasping for breath, even when going last. The leadership role was adjusted, and Nima and Naga led the rest of the way. As we slowly ambled upward, clouds swirled in. For a period, we were in a surreal world, with a carpet and ceiling of clouds. We could only see a narrow band of the other three twenty-thousand-foot mountains in the range. I was aware that Shey Shikar was meant to be 20,141 feet and that my Avocet watch altimeter already read 21,588. Still, I had never been impressed by the accuracy of the watch. We continued upward.

The clouds darkened and my thoughts briefly floated to my friend and fre-quent partner, Rob Slater, who had recently perished on K2 because he continued climbing in an approaching storm. We were six thousand feet lower than he'd been, however, and I was certain that we could deal with the consequences of plodding on to the summit. We reached the top just as the cloud layers merged and it began to snow. We took out Nepali and American flags for a summit photo. I was posed next to Naga Dorje and Nima Tashi when we heard a loud *whump!* A crack appeared two feet downslope. It was as if we were in a cartoon in which Wile E. Coyote is suspend-ed for a moment before dropping—in the next instant, the earth fell from beneath us. We dived forward in desperate unison and firmly swung our ice axes into what remained of the summit. Our legs dangled over a sheer six-thousand-foot drop. The sound of the falling cornice thundered over my pounding heartbeat as we crawled back to safety.

The storm intensified as we started down. Soon a whiteout swirled around us and our upward track was obliterated. Traveling by instinct and taking advantage of any slight clearing, we struggled downward. Every time I decided we should dig a cave and wait things out, we got a glimpse of a short section below and dashed a bit farther. Using all of our combined experience, and quite a bit of luck, we eventually found a way down, winding among icefalls that looked suicidal from below.

The next day the storm cleared. We gazed about our plateau and saw that there were two other, slightly lower peaks that would have been closer in altitude to Shey Shikar, if it really was 20,141 feet high. Moreover, one had a spectacular-looking knife-edged North Ridge. Billy, Steve, Bruce, and I decided to climb it. "Shey Shikar 2," or Bahini Kang, gave us classic mountaineering at its best. The knife edge twisted among ice, snow, and rock with steep drops on both sides. The views from the top were spectacular—and this time the summit remained intact.

After extensive first-ascent photos, we headed down the ridge. Two-thirds of the way back Steve, who was leading, elected to head down a steep snow gully that would provide a much quicker descent to the glacier. I questioned his choice, because the slope was about forty-five degrees and could slide. Steve pushed a few ice boulders down the path. After watching them tumble safely, he started descending. When the rope became taut, I also began downclimbing. Twenty feet below the ridge, I heard a disturbing *whump*. A big crack spread across the snow in front of me. Steve and I desperately crabbed sideways, and Billy hurled himself off the other side of the ridge. The avalanche gained momentum. Steve and I reached the edge of the slab simultaneously, and the rope from above jerked tight. The avalanche cleaned the slope, but Steve and I were left without a scratch. Billy regained the ridge, and we all safely descended along the avalanche's path.

The next day Billy, the Sherpas, and I descended back to base camp. Steve and Bruce remained high to attempt a harder route on Shey Shikar 1 (Tso Karpo Kang). Mike and the two Georges were all feeling great and wanted to attempt a climb. I joined them on an attempt at another beautiful peak that dominated the next valley to the north. Two of the maps labeled the mountain as "Kang YaJa." The altitude was about right, and we decided someone might call it "Shey Shikar."

Nima Tashi and Naga Dorje joined us. We packed up and headed down our valley to "Shey Shikar 3." Meanwhile, Steve and Bruce climbed the best route of the trip, ascending very steep ice up the direct "North" Face of "Shey Shikar 1" (Tso Karpo Kang).

The next morning dawned clear and windless and we enjoyed a perfect day. The route up "Shey Shikar 3" (Kang YaJa) was always interesting and never overly difficult. The weather was perfect on top, and we soaked in the views of the Kanjiroba Himal on one side and the Tibetan plateau on the other.

We had now climbed three peaks called Shey Shikar, by four northern routes. Everyone had reached a virgin Shey Shikar summit. We decided to walk out via the famed Shey Monastery, glorified in *The Snow Leopard*. We followed a spectacular, narrow canyon that wound to the top of the Kang La pass. A harsh wind gusted into our faces, and we ventured into an area that looked like a barren moonscape. The land was arid, devoid of any sign of life. The peaks were now only sixteen thousand feet high and without snow. We walked down to the monastery and its cluster of tumbledown stone huts. A football-field-sized pile of intricately carved *mani* stones attested to the years of monastic life and tradition that existed here. One elderly caretaker monk was all that remained of life at what was once a center of Tibetan Buddhist thought. We toured the monastery. Golden Buddhas and antique *thanka* paintings were heaped upon each other in a clutter of precious art mixed with ancient musket guns and lances—perhaps remnants of the days when bandits roamed the Tibetan plateau.

Across the valley shone the sacred "Crystal Mountain." This peak was the focus of the great philosopher and poet Milarepa during his twelve years of silent meditation at the Tsalkang Refuge in the thirteenth century. Billy and I began to walk to the Tsalkang Refuge, a few hours away. Forty-five minutes down the trail, I spotted a building clinging to the side of a rock wall. I led Billy on a death route to reach the refuge. After negotiating four crumbling vertical cliffs of rubble, we arrived at a small red stone building in front of a cave. We also saw the easy trail we had missed winding back down to Shey. Two novice monks, both about ten years old and dressed in heavy red robes, smiled widely at our arrival. They showed us the refuge with its golden figures, which were even more impressive than those at Shey. They then led us along a path for another hour to a second refuge hidden on a ledge in the middle of a sheer, fifteen-hundred-foot cliff.

We basked in intense sunshine on a ten-foot-wide perfectly flat ledge. The only sight visible in any direction was Crystal Mountain. We were seated on a Tibetan carpet, and the novice monks brought out yak butter tea and dried yak cheese. A magical feeling engulfed us. A few minutes later the reincarnate Lama for the Shey region appeared from the small monastery at the edge of the platform. He sat placidly beside us, his broad, serene smile emanating a deep feeling of peace. We basked in the calm silence drinking tea and nibbling cheese.

After several cups of tea, I broke the reverie and asked the Rimpoche, "What is the meaning of life?" Sadly, he did not speak English. Yet by the time we rose to start the long trek back, I was clear about one thing: We must always continue to seek out and climb our own Shey Shikars. Adventure is facing the unknown, and life must remain an adventure.

26

Northern Pakistan

Our eye program in Nepal was picking up momentum, and word of our eye camps had slowly begun to spread through the climbing community. A few of my climbing friends looked in on our cataract surgery while visiting Nepal. One who showed particular interest in the project was Greg Mortenson.

In the spring of 1997 I received a phone call from Greg, who suggested we bring our eye program to northern Pakistan. Greg is a tall, affable climber from Montana who has recently cut a swath through central Asia with the patina of a modern-day Lawrence of Arabia. He has a tendency to wear native garb. His bright smile flashes above long, flowing white robes as Greg works tirelessly to improve conditions in Baltistan and the regions stretching from Mongolia to Pakistan.

Greg was on a K2 expedition in the early 1990s and became trapped high on the mountain in a storm. A desperate retreat followed. After three days without food he staggered into base camp to find it abandoned. His teammates had given him and his partner up for dead. With no food, Greg and his partner crawled from the mountain. Emaciated and exhausted, with their last waning strength they managed to reach a poor Baltistani village. They were taken in by a Baltistani family and nursed back to health. The family lived in a destitute state with the entire clan sharing a single mud-floored room. The peasants gave Greg everything they had. When he recovered, the family refused his offers of cash or gifts. They just smiled, saying they had helped him because he was their friend. Greg asked if there was anything he could do—anything they wanted or needed. The family finally admitted that they needed a school for their children. There was none in the village, and they were cut off from the main Baltistani town because there was no bridge over the gorge separating their home from the nearest trading center. Greg returned to the United States having found a new direction for himself. He was determined to raise money to start a school and build a bridge for the family that had saved his life.

Greg came home during the immediate post–Gulf War period when American resentment against the Islamic world was running high, as it is now. He tried to extol the virtues of the Baltistani people of northern Pakistan without much success. Then he met a Swiss physicist named Jean Hoerni who had also been trekking in Baltistan and shared Greg's admiration for the tough mountain people of the Karakoram. He, too, felt the need to help some of the most underserved people in the world and was immediately taken with both Greg and his project. Fortunately, in his earlier life Hoerni had been at the forefront of the development of the microchip and had invented and patented a related processing system. He was also one of the founding directors of the Intel Corporation and had made a large amount of money. Hoerni immediately signed on as Greg's benefactor. Greg returned to northern Pakistan to supervise the construction of his bridge and the building of the first school for the children of the Hushe Valley. Greg worked with the local ayatollahs to find teachers. Similar to the efforts that Sir Edmund Hillary extended for the Sherpa people in Nepal, Greg's work took place on every front, from fund-raising, to construction, to supervision. He followed his initial projects through to completion, and then began discussions with the ayatollahs and village leaders about other projects that could improve the lives of the Baltistani people. Overwhelmingly, he hit on improvement in eye care.

At the time, in all of Baltistan, there were only four people with basic medical degrees, none of whom had advanced training in ophthalmology. One physician, Niaz Ali, expressed an interest in learning eye surgery. Everywhere that Greg went, he was impressed by the number of middle-aged and elderly people who were totally blinded by cataracts. While traveling through Nepal, Greg watched one of the Himalayan Cataract Project's eye camps and became excited about expanding the project to improve eye care in northern Pakistan.

Greg approached me and said that the Hoerni Foundation would fund our efforts to bring eye care to the Karakoram. They would buy the microscope for Niaz Ali and all the required equipment and surgical instruments. Greg wanted me to come and perform an eye camp as soon as possible. I immediately began preparations. I told Greg the first step would be to send Niaz Ali to Kathmandu for instruction in microsurgery and basic cataract diagnosis. We arranged to send an ophthalmic assistant as well as Dr. Ali for tutorials. Dr. Ali would return to Skardu, where he would prescreen a large number of patients who were bilaterally blinded by cataracts. I would then arrive with Greg and do surgery on the first eye of all of the patients while Dr. Ali assisted. Then I would assist Dr. Ali while he restored sight to each patient's second eye.

I wanted to talk to Dr. Niaz Ali after his return from the course in Nepal. I obtained the phone number of the hotel he was staying at in Rawalpindi, the old city adjacent to the capital of Islamabad. Giving this number to the hospital operator at my office in Vermont, I asked her to please get Dr. Ali on the phone. A few moments later the operator called me and said, "Dr. Tabin, I'm sorry, but they tell me Dr. Ali is in the shower." I suggested we call back in ten minutes. Fifteen minutes later, the hospital operator called me again and said, "Dr. Tabin, they say Dr. Ali is still in the shower." I thought, well, these people from Baltistan probably don't get much of a chance to bathe. Most likely he is just taking a long shower. I suggested we call again in fifteen minutes. Fifteen minutes later, we again telephoned, and the operator again said, "Dr. Tabin, they say he is still in the shower!" Trying to sound like I understood what was going on, I explained to the hospital operator that there are some places where people don't often get regular showers. Perhaps Dr. Ali had gone to the public bath down the street from the hotel. We should try again in one hour. In one hour's time, the operator, now sounding exasperated, said, "Dr. Tabin, they keep telling me he is still in the shower!" I asked to have the operator connect me to the front desk of the hotel. For the eighth time that morning, she called Pakistan. I was greeted by the person at the desk who said, "And how am I helping you, sir?"

"I need to speak with Dr. Niaz Ali."

The man screamed into the telephone, "Dr. Ali is in Peshawar!"

It turned out Dr. Ali had gone to visit relatives in Peshawar, a large city about two hours from Islamabad on the border with Afghanistan.

I never was able to speak with Dr. Ali. I had to hope that everything would be prepared when we arrived.

—

When I began planning to make an eye camp expedition to northern Pakistan, I counted on bringing my ophthalmic assistant from the University of Vermont, Ray Brassard, to assist in managing patients during pre- and post-operative care. Ray is a superbly competent and intelligent ophthalmic technician who had previously spent time in Saudi Arabia running the contact lens service at the King Khalid Eye

Hospital in Riyadh. He understands the Islamic world. I had purchased a plane ticket for Ray, and we were set to depart for Pakistan when, in an inspired moment of wisdom, middle management at the health-care company running the University of Vermont hospitals decided that Ray could not accompany me unless he used up all of his vacation time for the upcoming two years. I tried to explain that I really needed Ray in Pakistan. Ray worked with me all the time, and if he stayed in Vermont while I was away, he would only be kept busy doing little odd jobs of minimal consequence. It seemed to make sense that since I considered the trip as part of my job, Ray should be allowed to come to northern Pakistan as part of his job. They did not understand, however, and did not consider the project worthwhile. They insisted Ray could only participate as part of his vacation. There was nothing I could do.

Ray's absence from the trip left me in need of an extra pair of hands for patient care. It also left me with a free plane ticket to Islamabad. While I mulled over what to do, my adventure buddy Neal Beidleman was being engulfed by the media hype caused from the publication of Jon Krakauer's best-selling *Into Thin Air*. Neal was the guide who had huddled with clients during the night, saved many lives, and emerged as one of the heroes in the 1996 Everest disaster. On a whim, I suggested to Neal that he might want to take a break from the publicity to come along as my ophthalmic assistant in Pakistan. I told him there was a chance he might even be able to perform eye surgery. The trip was being funded by the Hoerni Foundation. I told him that this would be an official "Hoerni [pronounced *horny*] expedition" to northern Pakistan. Despite the fact that Neal's wife was seriously pregnant, he immediately signed on.

We flew via London to Islamabad where we were met by Greg Mortenson's driver and streetwise all-around helper, Suleman. Suleman has a seemingly ageless face, a wide squat body engulfed in Islamic robes, and hair plagued by the worst dye job I have ever seen. Sitting on top of a quarter inch of gray roots is a thick mat of jet-black hair that seems to have been smeared with something akin to india ink. Suleman perpetually wears a quizzical smile, yet he radiates an air of both obsequiousness and confidence. He immediately greeted us by saying, "I am thanking you so much for your coming for helping my people sir," and whisked us into a car to bring us to our guest house. Greg had left a comforting note waiting for us in the car. In it he assured us that there wasn't much gunfire in the region we were going to and that we could make it safely.

After a few days of exploring the bazaars and back streets of Rawalpindi, the old city of narrow, winding, crowded alleyways adjacent to the wide avenues of the newly created capital, Islamabad, we met Greg and prepared to head north.

Before leaving Islamabad, we stopped at the Al Shifa National Eye Hospital. We walked in and I was immediately impressed with the cleanliness of the hospital and the quality of the equipment. I met with the director, who bragged about the high-quality modern care that was delivered. I asked him about any outreach programs or training for doctors in outlying areas. He bristled and said no, they had a full residency training and only the most qualified people in Pakistan were able to attend his training program, which was second to none in the country. He knew nothing about eye conditions in northern Pakistan, but this was not his concern. Eye care in northern Pakistan was the concern of officials in northern Pakistan. His priority was providing top-notch care to the people of Islamabad. He had never heard of Dr. Niaz Ali, and when I suggested the possibility of Dr. Ali coming to his institution for further training, the director was not receptive.

I soon found that the hospital director's abruptness was the result of schisms among the different Islamic sects in the country. Three sects of Islam divide the Islamic Republic of Pakistan. The majority of the country and all of the power and wealth sit with the Sunnis, who control the government, foreign policy, and most of the religion in the country. A tiny minority belongs to the Ishmaeli sect of Islam. They tend to be centered in the Hunza region in the center of the country and are fortunate to have the support of the very wealthy Aga Khan Foundation. Finally, there is a 15 percent minority who follow the doctrine of the Shiite Islamic world. The Shiites tend to be more fundamentalist than the Sunni.

The Baltistani people are an interesting blend. They are high-mountain people who combine Shiite Muslim values with a Buddhist philosophy and Buddhist tradition. They are discriminated against by virtually everyone, including my Sunni friend at the hospital in Islamabad.

Northern Pakistan is home to approximately four hundred thousand people. Because of religious prejudices, the amount of aid and support given to the area is virtually nil. Greg outlined our plan. The first leg of our trip would be a drive to Gilgit in the Hunza region following the Karakoram Highway. Neal and I packed our equipment into a rusting, run-down jeep—one microscope, surgical instruments, five hundred intraocular lenses, and food for the journey—and squeezed in among the supplies. We picked up a final few items at the crowded Dilly Bazaar in Rawalpindi before setting out along the Karakoram Highway, a thin ribbon of flat dirt track hugging a dramatic gorge that coils above the mighty Indus River. It is an amazing feat of engineering. The road is washed out every several hundred yards, with no barrier to prevent cars from tumbling between three hundred and two thousand feet into the raging river. The Karakoram Highway has, perhaps, the highest fatality rate of any roadway in the world. Festive Pakistani trucks adorned like carnival wagons with ribbons, banners, and slogans barrel along in both directions. The prevailing attitude is *inshallah,* which means, "It shall happen if it is Allah's will." *Inshallah* was the main mantra we heard throughout our time in northern Pakistan. "It just doesn't get any better than this" became the mantra Neal and I adopted for the Hoerni expedition.

Our broken-down high-performance sports jeep was being driven at a breakneck speed along the winding, bumpy road. I have always had a cast-iron stomach, but on this ride I badly needed a dose of Dramamine. We raced around corners, silently barreling past trucks with the large blazing slogan: HONK YOUR HORN AROUND BLIND CORNERS. We continually beseeched the driver to slow down, but he always answered, "*Inshallah,* we will be okay." We continued along the bumpy road for twelve hours, and just when Neal and I decided that "it doesn't get any better than this," the skies clouded over and it began to pour. The monsoon rains pounded down on the car, creating poor visibility, which only inspired the driver to go faster on the now very slippery path. We began skidding on every turn, veering closer and closer to the fatal drop into the river. Again, just as we began to think that it certainly "couldn't get any better than this," we began to notice rather large stones bouncing down from the slopes above and smashing onto the roadway.

Greg, Neal, and I began to think the better part of valor would involve stopping overnight to sleep; the driver had already kept the pedal on the metal continuously for fourteen hours. Now, however, we were given no other option. A massive landslide blocked the entire road. Rocks the size of small Volkswagens continued tumbling down all around us, and finally he agreed to retreat to the last village, which we had passed forty-five minutes before. We turned around and drove for less than five minutes before finding that the road was completely blocked by a landslide in this direction as well. We were now trapped between two landslides in the pouring rain. "It doesn't get any better than this!" Everyone tried to sleep for a few hours while curled inside the back of the jeep.

We woke to pouring rain. It continued to rain for twenty-four hours before temporarily stopping. A few hours after the rain ceased, work crews appeared at the opposite end of the slide and, using only brute force, began maneuvering the rocks and dirt from the road. In less than three hours, the road was clear and we were able to recommence our joyride toward Gilgit. The views became more spectacular as we progressed. The shifting moonscape above the Indus River extended as far as we could see in either direction, with occasional clearing of the clouds and glimpses of high snow-covered peaks. Just before reaching Gilgit, we passed under the enormous mass of Nanga Parbat.

Although Nanga Parbat is only the world's seventh highest mountain, its vertical rise is second to none. We were driving along the Karakoram Highway at approximately four thousand feet above sea level. Above us, Nanga Parbat towered at nearly twenty-seven thousand feet. We were looking up at a vertical relief of more than four miles. We then moved down into the Hunza Valley, fabled for its sweet apricots and inhabitants who, according to rumor, routinely live until the age of 120.

When we finally arrived at the missionary eye hospital, we wobbled out of the tattered jeep and onto a fastidiously manicured lawn and garden. The hospital was spotless. Neal, Greg, and I spent a wonderful evening with the American missionary doctor, Mitch Ryan, and his wife and children. They projected a perfect image of American Christian missionary efforts. Their neat clothes and all-American fresh-scrubbed look were sure to send church donors scurrying to support their project. Unfortunately, the hospital's patient volume was much lower than expected. Mitch had gone to England and learned to do microscopic surgery with lens implants, which had previously never been performed in this region. The local ayatollah, however, was saying that the Christian doctors were putting Christian eyes into the people. Clearly, no Islamic person should have Christian eyes.

Greg produced an ingenious idea for resolving Mitch's difficulty in recruiting patients. A copy of the precious Islamic book, gilt in red and gold cloth, was placed in patients' hands just before their patches were removed. When the patches were taken off, they could see for the first time in years. Tears of joy washed down their faces, and the first sight they beheld was the Koran. Certainly their Islamic eyes were restored. From then on, we received only support from the local clergy. Greg had arranged for a busload of patients to come from the Hushe Valley for us to treat in Gilgit. These patients arrived, and I spent a day in the operating room with Mitch, showing him my technique for cataract surgery. Mitch had already become a skilled cataract surgeon and after one more pleasant evening, we planned to see our postoperative patients and then continue with Niaz Ali to Skardu.

The snaking, dusty road from Gilgit swung back under the massive bulk of Nanga Parbat as we rejoined the Karakoram Highway along the Indus River back toward Skardu. The road continued to wind and weave with long drops down to the Indus River, often littered with trucks that had failed to negotiate turns. Our driver continued to speed along repeating the mantra, "*Inshallah*." Neal continued his mantra that "it just can't get any better than this," and smiled as the road fully eased away from being a thin ribbon above.

After another long day's drive, we finally rolled into Skardu. A flat, broad valley led to a dusty, sprawling village of crude, unpainted wooden shanties. It was like pulling into a Wild West boomtown. A one-story sprawl spread from the center of the village. Across the main road at intervals of every few hundred feet were large red and black banners proclaiming, in English and Urdu, our free eye surgery camp. Neal and I would be staying at the K-2 Hotel, and as our beaten-up jeep rumbled through the dusty city streets we passed crowds of bicycles, pedestrians, and goats. Open-air markets dominated the central downtown area. Disorder was everywhere. From each market stall came the raucous sounds of anxious shoppers and vendors haggling over prices. The concept of forming lines was completely foreign here; everyone simply pressed forward in swarms. I would soon find that this type of disarray was not limited to open-air markets.

At the hotel Neal and I checked into comfortable rooms and ran into some old climbing friends from the East Coast who had just returned from an attempt on Latok's North Ridge. Barry Rugo, Tom Nonis, Mark Ritchey, and John Bouchard had just returned from a seven-week struggle on the mountain. They hadn't gotten very far, having been plagued by considerable danger from rockfall throughout their attempt. The team was eager to go home. Neal and I were eager to begin our eye camp. Neal had been doing some extensive reading about the anatomy and physiology of the eye and felt he was ready to take an active role in the camp. I mentioned that, because of the sheer number of patients, it might even be necessary for him to perform some surgery. To prepare, Neal raided the fruit bowl in the hotel restaurant and began practicing his surgical techniques on a peach. He assaulted the fruit with a surgical knife and attempted to sew the fleshy pieces together again. Although he was unable to bestow sight upon any of the peaches, his suturing technique was reasonably good.

The next morning we set out early for the hospital. As we approached, we found hundreds of patients and family members squatting, staring at us. Many were praying to Allah. A number of the seemingly well-to-do patients accosted us as we walked forward, pulling down their lower eyelids, yelling in Urdu and pointing at their eyes. Others tugged on our shoulders and pointed at their eyes. Greg tried in vain to assemble the masses into something resembling a line. Mass pandemonium reigned. Dr. Niaz Ali led the way to his small examination area where he had a modern slit lamp microscope, the only one in all northern Pakistan, a region the size of New England. I asked Greg to continue his efforts in organizing the patients so that we could examine them one by one. In the meantime Neal and I set out to find the room where we would be performing surgery.

We walked through hospital corridors overrun with diseased and dying patients. The acrid odor of human excrement and urine mixed with antiseptic hung heavily in the air. The operating room, which Neal and I finally found at the end of a dank hallway, took us aback. Shards of glass from broken I.V. bottles littered the floor, and filthy surgical instruments collected dust in corners. Against one wall, a row of wooden and cardboard boxes rotted from the inside out. This was far from the sterile work space I needed. I spoke with Greg and Niaz Ali, explaining that the room had to be made absolutely clean before any surgery could take place. I asked that every last piece of furniture be removed. The floor needed to be swept and then cleaned with sterilizing soap before anything could be reorganized.

I left the cleansing of the operating room in the hands of Dr. Ali's staff. Accompanied by Neal, I returned to the examination area, where the bedlam and pandemonium had not improved. Niaz Ali had managed to form a line of many of the poorer patients; the wealthier patients, however, and those who felt they had connections, continued to push to the front, grabbing at our shoulders, pulling down their lower eyelids and pointing at their eyes.

When we were finally able to begin examining patients, the array of pathology we found was amazing. Many people had symptoms from the end stages of diseases that, in the Western world, are treated in their earliest phases. We had hundreds of cataract surgery patients as well as many patients with eyelid tumors and other eyelid diseases. Neal was pleased to find out that, while I taught Niaz Ali microsurgical cataract surgery, he could step in as the eyelid surgery specialist. After an exhausting six hours of examining the seemingly never-ending line of patients, Dr. Ali, Neal, and I walked back to the operating room to see how the cleaning had progressed.

Nothing had been done. I was appalled. Every shard of glass and rotting box lay exactly where they had been six hours before. "Didn't I ask for someone to clean the operating room?" I asked Dr. Ali.

"Yes sir, but who is for cleaning? Unfortunately, the ayatollah has said that no women are now to be working here and it is a well-known fact that women are better cleaners than men, so what are we to do?"

I tried to control myself. "Find someone to clean this operating room!"

"But who is for cleaning? *Inshallah*, someone will come for cleaning tomorrow."

"Dr. Ali, we are supposed to start surgery tomorrow!" I said.

"*Inshallah.*"

"We need to find someone to clean *today*. What about all of these people standing around?" I pressed.

"Oh no, sir! These are families of the patients. They are not here for cleaning. But *inshallah*, someone will be here for cleaning tomorrow."

Neal, who had been following the exchange, rolled up his sleeves and began moving the boxes and sweeping up glass. I moved to help Neal, but Dr. Ali stepped in my way.

"No, sir, it's not for doctors to clean. *Inshallah*, someone will clean tomorrow."

Again I said, "Dr. Ali, we need to have this room spotless *by* tomorrow."

—

While I finished the examination and preparation of the patients, Neal undertook the enormous task of completely cleaning and sterilizing the operating room. Thanks to Allah, Neal was there.

The next morning we returned to the hospital bright and early for surgery. Dr. Ali was supposed to assist me for the first several cases. Neal acted as our circulating nurse and technician, while Greg Mortenson helped handle the flow of patients. The first several surgeries went very well, but during the third case, I felt something moving near my foot. Something sharp pierced my ankle, and I let out a scream. I looked down in time to see a huge rat scurry across the operating room floor. Nurse Neal swiftly ended the rat's life using one swift blow with the handle of a broom, like a true Aikido master. During the next few days he killed three rats that visited the operating room during surgery. I later spoke to the head of the hospital about the rat infestation. He agreed that, yes, this was a problem, but, "What are we to do? We have tried traps but it is not working." In search of a solution, he asked, "What are you doing to keep rats out of your operating room at home, Doctor?" I explained that in the States we keep our operating rooms and hospitals clean, and rodents don't usually live on our ward.

—

The next day we had the pleasure of checking post-operative patients who could now see, many for the first time in years. The devout Pakistanis immediately went down on their knees and thanked Allah for restoring their sight. With big smiles we returned to the operating room, where I continued to operate with Dr. Ali assisting.

On the third day of camp, Dr. Ali started doing cataract surgery with me as his assistant. He was a slow learner, and began by performing parts of each case while I took over on the rest. We switched back and forth when the surgery became difficult. In one particularly complicated case, the iris prolapsed out of the wound, and

Dr. Ali began to have some serious difficulties. I suggested that we quickly change seats so that I could continue the surgery. As I took over the case, I began to explain why things had gone wrong and how they needed to be corrected. "Dr. Ali, the problem is that there is posterior vitreous pressure. You have applied too much pressure with your hands on the side of the globe, which put pressure on the vitreous, and now there is more pressure in the vitreous than the forward chamber of the eye. Before we do anything else, we need to equalize the pressures, so I'll put a stitch in the superior part of the wound and push the posterior capsule of the lens back with an air bubble. Next I'll—"

"Geoff?" a voice asked from across the room, "Who are you talking to?" It was Neal.

I looked up from the microscope at Dr. Ali's now empty seat. I quickly returned my attention to the surgery and finished the case. Then I performed a second surgery and a third without hearing from Dr. Ali. Forty-five minutes later he finally stepped back into the operating room.

"Sir, how is our patient?" Dr. Ali casually asked.

"Fine," I said, "but why did you—"

"Oh, I am so happy, sir! I am so happy! I was so worried I went to pray to Allah. I prayed and prayed to Allah. I knew if I prayed to Allah, the patient would be okay. He is okay, sir?"

"Yes."

"Oh, all praises be to Allah!"

"Okay, now I need you to go slowly in your surgery, and this time you will put in the intraocular lens."

"*Inshallah!*"

"No, insha-*Ali*," I corrected.

Despite my best efforts, I never could convince Dr. Ali that a surgeon's skill is more important than his faith.

—

The eye camp slowly found its form. Sight was restored to more and more patients, and word spread that the Western doctors were curing the blind. In addition to the blind, all manner of diseased people crowded our small eye clinic. It didn't matter whether someone had eye disease, kidney disease, heart disease, or a tumor on his leg, our camp seemed to be the place to come if you needed a "miracle." People flocked to the clinic and pressed forward, pointing at their ailing parts, demanding to be seen and cured. Those with non-eye problems we had to dismiss, explaining that it was not Allah's will that they be seen.

Dr. Ali needed some time to learn several of the surgical steps, but he slowly became more adept. While he perfected his skills, Neal preformed surgery for the first time. I put him to work repairing eyelids that had been scarred from trachoma, a condition in which the lashes turn in and rub against the cornea.

Dr. Ali asked me to perform surgery on the daughter of a very important man in the local military. He was a big general, and Dr. Ali made it clear that I must do the surgery and that it must go well. The girl was suffering from blocked tear ducts, which caused her tears to well up in her eyes and run down her face. It was not a blinding condition, and I did not want to spend the time needed for her surgery when we could restore sight to people blinded by cataracts. But Dr. Ali insisted, and I reluctantly agreed. The surgery to create a new tear drainage channel is easy, but fraught with hazards. You must create a new hole from the edge of the eye into the nose that passes near several large blood vessels. In America the surgeon uses a head-mounted spotlight to aid his vision. Here I depended on the hospital's over-head spotlight. The surgery proceeded smoothly until the point at which I dissected the large angular vein. The power went out. It was pitch black. The auxiliary genera-tor was switched on, and I nervously continued. I was just cutting the new tear channel in one of the girl's eyes when the auxiliary generator blinked off, leaving us at the most critical stage of surgery—without any lights. I had created a small cavity in the woman's face, blood was oozing, and I couldn't see what I was doing! Salvation came in the form of a penlight, which Neal held over the eye as I worked. Miraculously, I finished the surgery without a disaster.

—

Despite the hardships we had to maneuver around, the surgical camp in Skardu was a success by any objective or subjective measures. The community found amazement and joy in the restoration of sight, and we had no major compli-cations with any surgery. To celebrate, the hospital administration and local govern-ment asked if they could put on a special dinner in our honor. Neal and I gratefully accepted. Before dinner, our hosts asked Neal and me if we liked goat. The Pakistanis exchanged small smiles and winks, intimating that something very special was going to happen. Neal and I agreed that, yes, we did like goat. This triggered more smiles, nods, and winks, and exclamations of "They like goat! They like goat, good goat!" Neal and I grinned at each other, nodded and smiled.

In anticipation of our celebratory banquet, we dressed in our best and cleanest clothes. At the district head's house we were escorted into a plush living room where handwoven mattresses adorned the floor. We sat on these mattresses, which were covered in ornately embroidered silk, and dinner conversation began. The seven officials at the table spoke in Urdu and drank the local water, which Neal and I could not touch for fear of parasites. We knew that because this was a Muslim country, alcohol would not be served. Still, we were expecting that Coke, Fanta, or bottled water (available in every stall in town) would be offered. None was forthcoming. Neal and I had just completed more than ten hours in the hot operating room and were both very hungry and very thirsty. We sat and smiled, listening to animated Urdu chattering while fantasizing about cool beverages. After this had gone on for a few hours, our hosts brought out a game of Skittles. Neal and I played against the district commissioner and hospital chief—and lost miserably. The Pakistani audience cheered joyously as Neal and I lost one Skittle game after another.

Finally, at nine o'clock, a servant brought out a large steaming bowl of what appeared to be water covered by a thin film of floating fat. We were each given a bowl. I peered into mine and saw a few appetizing strands of stray goat hair drifting in the "soup." We had no spoons or utensils. Everyone put the bowls to their mouths and made hearty slurping sounds. I gingerly tipped some of the liquid into my mouth and found that it consisted essentially of goat fat floating on boiling water— no seasoning or salt. Thankfully, we had also been given some chapatis—thick, flat bread. Neal and I were so thirsty and hungry that we ate a considerable amount of the bread and managed to drink a small amount of the soup. I was finishing my fourth chapati when a servant entered the room carrying a large steel bowl. He labored under its weight, using two hands to support the abundance of roughly chopped goat meat with which the bowl was laden. A femur bone protruded from the top, little bristles of hair still clinging to its distal end. I envisioned one of Fred Flintstone's prehistoric drumsticks. The servant plopped the entire bowl down in front of me. Trying to grin enthusiastically, I took a large piece of the goat meat, probably twelve ounces or more, and passed the bowl to Neal. Everyone immediately became very agitated. "No, no, no!" they shouted, pushing the entire bowl back to me. I stared down at the mountain of goat meat, and then looked up to see a servant staggering from the kitchen with a second steel bowl piled even higher than mine. This he plopped in front of Neal. During the next few minutes, an entire goat's carcass was distributed among the seven people at the meal. Approximately ten to fifteen pounds of goat meat plus an assortment of bones was placed in front of each man. We began to gnaw tentatively at our meat. There was no sauce, no condiment, no salt or pepper. There were also no forks, no knives, and no napkins. And there was still nothing to drink except the local water. We were left with just the essential—goat—and what a lot of goat it was. Neal and I gnawed on our bland, boiled goat meat while the officials smiled broadly, indicating that the animal had been slaughtered in our honor. They were most pleased to have a meal of "good goat" and chewed happily.

Just when I had resigned myself to plowing through the goat meat, a new plate was brought and placed in front of me, the most-honored guest. This dish contained the heart, the liver, the intestines, and the brain of said goat. The Pakistani made a very large show of the fact that it was in my honor that the goat had been sacrificed, and now it was my honor to have all of the entrails. Neal and I glanced at each other, attempting to hold our laughter in check. I looked away and bit my lip. My stifled laughs escaped in the form of tears. I glanced at Neal again. He was having the same problem; tears streamed down his face. We knew it would be impolite to laugh, but how does one respond when presented with fifteen pounds of goat and entrails? Not to mention being given the first chance to eat the brain as a token of the gratitude of people who don't speak your language. As tears came down our faces, Neal and I continued to fight our laughter. Our host assumed these were tears of joy, and a happy evening was had by all.

As Neal and I rode back to our hotel that evening, Neal reiterated his mantra, "It just doesn't get any better than this." For once, he was right.

—

In 1998 I was prepared to return to northern Pakistan to continue working with Dr. Niaz Ali. After our initial cataract camp, he had continued doing cataract surgery and by all reports had markedly improved his skills. We had also sent him to Peshawar for a one-year course in public health ophthalmology to improve his diagnostic skills. It seemed to be the perfect time to return to work with him on advanced cataract surgery techniques and full ophthalmologic care.

About two weeks prior to my departure for Pakistan, the American embassies in Kenya and Tanzania were bombed. Three days before I was scheduled to leave, I received a phone call at home. On the other end of the line was Suleman, my driver from Rawalpindi.

"And how are you sir?" Suleman asked. "Most Salaams to your family, sir."

"I'm fine thanks, Suleman. Greetings to you as well."

Suleman quickly cut to the point of his call. "I am hearing you are coming for working in Pakistan, sir. I am hearing, sir, that America will soon be bombing into Afghanistan. If American is bombing into Afghanistan, I think maybe it is not so good for you to be coming to Pakistan. Please sir, maybe you should be coming later because I am not wanting to be driving if America is bombing to Afghanistan."

This was the first I had heard of any planned American retaliation. As soon as I had thanked Suleman for the warning and ended the conversation, I telephoned the American State Department. They told me that they had just issued a new warning cautioning as strongly as possible that Americans not travel to Pakistan. They had also recalled all nonessential American embassy personnel and families from the area. I asked the State Department expert on Pakistan if America was planning on bombing Afghanistan. He said this was absolutely not the case. He had heard nothing of the sort. The reason for the warning, he said, was purely because of threats from militant groups within Pakistan. It had nothing to do with other parts of the world.

Because of the strength of the State Department warning, I canceled my trip to see Dr. Niaz Ali. Instead, I altered my plans so that I could visit doctors in Sikkim. Two days after Suleman's phone call, America did indeed send missiles into both Afghanistan and Sudan. I could not help but wonder how the American government and the State Department had possibly imagined that Osama bin Laden, their stated target, had not figured out the impending missile attack if my friend Suleman, a taxi driver on the streets of Rawalpindi, knew about it a full two days in advance.

27

SEILSHAFT

Did Dan Reid have a death wish? Do I have a death wish? The answer to both questions is emphatically no! It is a joy of life that we shared. Dan Reid exuded and savored life. An old Hindu expression states, "It is not how many Dawalis you have seen, but how many firecrackers you have lit." It is more important to have lived much than to have lived long. Dan Reid maximized his life. He was constantly turning blind corners to face new challenges. He lived his life with passion. He threw himself fully into every moment of his time on earth. I do feel sad about Dan's death and those of my other climbing partners who have died—I miss their company and am sorry that we will not share future adventures—but I would not have changed the way Dan Reid lived his life in order to prolong his existence. I do not believe in reincarnation or an afterlife, but I know that some of Dan Reid lives on in those of us who knew him. His spirit will be passed on to my children, as is his name. My son, Daniel Reid Tabin, was born in 1999.

—

I have had more than my share of close calls, and each has heightened my appreciation for life. My many scrapes in the mountains and elsewhere have helped me become more cognizant of the small joys of everyday life. They have increased my desire to experience, feel, and savor every moment of my life. Being willing to fully commit to an adventure—and fail—has helped me to take risks in other areas of my life. This mentality also leaves me with a healthy level of fear when appropriate. I am keenly aware of my own abilities and limits. I now have a better sense of how close to the edge I can push. I no longer climb as well as I did twenty years ago. My enthusiasm, however, remains just as strong. I still love to climb rock, ice, and mountains as well as hike, ski, and just spend time in the high peaks. Despite a day job and family, I still head for the hills at every opportunity and train at my local rock climbing gym or home bouldering wall several times each week. The routes I climb are no longer major first ascents or cutting edge by world standards. All that matters, however, is that they are cutting edge and first ascents for me and that they keep my fun-o-meter in the red zone.

I cannot explain why I am alive while many of my friends, who were much finer mountaineers than myself, are dead. Part of the explanation is pure luck. Certainly many of my friends who have died were careful, cautious, and skillful mountaineers. Many were much more talented. I was very lucky to survive my teens and twenties. In fact, I was lucky to survive my thirties. On many occasions I thought I was going to die for certain. I watched several large avalanches and rockfalls descend directly upon me. Had my position been altered by only inches, I would have been squashed like an ant under a shoe. There have also been innumerable other situations in which a combination of pure luck and my partners' skill kept me barely alive. One such occasion occurred on Castle Rock in Boulder Canyon, Colorado, when I was leading high above my last point of attachment to the rock. I was fifty feet above my last point of attachment and ninety feet above a large rock ledge where my partner, George Lowe, was belaying the rope. When I fell, George sensed the dire consequences of my fall and began playing in the extra slack in the rope. Seeing the length of my fall, he untied from his belay stance and jumped to take in my extra slack. The rope jerked me to a halt—headfirst, less than a foot from a large rock ledge. Had I gone an additional few inches, I would have exploded like a watermelon falling from a skyscraper.

That fall was one of many times during which I wished I were somewhere else. When I was a child one of my favorite cartoons featured a little turtle, Tudor, who begged a wizard to allow him to experience various adventures. Invariably he got into trouble. Each episode ended with him screaming, "Mr. Wizard! Mr. Wizard! I don't want to be a knight of the round table anymore!" Mr. Wizard would then say, "Dreezle, drizzle, drazzle, drome, time for this one to come home," and Tudor Turtle would be whisked to safety just before the Black Knight's lance skewered him. Alas, I have no wizard. My cries of "Mr. Wizard, I don't want to be a mountaineer anymore!" have been in vain. I have had to rely on my own skills, a bit of luck, and my partners for survival. Taking responsibility for the outcome is what makes an adventure.

Climbing a mountain gains meaning only from the experience, not the outcome. Notoriety is fleeting. But the friendships forged in shared adventures remains. The only tangible benefit that success on any mountain has given me has been that it helped me meet and share future adventures with some great climbers. One such encounter with fame came after an American Alpine Club annual meeting in Atlanta. As I staggered out from the bar late in the evening, a man approached me. His face was more weathered than any of the mountains shown in the slide shows. I instantly recognized Fred Beckey, a legendary figure in American mountaineering. Fred had been a full-time climber for most of his seventy-plus years and had pioneered more classic climbs than any other human alive. From Chouinard to Harrer to Lowe, every top climber for the past forty years has teamed up with Fred for first ascents of many of the greatest routes in the world. He is reputed to have a (perhaps mythical) little black book of all the greatest unclimbed routes in the world. Fred is so secretive about his destinations that he often makes his climbing partners call him on pay phones scattered across the country, where he gives clues and hints about where they might be meeting to climb, not wanting to reveal the destination of his coveted first ascent such that, if the trip fell through, the other person might snag the first climb of the rock, mountain, or spire.

Moving out of the bar, I heard Beckey's voice call out, "Tabin, Tabin, right?" I turned and he said, "Hey Tabin, I'm Fred Beckey. I've heard about the climbing you've been doin' and I think we oughta get together and do something. What are you doing now?" I sobered partway up with the prospect of Fred enticing me on an adventure and told him that I had no plans. He said, "Great. Come with me. We're goin' to the best place in America." He put his arm around me and flattered me by saying, "I've been following your climbs, yes sir. You've been doin' some good stuff. Come on, Tabin, we're goin' out tonight," and he pushed me into a cab. He ordered the driver to take us to the Cheetah Three Lounge.

A thirty-dollar cab ride later we got out and Fred commanded me to "Pay the man. Come on, pay him, pay him!" We then came to the entrance of the Cheetah Three Lounge, where a flashing neon light advertised 24 TOTALLY NUDE TABLE DANCERS. The admission was twelve dollars per person. Fred assured me it would be money well spent as he again commanded me, "Come on. Pay him, pay the man!" I paid both cover charges, and we walked in and sat at a table. The music was a bit too loud to carry on a conversation so we just admired the mountain scenery. Fred then became very excited and agitated, and commanded me, "Give me twenty dollars quick." I gave him a twenty-dollar bill and Fred disappeared.

A few moments later a gorgeous teenage girl was shuffling from her left foot to her right foot and back to her left, almost in time to the music, on our table. Fred began a nonstop banter, barely audible over the blaring music, saying, "Boy, you look like you're in pretty good shape. Yes sir, I'll bet with a shape like yours you probably do a lot of athletics. Do ya? Well, do ya ever climb? We're here for a climbing convention and I was thinking, there's actually a really good place to climb only three hours from here and well, if you can get a friend and a car . . . have you got a car, or maybe you got a friend who's got a car? If you could pick us up at our hotel at six o'clock in the morning on Sunday, we'll take ya climbing, 'cause we're here for a climbing convention. Do ya like rock climbing? I think you'd like it. You got the right body for climbing. So what do ya think? You and a friend, six o'clock Sunday morning . . ." A few moments later the song ended and the girl, twenty dollars richer, went to another table, where the patron had paid twenty bucks for her to adorn his view. Fred followed her to the other table and continued his rant. "So, Sunday morning, you'll pick us up at the hotel at six o'clock. Right? We're goin' to the Tennessee Wall, it's good rock . . ." The girl, who still had not responded to Fred with so much as a nod, continued to shuffle left foot to right foot to left foot, still almost in time to the music. An enormous mountain of a man came over and asked Fred to please not speak to the girl while she was dancing. Fred replied that he was just finishing making arrangements for going climbing on Sunday.

The next thing I knew a hand was securely gripped onto my belt and a second hand clutching my collar; an alley door materialized and opened. Fred and I found ourselves lying faceup in an alley staring at the stars. Although Fred and I have become good friends and stay in touch by e-mail, this remains the only outdoor adventure we have shared.

—

Sharing an adventure, and working together to survive, builds very tight bonds. All pretenses are stripped away. There can be no facade or games. This allows great insights into both yourself and your partner. The intensity of these interpersonal experiences has led to many of my closest friendships. I had the privilege of spending an evening with Heinrich Harrer, the great adventurer whose writings greatly influenced my life. The spry octogenarian—who skied in the 1936 Olympics, made the first ascent of the Eiger Nordwand, spent *Seven Years in Tibet* and became a tutor and friend to the Dalai Lama, made important first ascents in Alaska and the Andes, was the first outsider to encounter the highland Dani, the first to penetrate the

Carstensz Range, and the first to climb its major peaks—was warmly animated as he recounted anecdotes from his amazing life. I asked Heinrich what he felt were his most significant and satisfying accomplishments. He instantly replied, *"Seilshaft"*— the friendship of the rope, referring to the lifelong bonds he formed with his partners who shared the experiences.

My feelings of *seilshaft* are also strong. The bond of the rope, where you mutually trust your life to your partner's skill and judgment, has created enduring friendships for me. The mountain relationship is totally honest. You know exactly what both you and your partner are capable of; you must accept each other's limitations and work together to succeed. This leads to a relationship based on acceptance and trust and produces long-term, caring loyal friendships. I stay in close touch and still climb with most of the people mentioned in the pages of this book. Most of them have continued to live lives of adventure and are thriving as we reach our middle years. Bob Shapiro, my partner from Oxford, Mount Kenya, and Carstensz Pyramid, returned to America, where he shifted his focus from mountain to intellectual adventure. He now has more degrees than a thermometer and has joined me on the faculty at the University of Vermont College of Medicine. Bob lives just a few miles from me and continues to be one of my closest friends. Although he is no longer pushing himself in the mountains, he has ascended to the cutting edge of neurobiology research, specializing in the anatomic mechanisms of migraine headaches. He is also active in the adventures of his children.

Like Bob and myself, several of my other closest climbing friends have incorporated fatherhood into their adventures. I became an insta-dad to three daughters and have added another daughter and son. My responsibility to my family has not changed my attitude to climbing. I was already backing away from the edge in dangerous sports and working full time as a physician when I got married. My expeditions abroad had already shifted to teaching eye surgery, not climbing high peaks. But my love of climbing has not been lessened by my love for my wife and children. I had the good sense and good fortune to marry a tolerant partner who respects my need to climb. On my wedding day Carl and Nora Tobin, Neal Beidleman, Rich Romano, and I made the first ascent of an ice climb in Smugglers Notch, Vermont. In honor of the day, our friendship, and a vow to keep climbing, we named the route "Prenuptial Agreement." Less than two hours later, I shared my wedding vows.

Many of my friends have also been able to balance climbing and a family. Several married climbing wives. My oldest climbing partner, Henry Lester, still climbs hard. He and his wife, Peyton, have two sons. They live in Boulder, where he is a financial adviser. Neal Beidleman is married with two children and lives in Aspen,

Colorado. Neal uses his aeronautical engineering degree to consult on a diverse array of projects ranging from satellite communications, to a vest that keeps people alive in an avalanche, to extra-warm, moisturizing high-altitude mittens. Carl Tobin lives in Anchorage, Alaska, with his wife, Nora, a top adventure racer, and their two children. Carl teaches biology at Alaska Pacific University. Tom Dickey went back to school and became a physician's assistant. He and his wife have a daughter and live outside Boulder. George Lowe has two new daughters from a second marriage to a climbing orthopedic surgeon and lives in Golden, Colorado. Nobody mentioned above has slowed down in their enthusiasm for climbing or adventure.

Others, like Bob Shapiro, have shifted their focus more towards family and career. Sam Moses, who joined Bob and me in New Guinea, has gone on to become a very successful freelance writer after leaving his staff position at *Sports Illustrated*. He moved to Hood River, Oregon, where he has become a devoted sailboarder as well as a husband and father. Louis Reichardt has continued his meteoric rise through academia. Louis is one of the most prominent neuroscience researchers in the world and has lost none of his curiosity or wit. And—*like parent, like child*—all of Reichardt's brilliant children have matriculated at the world's most prestigious universities. Jim Morrissey, the leader of our 1983 East Face expedition to Mount Everest, has gone on to father enough children to populate a small town while continuing his cardiothoracic surgery practice. Every five years we have a reunion attended by all living members of the expedition at Morrissey's ranch near Yosemite.

Other friends have continued to devote much of their energy to climbing. Steve Ruoss has managed to combine his mountaineering with a career as a pulmonary specialist at Stanford. We still manage to get together and climb at least once per year. Jim Frush, the leader of my 1988 Everest expedition, is currently the president of the American Alpine Club and using his skills as a lawyer to promote environmental causes and conservation of mountain lands, both in America and around the world. The Burgess twins have continued living on the edge and have become much-sought-after speakers and guided trip leaders. Carlos Buhler remains a cutting-edge sponsored climber. Specializing in small, light expeditions, he continues to push the limits of technical difficulty in the Himalayas. Mr. Hong Gil Om from the Korean Everest team in 1988 has gone on to climb all fourteen of the twenty-six-thousand-foot peaks in the world and has become a national hero in Korea.

David Kirke and the Oxford Dangerous Sports Club moved to London and became just the "Dangerous Sports Club." David is still very much alive and has gone on to lead many more events ranging from walking across the English Channel in a large bubble to setting world records in ultralight aviation. My Sherpa friend

Dawa Tsering Sherpa returned to Nepal with the money that he earned working in America and built the Everest Summit Hotel in Lukla, which he runs with his wife. The Everest Summit is "the" place to stay on the approach to Everest, despite not having a wrestling arena. Dawa has become a top trekking and climbing Sirdar and is providing an education for his children at the best schools in Kathmandu. Nima Tashi Sherpa, my other Sherpa summit partner—who broke both of his ankles in an accident getting porter loads from a pass and wrote me his desperate letter stating, "I have broken the wrists of both feet"—has recovered from his ankle fusions. After living with me for six months during his convalescence he returned to Nepal and climbing. In addition to many other peaks Nima Tashi has gone back to the summit of Everest five more times. His partner on his latest Everest success in May 2002 was Peter Athans (making his seventh trip to the summit, the most by any non-Sherpa), who paid for his initial plane flight to America. Peter has also relocated to Burlington, Vermont, where his wife is now a medical student and Pete is one of my main partners on local rock and ice climbs. Ken Kammler, the orthopedic surgeon who joined me on the summit of Mount Vinson, helped with Nima Tashi's surgery and has been going to Mount Everest as a high-altitude doctor and researcher.

Over the past several years my personal adventures and travels have increasingly been for eye surgery. My partner in eye care in Asia, Dr. Sanduk Ruit, and I have vowed to work to eliminate all preventable and treatable blindness from the Himalayan region in our lifetime, a goal more audacious than setting out to make the first ascent of the East Face of Mount Everest. We formed our own tax-free nongovernmental organization, the Himalayan Cataract Project, in 1994. Since then I have been going on three eye surgery expeditions to Asia per year. The excitement of the first day's post-operative exam has not lost any of its thrills for me. In the same way that I get a tingle of excitement approaching a big rock wall in the mountains, my whole body becomes energized as I start a day of operating, knowing that we will be restoring sight to blind patients. The smiles and tears of joy from people freed from cataract blindness always give me a thrill—yet even more exciting has been seeing the progress made by the surgeons we are teaching in Asia. Dr. Biswas from Biratnagar has improved steadily every year. I remember returning after two years and asking Dr. Biswas how many surgeries he'd done in the previous year. He proudly told me, "Last year I am making 935 surgeries." Two years later he smiled and said, "1,647." Currently, Dr. Biswas is restoring sight to more than two thousand patients per year with absolutely perfect cataract surgery. As his skills have bloomed, his reputation in the region has also increased and more and more patients are flocking to the hospital. The Golchha Eye Hospital is now self-sufficient for its cataract surgery through cost recovery. In Nepal the number of cataract surgeries performed annually has increased from fifteen thousand and only 10 percent with modern microsurgery and intraocular lens implantation in 1993 to ninety-seven thousand and 96 percent with intraocular lenses in 2001. As we are beginning to overcome the cataract problem, Dr. Ruit and I are now turning our attention to training full ophthalmic subspecialists and also improving primary eye care in Nepal.

Similarly, Dr. Niaz Ali in northern Pakistan has changed eye care in Baltistan. He is currently performing a steady fifty or more cataract surgeries every month and providing excellent basic ophthalmic care for his region. We have trained more than a dozen cataract surgeons in Tibet, established an eye-care center in Lhasa, and have expanded our program into Sikkim, West Bengal, and Bhutan.

Through the generous support of Mark Daniel, one of my close friends at Oxford who is a successful businessman in Singapore, we have entered into an agreement with the kingdom of Bhutan to develop an eye-care program. Bhutan has a benevolent dictatorship, a system of government that works extremely well in Asia. King Jigme Wangchuck has issued an edict that he does not want to expand the gross national product of his country at the expense of the gross national happiness of his people. He has been very careful about which foreign groups he allows to work in his country. He began by developing a system of roads and primary health care, which provides basic health services for all of his people, and a transportation system that provides access for all of the people in the country to receive care, and free schooling for all small children. With Mark Daniel's financial support and the help of the government of Bhutan, we were able to design a model system for total eye care. We begin in childhood with basic eye health screening. Our program includes teaching all primary school teachers to test their students for eye disease and nutritional deficiencies. Next, we are training ophthalmic assistants for every primary health-care post to give basic eye care and recognize and treat infections, and to provide spectacles for all Bhutanese who need glasses. These primary centers then refer surgical cases to the doctors. We are training three Bhutanese doctors in cataract surgery and also sponsoring three young Bhutanese doctors in full three-year ophthalmology residencies. At the conclusion of our five-year plan, there will be basic eye care for all citizens, a referral ophthalmology service in the center of the country, and free cataract surgery for all Bhutanese citizens.

—

My partner in all of my Asian ophthalmological endeavors, Dr. Sanduk Ruit, embodies the spirit of blind corners. He has been willing to take great risks and has thrown himself fully into the lofty goal of ridding his region of needless blindness. We may fail, but not without giving it our best effort. Turning blind corners is more than just adventure. It is curiosity and remaining open to explore, take risks, and learn more about yourself and the world. The more I learn, the more I realize that there are no answers, only more questions. It is difficult to express the joy I get from climbing, adventure, and taking on new challenges. People can point to the risks and the hardships and question the use of the word *joy*. But it is joy. Joy in the discoveries, in the movement, in the travel, in the successes on the summits and in the operating room, in the focusing of energy in failure, and in the *seilshaft*. I climb more than simply "because it is there." I climb because I am here.

I am often asked, "What do you do after you conquer the seven summits?" My first answer is that I never conquer a mountain. I have been lucky enough to climb on some wonderful peaks and transiently coexist in harmony and feel like part of them for a while. Second, there are enough new climbs and adventures for me to explore in this world for many more lifetimes. I have also found a new area of adventure to pursue, changing the focus of my energy from climbing Himalayan peaks to eradicating blindness. All of us have our own Everest. Finally, I try not to dwell on what I have accomplished, but concentrate on what I am doing now, and what I can do in the future. If you are willing to turn blind corners, the horizons remain endless.

I remember Carlos Buhler saying, "The people who succeed and do not push on to greater failure are the spiritual middle classes. Their stopping at success is proof of their compromising insignificance. How petty their dreams must have been." As for me, I still have plenty of dreams left to fail on.